The Last Word

BEN MACINTYRE is a columnist and Associate Editor on *The Times*. He has worked as the newspaper's correspondent in New York, Paris and Washington. He is the author of six previous books including *Agent Zigzag*, which was shortlisted for the Costa Biography Award and the Galaxy British Book Award for Biography of the Year 2008. He lives in London with his wife and three children.

The Last Word

Tales from the Tip of the Mother Tongue

BEN MACINTYRE

BLOOMSBURY

LONDON · BERLIN · NEW YORK · SYDNEY

First published in Great Britain 2009
This paperback edition published 2010

Copyright © by Ben Macintyre 2009

The moral right of the author has been asserted

These articles have been previously published in
the author's column in *The Times*

Bloomsbury Publishing Plc
36 Soho Square
London W1D 3QY

www.bloomsbury.com

Bloomsbury Publishing, London, New York and Berlin

A CIP catalogue record for this book is available from the British Library

ISBN 978 1 4088 0435 3

10 9 8 7 6 5 4 3 2

Typeset by Hewer Text UK Ltd, Edinburgh
Printed in Great Britain by Clays Ltd, St Ives plc

For my mother

Introduction

THIS BOOK BEGAN LIFE as a column in the Books section of *The Times*. My brief was to write about words. I took this to mean I could write about anything linked, however loosely, with language: in other words, everything. I wrote about military euphemisms, nursery rhymes, the accidental poetry of electronic spam, the disappearing telegram and the lyrics of Abba.

No one stopped me, so I carried on.

I wrote about the words of Boris Johnson, Kenny Rogers, and Osama bin Laden, the words used by book reviewers, computer nerds, spies, cricketers, Scott of the Antarctic and the Piraha tribe of the Amazon, whose members only count up to three. I explored words for baldness, book titles, intellectuals, the credit crunch, literary smells and why there is no satisfactory word for the symbol @. I interviewed a fourteen-year-old pygmy chimpanzee, and set off on a fruitless quest in search of French jokes that could be regarded as funny.

Readers joined in, supplying mistranslations, malapropisms, neologisms, epitaphs, words that have vanished, terms in other languages inexplicably absent from ours and a torrent of loophemisms, words to disguise the act of going to the toilet.

There is a grumpy modern vogue for complaining about the supposed degradation of the English language: about sloppy spelling, incorrect grammar and misplaced apostrophes. This book heads in the opposite direction, celebrating the strangeness and adaptability of our language, its peculiar offshoots and unofficial accretions. This is not a defence of Correct English (which needs no defending) but a celebration of all the unexpected and delightful ways that English has adapted into such variants as Chinglish (Chinese-English, Spanglish (Spanish-English), Ponglish (Polish-English) and Geek-speak, the fast-evolving language of the internet.

Every day, the vocabulary of English is embiggened (a word coined by the greatest of modern culture-philosophers, the Simpsons). The collective noun for exhibitionists in public parks, I learned, is 'a phalanx of flashers'. 'Collyerism', or 'disposaphobia', is named after Langley Collyer, who was crushed and entombed by his own unstoppable book collection.

It has been a privilege to wander the tributaries, sources and oxbows of the language, to discover that the Hobbit was born on an empty page, to learn the deceptively gentle 'purr' is Scots Gaelic for head-butt, and to stumble on the greatest Country and Western song title of all time: 'Since You Bought the Waterbed, We've Slowly Drifted Apart'.

I am grateful to Erica Wagner, the literary editor of *The Times*, for commissioning and editing these pieces in their original form; to Richard Charkin of Bloomsbury for suggesting there might be a book in them; and to *The Times* for permission to reproduce them here.

There is no last word on any subject, because words never stand still. Words define and reveal, persuade and enlighten, but then move on. As Tom Stoppard once wrote, 'They deserve respect. If you get the right ones in the right order, you can nudge the world a little or make a poem which children will speak for you after you are dead.'

Living, evolving and mutating, words are little shards of immortality that will outlast us: famous last words.

Ben Macintyre
September 2009

Say it with flowers

IN THE SUMMER OF 1945 Mrs Irene Graham, of Thorpe Avenue, Boscombe, was told that a German prisoner of war from the nearby camp would be coming to help her in the garden. The hard-working young PoW 'seemed a nice friendly chap', Mrs Graham recalled, and she was sorry to see him go when, at the end of the year, he was repatriated to Germany. The following spring, the crocuses in her lawn came up spelling out, in large letters: 'Heil Hitler'.

The hidden message is an extraordinarily rich part of the language. Groups in society routinely develop shared codes, signs and symbols for secrecy, for bonding, and for the simple pleasure of passing on a message that some will see and decipher, and most will not.

Boy Scouts, stock traders, lonely hearts, gang members, obituary writers, homosexuals, spies, bookmakers, convicts, Nazi gardeners, Freemasons and footballers all send messages in code, in the belief that only those in the know will know. Sometimes this fails spectacularly: the footballer who recently made the handcuffs gesture in support of a team-mate convicted of killing two children while drink-driving apparently believed he was being subtle. On the day that Monica Lewinsky revealed her affair with Bill Clinton, the

President wore a tie she had given him – this was seen as a hint of complicity, intended to persuade her to keep quiet, which did not work.

Secret languages can be inclusive, or exclusive, or both. In Norway during the war, Norwegians opposed to the Nazi occupiers often wore paperclips attached to their lapels or some other part of the clothing. A Norwegian inventor, Johan Vaaler, had been granted a patent for a paperclip in 1901, and the tiny twist of metal became a national symbol, a visual memorial of people holding together in small ways.

Debutantes in British high society developed a sophis-ticated acronymic code, meaningless to their mothers and chaperones, to describe the various sorts of young men at deb parties: HD for Heavy Drinker, NQOCD for Not Quite Our Class Dear, NSIT for Not Safe in Taxis and VVSITPQ meaning Very Very Safe In Taxis Probably Queer.

In the same way, but at the opposite end of the social spectrum, hobos during the Great Depression would scratch or chalk symbols on gateposts as they wandered from place to place, to inform other tramps of the sort of reception they could expect within. This secret hobo language might advise of an owner with a gun, or a dog, or money; a top hat scratched in the gatepost meant a kind man; a cat sym-bol indicated a generous woman; a cross advised the visiting hobo to 'talk religion and get food'.

Perhaps the most telling symbol of all was a single wavy line, which indicated that the owner of the house was also poor, and that the wanderer should keep moving on.

Like spoken or written language, the code of signals can be misheard and misread, leading to all sorts of misunder-standings. During one speech, George W. Bush famously made the hand gesture – with raised index and little fingers – that in Texas indicates support for the Texas Longhorns teams of the state university. But that sign also represents *el cornudo*, the horned hand, symbolising the head of a goat and a mark of recognition between Spanish-speaking Satanists. Bush's one-man war with the language is well known, but it is quite a feat to be able to misspeak without saying anything at all.

A guide to reviewese

IN A RECENT ARTICLE, I described a book as 'magisterial', and promptly received a text message from my most critical friend. 'magisterial? u mean dull, no?' He was right. I had used the word to indicate that the book was long and scholarly, and to imply that I had read it all (which I had not). In reviewese, 'magisterial' means lofty, and dreary.

The book world is rife with such euphemistic terms. They are not exactly clichés, although they work as hard and for as little recompense as any hardscrabble cliché. Instead, they form a sort of literary shorthand, an easy vernacular for reviewers and readers, and they are highly contagious. They crop up throughout literary journalism and then gather in herds, as puffs on the backs of paperbacks: 'searingly honest', 'penetrating insight', 'achingly funny'.

The Times Literary Supplement has a splendid informal list of hackneyed words and phrases to avoid like the plague. These include: 'rich tapestry', 'consummate skill', 'peppered with' and 'I defer to no one . . .'

Some words, such as 'mellifluous' and 'coruscating', are seldom used outside book reviews; others, such as 'insightful', have been used so often that they mean nothing at all. But some have hidden meanings.

Here, then, is a brief glossary of literary euphemisms:

Mesmerising This word is traditionally deployed by the non-specialist reviewer to describe a specialist book, for example: 'Hawking's *A Brief History of Time* is quite mesmerising.' It translates as: 'I didn't understand a word, but I'm not going to admit it because I need the money, and I've already sold the book.'

Edgy Any author under the age of thirty, being reviewed by someone over thirty, is likely to be described as edgy. The edginess factor will increase in proportion to whether the author is non-white, female and attractive, and the reviewer is white, male and fat. Drugs, sex and racial conflict are also contributory factors. Edgy is also a synonym for glue-sniffing, necrophilia, lap-dancing and Michel Houellebecq.

Exquisite sensibility Gay.

Veiled sensibility Closet gay.

Shot through with mordant wit This phrase tends to be used by reviewers to describe books written by other reviewers. It means: 'Extremely nasty, but I don't want this bastard to work me over next.'

These are minor quibbles (mere cavils) . . . This is a favourite of the weedier academic reviewers. It usually crops up towards the end of the review, when the reviewer has suddenly realised that he may have put the boot in too hard at the start, and feels guilty.

Writing reminiscent of Probably plagiarised.

It is a truth universally acknowledged . . . that any review touching, however tangentially, on the life, times, writing or recipes of Jane Austen must begin with this knackered introduction.

X meets Y This is the single greatest contribution of publishers' marketing departments to modern literature. It shackles together two more famous authors or books in the hope of making a hybrid, and can lead to some unlikely couplings: 'Henry James meets Hunter S. Thompson' or 'Virginia Woolf meets Naomi Wolf meets Steppenwolf meets Peter and the Wolf'. The offspring of such unions are almost always still-born. (See the next Dan Brown/*Brick Lane*/Shakespeare etc.)

Exhaustive Exhausting.

Wears its scholarship lightly Author is not a real scholar. But I am.

Triumphant return to form I was expecting this to be as abysmal as the last one, but it was only mildly disappointing.

Gnomic Baffling.

Imaginative Fiction reviewers use this to describe a book that they wish they had written; non-fiction reviewers use it to describe a book they do not believe.

Compelling I managed to finish it.

Painfully/funny/sad/poignant/long Demonstrates the deep sensitivity of the reviewer. A health warning also attaches to any book described as achingly, eye-wateringly or heart-stoppingly anything.

Arch I'm not sure if this is funny.

Detailed Has footnotes.

Richly detailed Has lots of footnotes.

Densely detailed Has footnotes, endnotes, acknowledge-ments, epigrams, foreword, preface, bibliography, appendices, indices and marginalia. Translation: unreadable. (See pano-ramic, workmanlike, painstaking, extensively researched.)

Quaint Eccentric.

Eccentric Author should be sectioned immediately.

Vertiginous So clever and showy that it made me feel a bit sick.

Vibrant Usually used to describe a young author that the reviewer met when drunk at the Martin Amis launch and thinks he might have fancied. (See also *accomplished debut*.)

Important Worthy.

Crucial Worthier.

Seminal Worthiest.

A colourful cast of characters The author is trying to be P. G. Wodehouse.

This curate's egg of a book ... The telltale mark of the indecisive reviewer.

Whips along, zips along, rattling yarn, high-octane, page-turner I usually review books about classical music, but the literary editor has given me this ghastly potboiler and I am putting a brave face on it.

Smorgasbord, potpourri, salmagundi, etc. are typical literary show-off terms intended to demonstrate the international learning of the reviewer. Translation: mixture.

Schadenfreude 'The book of mine enemy hath been remaindered, and I am glad' (Clive James).

Tightly plotted Has a beginning and a middle, and you find out whodunnit at the end.

Mayonnaise, a word cooked up by war

THE FIRST CASUALTY OF war is language. Wave upon wave of euphemisms, neologisms and fresh slang come marching into the dictionary at times of conflict. Wars in Iraq and Afghanistan have popularised terms such as 'shock and awe', 'green zones', 'friendly fire' and 'collateral damage', military-speak for killing civilians. Such words are the equivalent of armies of occupation: once installed in the lexicon, they never leave.

But war is also an astonishing engine for creating new words and phrases. On the battlefield soldiers are thrust into new situations that must be put into words, they encounter sights and languages to be absorbed and adapted into their own, while new technologies and tactics demand new terminologies.

Mostly, however, soldiers are bored, sitting around for long hours passing the time: countless words have their origins in military chat, including the word 'chat'. A 'chat' was a slang word for 'louse', widely used by British soldiers in the First World War. In quiet moments on the Western Front, the men would sit around picking lice out of their uniforms and talking, an activity that became known as 'crumbing up' or 'chatting'.

Some of the most benign words have the bloodiest origins. 'Mayonnaise', for example, was born out of bloodshed and near-starvation. In 1756, French forces under the duc de Richelieu finally ousted the British from Port Mahon, on the island of Minorca. (Mahon, Maó in Catalan, is named after Hannibal's brother, Mago Barco, who took refuge there in 205 BC.) But the siege had lasted so long that the Duke's chef had few ingredients left with which to furnish the victory table: he did his best and whipped up a basic sauce from eggs and oil, which he called 'Mahonnaise'.

This seems like an ideal word recipe: take one obscure Carthaginian general, a forgotten British defeat and an inventive French chef. Stir together and leave to set.

Morris dancing, the much-mocked activity involving grown-up men wearing funny hats and knee-bells, was once a thrillingly dangerous martial ritual brought to Britain in the fourteenth century by John of Gaunt. On his Spanish expeditions, John of Gaunt had witnessed a Moorish sword dance of such extreme violence that one mistake could deprive a dancer of a limb or head. ('Morris' is derived from the Spanish word for Moorish, 'Morisco'.) Imported to Britain, the dance was gradually civilianised and rendered safe.

Deadlines, as every journalist know, are brutal things. The first deadline was drawn around the Confederate prison camp at Andersonville (now Fort Sumter) in Georgia. It was a light fence, 4ft high and about 25ft from the edge of the stockade wall: any Yankee prisoner crossing the line was liable to be shot dead by sentries on the orders of the exceptionally nasty prison governor, Heinrich Hartmann Wirz, a Swiss mercenary.

The trial of Wirz after the Civil War (he was executed in 1865) brought the term 'deadline' into common parlance and writers, taxpayers and others have been scrambling to meet the damn things ever since.

Squaddies have a particular knack for inventing new words to describe the enemy, their officers and their hosts. British troops in the Falklands in 1982 referred to local inhabitants as 'Bennies', after the faintly dim character in the television series *Crossroads*. In reply, the Falkland Islanders called their liberators 'Whennies', since all their anecdotes tended to start with the words 'When I was in Germany/Afghanistan/Aldershot etc . . .' Senior officers attempted to damp down the word war by banning the word 'Bennies', so the troops began calling the Falkland Islanders 'Bubs', an acronym for 'bloody ungrateful bastards'; when that, too, was banned, they resorted to calling them 'Stills', short for 'still bloody ungrateful bastards'.

And 'bastard', too, springs etymologically from wartime. A 'bast' was a species of pack-saddle used in the baggage-trains that followed medieval armies. On the march, this saddle could be spread out to form a sort of rustic bed. A child produced on top of one of these in the middle of a war was likely to be illegitimate, hence bastard, which just goes to show that words can be conceived in the most unlikely and uncomfortable places.

The lost language of now

IN 1980, DANIEL EVERETT, an American missionary and linguist, set off into the heart of the Amazon to track down some of the world's most elusive words: the language of the Piraha, a small tribe of Amazonian Indians living on the banks of the Maici River in Brazil.

For the next twenty years Everett, the son of a California cowboy, tried to hack his way through this impenetrable language, coming across verbs that grew into the most contorted shapes, a complete absence of subordinate clauses in sentences and forests of nouns that seemed to change without reason or pattern.

Piraha, now spoken by fewer than 400 people, is not related to any other known living language; the people who speak it are monolingual and no outsider had ever mastered it before. The language has no simple colour words, no comparatives, no abstract concepts, no stories of the past, nor visions of the future. The Piraha have no history, no fiction, no creation myth and no folklore.

Intending to shed the light of Christianity on the tribe by translating the Bible into Piraha, Everett found himself lost in an alien tongue.

The language has three vowels and eight consonants for men, and the same number of vowels but only seven consonants for women. There is a supply of nouns, but each verb has up to sixteen suffixes, which may be present or absent: thus, two to the power of sixteen, making 65,536 possible forms for each and any Piraha verb. To complicate matters further, there is hum speech, musical speech and whistle speech. Struggling through the linguistic undergrowth was only one challenge, alongside anacondas, tarantulas and river pirates. Everett's wife and daughter caught malaria and almost died. He watched in horror as the Piraha killed an orphaned baby, on the grounds that the child would soon die anyway.

As his command of Piraha grew, he explored deeper into this linguistic *terra incognita*. Here was a people so in tune with their surroundings that they had no north or south, no left or right, but merely 'upriver' and 'downriver', a direction hard-wired into their speech, like a GPS. They had no need of numbers, and thus no quantifiers – no words meaning all, each or every. For eight months, Everett tried to teach them to count, entirely without success.

Piraha, he concluded, was predicated on the 'immediacy of experience'. The language consisted of questions, declaration, or commands, all directly related to the tribe's visible world. 'The Pirahas only make statements that are anchored in the moment,' he writes. 'Declarative Piraha utterances contain only assertions related directly to the moment of speech, either experienced by the speaker or witnessed by someone alive during the lifetime of the speaker.'

This is a language of the here and now. The Piraha and their language live from day to day. 'Pirahas don't store food, they don't plan more than one day at a time, they don't talk about the distant future or the distant past – they seem to focus on now, on their immediate experience.' Everett's most astonishing find was that the Piraha lack the grammatical principle of recursion, thoughts collected together in sentences with more than one clause. Noam Chomsky held that recursion is common to all language, and that the ability to use grammar is what sets humanity apart from all other terrestrial life forms. But recursion requires abstraction and generalisation, which contravene Everett's 'immediacy of experience' principle.

'It is not simply that Piraha accidentally lacks recursion. It doesn't want it; it doesn't allow it because of a cultural principle.'

Like most explorers, and many linguists, Everett is plainly an obsessive. After years of living in the Amazonian jungle, he found himself drawn to the Piraha way of seeing the world: his marriage and his faith collapsed. 'The Pirahas simply make the immediate their focus of concentration, and thereby, at a single stroke, they eliminate huge sources of worry, fear and despair that plague so many of us in Western societies.'

Everett came to the jungle intending to teach and convert though language, but was converted to a new way of thinking.

'Do not sleep there are snakes' is a Piraha saying. Members of the tribe sleep little, and tend to chat through the night, but the expression is more than just a warning. Everett translates it as 'Life is hard, and there is plenty of danger. And it might make us lose some sleep from time to time. But enjoy it. Life goes on.'

The Piraha live, and speak, for now, and in their strange tongue they have retained something we have lost.

How to talk to American voters

'YOU CAN PUT LIPSTICK on a pig, but it's still a pig,' Barack Obama said, opening up a real can of worms, or piggery of cosmetics, or something.

Republicans accused the Democratic presidential candidate of insulting the Republican vice-presidential candidate Sarah Palin, who had just referred to herself as a 'pitbull with lipstick'. Why comparison with a pig, an intelligent and delicious creature, should be so much more hurtful than aligning oneself with a particularly aggressive breed of dog, defeats me.

Obama was simply indulging in a long-established tradition, by introducing a folksy colloquialism on to the campaign trail, something that presidents and would-be presidents have done for decades.

A touch of downhome language works wonders with the US electorate. Ronald Reagan was a dab hand at introducing obscure Americanisms into formal occasions. Bill Clinton was equally adept at Arkansas slang, usually about dogs. 'I don't have a dawg in that fight,' he used to say about legislation that did not interest him. So, far from being a calculated insult, the pig (or hog) in lipstick is a familiar idiom in US politics, car sales and urban building projects, used to describe anything unpleasant that is gussied up to look smart, expensive and clever.

According to the American lexicologist Ben Zimmer, in 1985 a San Francisco radio host used the phrase to condemn a plan for a new sports stadium. In politics, the first recorded use was in 1986, when the Texas Democrat Jim Hightower used it to describe a reshuffle of Ronald Reagan's Cabinet.

But it was the late and linguistically delightful Governor Ann Richards of Texas who put pigs in lipstick firmly in the American political dictionary. In 1991, when producing her first budget, she declared: 'This is not another one of those deals where you put lipstick on a hog and call it a princess.' The following year, at a barbecue in South Dakota, she gave the overdecorated pig a name – hammering the Republican Government for deploying warships to protect oil tankers in the Middle East, effectively subsidising foreign oil, she said:

'You can put lipstick on a hog and call it Monique, but it is still a pig.'

The English expression 'you cannot make a silk purse out of a sow's ear' dates back to the sixteenth century, and in 1732, long before the invention of lipstick, Thomas Fuller noted that 'a hog in armour is still but a hog'. This was apparently a reference to poor, ill-dressed or elderly folk dolling themselves up in expensive kit (i.e. armour) to appear above their station. 'An awkward or mean-looking man or woman, finely dressed', is how a 'pig in armour' is defined in Francis Grose's *A Classical Dictionary of the Vulgar Tongue* (1796). To mix our barnyard idioms: mutton dressed as lamb, with lipstick.

The problem with introducing obscure idioms into American political parlance is the sheer regional variation of so much slang.

Alan Simpson, a Republican from Wyoming, flummoxed journalists when he compared the flamboyant demonstrations of politicians to the 'sage chicken dance', a term used to describe the mating rituals of that bird. A sage chicken is a rare prairie fowl, noted for its extravagant waddling and waggling when over-excited; but only Senator Simpson and a handful of Western ornithologists knew this.

George W. Bush caused a similar flutter of linguistic panic when he told reporters in 2002 that 'Saddam Hussein has sidestepped, crawfished, wheedled out of any agreement he had made ... he is stiffing the world'. Was crustacean-imitation to be added to the litany of Saddam's crimes? Stiffing sounded very painful indeed.

'To crawfish' is a Southern term meaning 'to wriggle, retreat or back away', reflecting the behaviour of the fresh-water aquatic arthropod sometimes called a crayfish or crawdaddy, related to the lobster and the shrimp. In the way that idioms sometimes do, it caught on immediately: in a few days everyone in Washington was talking about Saddam's tendency to crawfish. 'Stiffing' is even more obscure. Meaning 'to do someone down', today it has a sexual connotation, but originally the phrase referred to a passenger on a cruise liner too mean to leave a little extra cash for the ship's staff. Iraqi interpreters must have been utterly baffled as they tried to tease out meaning from a small lobster that fails to leave a tip.

Pigs, pitbulls, sage chickens, hogs, dogs and crawfish: the strange bestiary of idiomatic politics and diplomacy is one of the joys of covering US politics. Every word counts in this most brutal contest. It's dog eat dog out there, and no amount of sage-chicken dancing should obscure the point of the exercise: to crawfish out of danger, stiff your opponent and decorate the pig with multiple layers of lipstick.

An author in search of an adjective

I ONLY MET THE late Harold Pinter once, at a dinner party, and I don't think I have ever encountered anyone less Pinter-esque. There were no ominous pauses in the conversation. There was no oblique and enigmatic dialogue. The atmosphere could not have been less sinister.

Pinter spent much of the evening ranting with happy profanity about the sins of Tony Blair, George Bush and all Americans, and gently reminiscing about cricket. (He recited the short poem he had written about the world's finest sport: 'I saw Hutton in his prime / Another time. Another time', and recalled how he had sent this little gem to his friend the playwright Simon Gray. After several weeks without a response, Pinter said he sent an angry note to Gray demanding to know what he thought of the poem, and got the reply: 'Harold, I haven't finished reading it yet.')

Pinter was hilarious, mischievous, voluble and entertaining. But he was not remotely Pinteresque.

I wonder if Pinter felt saddled by his own adjective – an adjective, moreover, that does not so much describe his writing as the spaces between his writing. Sadly, it is now too late to ask him.

In the same way, I doubt Charles Dickens would have struck one as Dickensian. He was amusing, energetic and good company, yet his name has come to denote all that is grim, decayed and doom-laden.

Few writers earn the distinction of morphing into an adjective, and Pinter is the only modern playwright to have done so during his own lifetime. Indeed, the process by which a writer become an adjective is a sort of linguistic alchemy, a combination of fame, stereotyping and chance.

Most auctorial adjectives are formed simply by adding '–ian', '-ean', '-esque', 'or –ic', and hoping the word sticks. Hence Brechtian, Kafkaesque and Byronic. But why not Byronesque, Brechtic or Kafkean? Some writers who surely deserve the honour never win eponymous adjectival status. Others have been eclipsed by their own literary creations: we have Sherlockian and Holmesian, but not Conan Doylean, Doylesque or Doylish.

Perhaps because they cannot be easily pinned down to specific literary characteristics, writers such as Eliot, Le Carré and Austen have somehow escaped adjectival capture.

George Bernard Shaw, partly though his own efforts, managed to ensure that his adjective would be for ever Shavian. (Not to be confused with 'the Shavian adjective', which was the euphemism used by the English press to avoid having to use the word 'bloody', after Shaw dared to have Eliza Doolittle say 'Not Bloody Likely!' in *Pygmalion*.)

Shavians insist the word 'Shavian' means a 'mixture of quixotic seriousness and harsh laughter'. To me the word means 'Not nearly as funny as it was when it was first written'.

By the same etymological principle, the Marlovian theory holds that Christopher Marlowe wrote the poems and plays of Shakespeare, and the writing of Henry David Thoreau is sometimes described as Thoreauvian. But otherwise the Shavian precedent has never really caught on. In theory, Saul Bellow's style should be Bellovian. The works of Michael Moore should be Moorvian, or possibly Moravian. But would anyone seriously describe the style of Evelyn Waugh as Wavian?

Writers unfortunate enough to have names that are already words are doomed never to have their own adjective. Graham Greene's writing cannot be described as Greenish. Alexander Pope was a Roman Catholic, but his legacy is hardly Popish. Thomas Mann was definitely not Mannish. And how to adjectivise Edgar Allan Poe? Polish?

Political names that evolve into adjectives almost invariably end in '–ite': Blairite, Thatcherite, Reaganite – which can double up as nouns. Eponymous political adjectives imply a specific set of beliefs, a degree of partisanship, but on very rare occasions a politician rises above politics in the public mind, and is accorded a grander ending to his adjective. I can think of only two examples of this in modern times: Kennedyesque and Churchillian.

Eponymous adjectives, on the whole, are dangerously overused, a portentous way of saying something very simple, lazy literary shorthand boiling down an entire writer to a single trait. Lawrentian is often used to mean 'sexy' and Platonic is a pretentious way of saying 'unsexy'. If a writer makes up words, and he gets a sympathetic reviewer, he is Joycean.

A run-in with a traffic warden may be Orwellian – a way of describing anything we dislike done by someone in authority – whereas a battle involving government bureaucracy, the tax office or doctors' waiting rooms is another grade up: i.e. Kafkaesque.

Shakespearean has come to mean anything that involves a powerful figure getting into trouble. American political commentators insisted that Bill Clinton's imbroglio with Monica Lewinsky was Shakespearean, when it was really Pythonesque.

But perhaps the most unlucky victim of the simplified auctorial adjective is poor Proust: the greatest novelist of the twentieth century, 3,200 pages of monumental prose with more than 2,000 literary characters, reduced, in common parlance, to a smell.

Whenever anyone of literary bent sniffs something that reminds them of something, it is all but obligatory to describe the experience as Proustian.

Absinthe made many poets drunk, but not many drunks into poets

IN 1905 A DEPRESSED Swiss farmer named Jean Lanfray sucked down an industrial quantity of absinthe, and then shot dead his wife and children. There was outrage across Europe and many countries, including Switzerland, banned the drink. Exactly 100 years after Lanfray's famous bender, the Swiss Parliament has voted to legalise the most notorious literary tipple: *la fée verte*, the green fairy, has returned to the drinks cabinet of artistic acceptability.

There have been various absinthe imitations on the market for a while, including a Czech variety, tasting of liquorice disinfectant, which was briefly stylish in Britain. The Swiss stuff, by contrast, is probably closest to the original, since it contains up to thirty-five milligrams per litre of thujone, the psychoactive chemical in wormwood (*Artemisia absinthium*), the secret ingredient in the emerald devil along with alcohol and anise. The Swiss distillers expect to obtain an official appellation, to secure the exclusive right to make absinthe.

Thujone, according to artistic legend, is the mind-bending substance that left Hemingway juggling with knives after a heavy night on the green sauce, and encouraged Van Gogh to aural self-surgery. Under its influence, Oscar Wilde saw a bunch of tulips sprout out of a cafe floor. Many of the greatest French writer-roués drank it by the pint: Rimbaud, Verlaine, Baudelaire. It inspired paintings by Degas, Manet and Picasso. Vaclav Havel ordered up some for his sixtieth birthday party. Toulouse-Lautrec kept in the hollow handle of his cane half a bottle, which he mixed with brandy to create a cocktail which he called *tremblement de terre*, the earth-shaker. (After one particularly ferocious session, little Henri was found shooting at spiders which, he said, were preparing to attack him. His disapproving father remarked: 'Why doesn't he go to England? They scarcely notice the drunks over there.') No drink is more closely associated with literary and artistic inspiration. Wilde (shortly before the unexpected bouquet appeared out of the floor) declared that a glass of absinthe was 'as poetical as anything in the world'. The side effects (apart from extravagant inebriation) included melancholy, madness and early death.

Because being drunk, sad, mad and/or dead was considered the height of sophistication in *belle époque* artistic circles, writers continued to quaff themselves silly until the Swiss farmer came along and spoiled the party.

But does absinthe really make the mind grow sharper? In a splendidly detailed exploration of the subject, *Hideous Absinthe: A History of the Devil in a Bottle*, Jad Adams reports recent animal research suggesting that thujone 'excites the brain' by blocking certain chemical receptors that slow neural activity.

Wilde felt his absinthe-soaked thoughts spiralling in strange directions: 'The first stage is like ordinary drinking, the second when you begin to see monstrous and cruel things, but if you can persevere you will enter in upon the third stage where you see things that you want to see, wonderful curious things.'

In a more sober moment, Wilde conceded that he enjoyed the atmosphere of absinthe drinking more than the effect. Writers have always seen what they wanted to see in absinthe. In many ways, the myth was an artificial concept, an idea, symbolic shorthand for bohemian indulgence, artistic hedonism and chic misbehaviour in the stews of Pigalle and Montmartre.

The British writer George Moore came over all trembly when he saw Degas's masterpiece *The Absinthe Drinkers*, with its depiction of an elegant woman staring into her glass of ruin. 'Heavens, what a slut!' he panted. 'A life of idleness and low vice is upon her face.' You can tell that he would have loved to crawl inside the painting and get to know her better.

As with heroin, the paraphernalia of absinthe drinking added to the mystique: water poured over a sugar cube balanced on a spatula which would then drip into the green

milky and opaque. This was the 'louche
the mind of half-cut poets, symbolised the
of the imagination. The colour change added to
the magic: beautiful and transparent one moment, sinister
and cloudy the next.

While artists were building up the reputation of absinthe
as the green muse, a passport to artistic creativity and a
fashionably early death, late nineteenth-century reformers were busy condemning the drink as moral decay in a
bottle. One doctor described so-called absinthism (and the
absintheeism it caused in the workplace) as the cause of
'degeneracy in the entire French race'. Some believed that
the drink encouraged anarchist tendencies, homosexual-
ity, cowardice in the First World War, sterility and even,
in large quantities, spontaneous combustion. The French
prohibition movement adopted the snappy slogan: 'No
absinthe – no fits.'

From Adams's book, it is clear that the drink was neither
as inspirational nor as exotically bad for you as writers and
artists liked to claim. Most of those who suffered from the
effects of absinthe were victims not of any evil or mystical
qualities inherent in the drink, but of the high alcohol content (it was three times the strength of brandy). Like every
drug, it could heighten the senses, and then dull them hor-
ribly; it provided temporary elation, then addiction, and
often misery. Absinthe made many poets drunk, but it did
not make many poets.

Switzerland provides the proof. Here absinthe was
invented; here it was first banned, and here, a century later,
it has become legal once again (having been made illegally in
Swiss stills in between times). But a great Swiss poet is like
the green fairy herself: blink, and you miss it.

When one language eats another

WHILE CELEBRATING THE RESILIENCE and adaptability of the English language, it is easy to forget that other, more fragile languages are dying at a staggering rate, that the very strength of one tongue is a threat to others.

At the end of 2001, there were an estimated 6,912 distinct languages spoken worldwide. By the end of this century, that number will probably be halved, with a language dying roughly every ten days. While we mourn the erosion of other parts of our natural world, the destruction of languages, unprecedented in human history, seems to pass almost unnoticed, and unmourned.

Indeed, our flora and fauna are surviving far better than words: some 40 per cent of languages are endangered, compared with 8 per cent of plants and 18 per cent of mammals.

Languages thrive in isolation: a single community split into two and kept apart may take as little as one century to develop mutually incomprehensible languages. Today the islands of Vanuatu, with 205,000 people spread over sixty-five islands, support more than 100 distinct tongues.

Conversely, languages die fastest when crushed together. Densely populated Western Europe has very little language diversity, with every language a variation of Indo-European – the sole exception being Basque, a tiny island of language with no known relatives. The cultural loss from a dead language is incalculable: each encodes a distinct way of seeing existence, but also specific forms of knowledge about the natural world.

The 4,000 speakers of Kayapo in Brazil, for example, can differentiate between fifty-six varieties of bee, depending on flight patterns, honey quality and other factors. At a time when bees are dying, inexplicably, in huge numbers, the knowledge enshrined in Kayapo may be critical to the future of bees, yet the language may not live long enough to impart its secrets.

English, Russian and Mandarin are the linguistic sharks of the world, gobbling up the small fry through globalisation, emigration and urbanisation. By contrast, some 3,500 of the smallest languages are spoken by just 0.2 per cent of the world's population.

Like a stuffed, extinct animal in a museum, a language that survives only in a dictionary and not as a spoken tongue is a sad spectacle, but at least it stands as evidence of what has been lost, and what might yet be learnt from these silenced voices.

Take the Tofa people of Siberia, with a language spoken by only thirty elderly people. The language has been so eroded that no one can quite remember the creation myth that once bound the community together. The old people vaguely recall a tale involving a duck laying an egg which broke, forming the Earth from the shell and a lake from the yolk. But as the language died, so did the story.

The Tofa duck myth was once how a people made sense of the world: without it, and without the language to describe it, they are lost for words.

Everyone needs an aunt-seducer

THERE ARE 613,000 WORDS in the English language, according to the *Oxford English Dictionary*, and it simply isn't enough. True, English has more than any other language, and true, those 613,000 words work pretty well for most purposes, but there are so many things for which there is no English word, at least not yet.

Why, for example, have we not invented a word to describe the impotent fury one feels on being given an explanation by the plumber or mechanic that is plainly untrue and involves spending more money, but which one lacks the necessary expertise to refute? How should you describe that vague but intense feeling of disappointment when you know you are about to sneeze but, for some reason, don't?

Or the flush of anger/gloating/transferred embarrassment experienced when someone else's mobile phone rings in the theatre?

Adam Jacot de Boinod has made a career out of unearthing useful or unlikely words that exist in other languages, and ought to exist in ours, collecting them under the title *The Meaning of Tingo*. ('Tingo' is a word from the Easter Islands meaning 'to borrow objects from a friend's house, one by one, until there is nothing left'.)

I am not sure how I have got through life so far without knowing there is a word to describe 'a young man of excessively good manners whom you suspect of ulterior motives'. In German this is a *Tantenverführer*, literally an 'aunt-seducer'.

Similarly, the planet is presumably full of people who 'try to curry favour or draw attention to themselves by doing lots of work, but doing it badly'; yet only in Malawi is there a word for such a person, *jijirira*.

Such terms often encapsulate some attribute or concept that is oddly familiar, even though we have no word for it. Take *kokobijin*, a Japanese word for 'the sort of woman who talks incessantly about how she would have been thought of as a stunner if she had lived in a different era, when men's tastes in beauty were different'. Every workplace is full of *neko-nekos*, an Indonesian term for 'one who has a creative idea that only makes things worse', but we never knew what to call them before.

The Germans are particularly adept at inventing words to describe particular sorts of people or embarrassing social occasions. *Trittbrettfahren*, for example, means 'to take advantage of someone else's efforts without contributing anything' (literally, it is 'the person who rides on the stepping-board of a train without buying a ticket'). 'Freeloader' seems pallid by comparison. Who has not bridled at the behaviour of the *Spensenritter* (literally 'expenses knight'), the executive who shows off by settling the bill with maximum ostentation, even though his company is paying and it costs him nothing. The echoes of bogus chivalry in the behaviour of the 'expenses knight' are particularly apt.

German is the only language to boast an expression meaning to 'make up a new word on the spot in a moment of need': ad hoc *Bildungen*. There is even an invented German word that means a fear of palindromes (words that read the same backwards and forwards), which is, of course, a palindrome: *Eibohphobie*.

Sadly there is no word in English for 'an act someone does for you thinking they are doing you a favour, but which you really didn't want them to do'. But the Germans have one: *Bärendienst*. The Japanese, however, have gone one better (or worse, in terms of tortured social behaviour), with *arigata-meiwaku*. This means 'an act that someone does for you thinking they are doing you a favour, but which you really didn't want them to do, and for which, according to social conventions, you now have to express suitable gratitude that you don't actually feel, to avoid giving offence'. Think of the sensation you get at Christmas when your mother gives you yet another set of matching handkerchiefs, and you know the meaning of *arigata-meiwaku*.

There may be few occasions when you can successfully deploy the Inuit word *areodjarekput*, 'to exchange wives for a few days only', unless you are planning to move to Alaska or go on *Wife Swap*.

But such terms provide a fascinating insight into different cultures. Tsonga, the language of the Limpopo province of South Africa, has two crucial words that no one should be without: *dlanyaa*, 'to lie on one's back with legs apart gorged with food', and *rhwe*, 'to sleep on the floor without a mat, and usually drunk and naked'. I have never been to Limpopo, but it is clearly a wonderful place.

Reassembling Humpty Dumpty

CONTRARY TO WHAT SCHOOLCHILDREN have been led to believe for more than three centuries, it might just be possible to put Humpty Dumpty together again. It would not even require all the king's horses and all the king's men to do it: an archaeologist, a large metal detector and an expert in seventeenth-century guns should do the trick.

The hapless Humpty, it appears, was not an egg (that notion did not take root until 1871, with the publication of *Through the Looking Glass* and Sir John Tenniel's illustration of Humpty as an egg). The original Humpty Dumpty was really a large cannon, used by Royalist forces to defend besieged Colchester in 1648. Royalists under the command of Sir Charles Lucas defended the town against the encircling Parliamentarians for eleven weeks, largely thanks to 'Humpty Dumpty', the nickname for the cannon expertly operated by a

Royalist gunner, 'One-eyed' Thompson, and mounted on the church tower of St Mary-at-the-Walls.

Eventually, however, the Roundheads managed to score a direct hit on the tower, and Humpty (and Thompson) had a great fall. According to Albert Jack, in his new investigation of nursery rhymes, the shattered cannon 'buried itself in deep marshland' outside the city walls. The reason all the king's men could not put the weapon back together again may have simply been that they could not find all the pieces buried in the Essex mud. In all probability the remains of Humpty are still there.

The rhyme was pure Parliamentarian propaganda, a mocking ditty to show that the most effective weapon in the Royalist armoury had been neutralised, destroyed beyond repair. Putting Humpty together again, albeit 360 years late, would be a pleasing counter-coup for those of us still rooting for the Royalist cause ('Wrong but Romantic').

One of the oddest aspects of nursery rhymes is their specificity. The names of the protagonists have been perfectly preserved down the ages: Dr Foster, Jack Horner, Old Mother Hubbard have been handed down from child to child without alteration and often without curiosity. Yet all of these nursery rhyme characters can be traced into history, albeit tentatively.

The Grand Old Duke of York was probably James II, who marched his troops to Salisbury to do battle with William of Orange in 1688, and then marched them back again when he realised how many of his former allies had defected. Three problems: James II was not Duke of York, although he had been; he was fifty-five, so not particularly old; and Salisbury Plain is pretty flat.

An alternative candidate is Prince Frederick, the unwarlike son of George III. The hill down which he marched may have been Mont Cassel, the hill near Tourcoing where the Prince's forces were soundly beaten by the French in 1794. On the other hand, the '10,000 men' may refer to the workers toiling up and down hill at Frederick's mansion near Harrogate in order to build his (not strictly deserved) Temple of Victory on a nearby hillock.

The history behind nursery rhymes is not only highly specific, but often splendidly grim. Take 'Mary, Mary, Quite Contrary', an apparently simple tale of one girl's taste for elaborate horticulture that is really about torture. 'Mary' may be Mary I, and the 'garden' may be Steven Gardiner, her brutal Lord Chancellor. When the devoutly Roman Catholic Mary and Gardiner set about purging Protestants, imprisoned dissenters were tortured with a grisly array of implements: 'cockleshells', a device for crushing the genitals; 'silver bells', the nickname for thumbscrews; and 'maids', a sort of early guillotine.

In this reading, Mary was not just contrary, but fabulously cruel. Her growing garden is, in fact, an expanding graveyard.

'Little Jack Horner' may have been steward to the Abbot of Glastonbury, Richard Whiting. It is said that Whiting, attempting to protect his abbey from the dissolution, sent Horner to Henry VIII with the deeds to numerous properties, concealed beneath a pie crust, as a bribe. Horner, however, 'pulled out a plum' – the deeds to Mells Manor House in Somerset. Whiting was hanged, drawn and quartered for his failure to obey the king without question; the descendants of Thomas Horner, who deny the legend, still live at Mells Manor House.

'Georgie Porgie' may have been George Villiers, Duke of Buckingham, James I's favourite and possible lover, who was notorious for having affairs with women at court but 'ran away' (i.e. survived retaliation from the weeping ladies' husbands) because he enjoyed the king's protection. Mother Hubbard was probably a joke at the expense of Cardinal Wolsey, who went to Rome (the cupboard) to get the dog (Henry VIII) a bone (a divorce), and failed.

Nursery poetry is a tribute to the English oral tradition, and a reminder of the riches beneath the surface of the playground rhyme: characters, jokes, events and stories, perfectly preserved and awaiting excavation from history, like the bits of Humpty Dumpty himself, waiting to be reassembled from the Colchester marsh.

The charm of Chinglish

AS THE BEIJING OLYMPICS kicked off, another intense competition was under way: a bitter battle between opponents and devotees of Chinese signs in mistranslated English.

Before the Olympic Games began, the Chinese Government had vowed to eradicate the thousands of signs in 'Chinglish', the strange, mangled hybrid of English and Mandarin that visitors to China love, and Chinese officials hate.

The Committee of the Beijing Speaks Foreign Languages Programme claims to have removed 4,624 examples of mistranslations, and replaced these with standard English. For several years, teams of linguistic monitors have been scouring Beijing's restaurants, parks, museums and underground stations in the hunt for grammatical or linguistic gaffes.

Disabled toilets no longer advertise themselves as facilities for 'Deformed Man'. Signs on public lawns urging pedestrians to 'Show Mercy to the Slender Grass' have, sadly, vanished. Even the unmistakable 'Dongda Hospital for Anus and Intestine Disease' has been changed to the 'Hospital of Proctology'. The food on Chinese airlines is no longer described as 'Airline Pulp', although that is still an accurate description of what appears on your tray.

The head of the BSFLP, Chen Lin, is adamant: 'We want everything to be correct, We don't want anyone laughing at us.' Some of the laughter was undoubtedly patronising and offensive, but many of the best examples of Chinglish are delightful, reflecting the inventiveness that results when two such different languages collide.

Many Chinese words express concepts indirectly, and can be interpreted in a multiplicity of ways, thus making precise translation into English extraordinarily hard.

One of the pleasures of eating out in China, for example, is the challenge of trying to determine what the menu translator (or, for that matter, the chef) may be getting at.

A diner may have some idea of what is coming when ordering 'corrugated iron beef', but the ingredients of 'government abuse chicken' or 'the fish explodes the oil' are harder to predict. Some Chinese menus simply make promises, such as 'pleasant aftertaste' or, more lyrically, 'this tastiness cannot be carried, even with both hands'. There is also a tendency towards indigestibly literal translation: 'worm pig stomach', 'young chicken without sex' or 'ovary and digestive glands of a crab'.

As Abigail Lavin has observed, mistranslated signs tend to fall into two categories: those that are designed to convey information to English-speaking visitors (and fail), and what she terms 'Ornamental Chinglish', in which the translator has simply become carried away with the pleasure of deploying English, or nearly-English, and has no idea how to apply the brakes. In much the same way, Westerners like to adorn their bodies with tattoos in Chinese characters without knowing, or much caring, what they mean.

For some reason, the translations tend to get out of hand when advising foreigners on how to treat the environment: 'People and flowers, plants help each other in breath, if you pick the flowers they will die, and you will reduce your life too' advises one sign, while another admonishes 'Let us do the birds friend.'

My favourite in this genre is a sign at the entrance to People's Park in Shanghai: 'Visitors are not supposed to tease, scare, or capture bird, cricket, fish and shrimp or cicada (except those for community purposes).' This seems to me a quintessentially Chinese Communist concept: cicada-teasing is not supposed to happen except in the service of the greater community, when it is just fine.

There is something uniquely hospitable about Chinglish, with its generous extravagant determination to get to grips with the foreign tongue. No sign could be more welcoming than the one that still adorns many Beijing hotel rooms, inviting visitors to: 'Please Take Advantage of the Chambermaid.'

The pidgin has landed

THE GREAT POLISH INFLUX has brought to Britain improved plumbing, kielbasa (that terrific Polish sausage) and a new hybrid language: Ponglish, a curious admixture of English and Polish that has become everyday slang among young Poles in Britain, and exported back to Poland as part of the cultural baggage carried by returning Poles.

The word 'driving', for example, is rendered in Ponglish as 'drajwnic', and pronounced 'driveneech'; 'taxes' are 'taksy'. A young Polish driver in Britain may be taking his kara along the strity, and slowing down at the kornerze or, more likely, accelerating. On his dzien offa, he may go for a drinkowac with his frendy. Ponglish is not hard to learn.

The intensive cultural exchange between Britain and Poland has resulted in many English words becoming absorbed into trendy Polish slang. A young Pole returning home with cash in hand may well indulge in some serious retail therapy, or szoping.

In many ways, emerging Ponglish is a classic pidgin tongue, the result of a sudden collision between very different languages, a reduced form of communication forged when two mutually incomprehensible languages live and work together.

Most usually, pidgins emerge from voluntary trade contacts, or from slavery; from the need to communicate on a mercantile basis, or because of physical displacement from the mother country. Speakers of Ponglish have often come to Britain to earn more money, and return home having earned it, taking along a new vocabulary; Poles thrust into an unfamiliar language landscape adapt their own language to fit English, and modify English to fit their own purposes and pronunciation.

Unsurprisingly, given the industry of the newcomers, most Ponglish words refer to working, driving, paying taxes, lunch breaks and drinking. An editorial in the *Daily Telegraph* sniffed that words in Ponglish 'exude an aroma of low commerce and lower consumerism'. True, Ponglish is not the stuff of high culture, but most pidgins are constructed this way: as simple language structures ensuring that different peoples understand one another sufficiently to turn a mutual profit.

Chinese pidgin English, for example, was originally spoken in coastal areas of China from the seventeenth to the nineteenth century. The British arriving in Guangzhou in 1664 could not get a grip on Cantonese, and the Chinese were equally baffled by English: the result was a simple hybrid that would eventually expand to about 700 words, specifically for the purposes of doing business. Indeed, pidgin derives from the way 'business' was pronounced in Chinese pidgin, the economic patois.

Like most pidgins, it is most easily understood through half-closed ears: 'Tumolo mai no kan kum', for example, means 'I can't come tomorrow' in Chinese pidgin. Although the trading tongue was largely replaced by standard English at the end of the nineteenth century, many pidgin words had already lodged permanently in English. When you take a 'look-see', or declare that you 'no can-do', or even enter a 'no-go area', you are expressing the remnants of a mercantile language formed by the origins of Anglo-Chinese trade.

Phrases such as 'long time no see', another Chinese pidgin construction, have a poetry that is peculiar to pidgin. With a restricted vocabulary, pidgin must work harder to say something for which there may be a single word in another, more established language, but the result is often delightful. Among the Koorie people in the Australian Outback, for example, a solar eclipse is 'Kerosene lamp him b'long Jesus-Christ gone bugger-up altogether'.

Traditionally, pidgins are languages of convenience: when a form of language is used from birth among a distinct group of speakers, it ceases to be a pidgin and becomes 'creolised'. Creole, in some ways, is established pidgin.

Tok Pisin, for example, is the creole spoken in Papua New Guinea, with sixteen consonants, five vowels and a vocabulary derived from English, but also German, Portuguese and Austronesian languages. The name 'Tok Pisin' comes from 'talk' and 'pidgin'.

Pidgin words are almost infinitely adaptable. 'Gras', for example, in Tok Pisin, is descended from the English word 'grass'; but 'gras bilong het' (literally 'grass belong hat') is 'hair'; 'gras bilong pisin' (pigeon: the bird and the language are the same in pidgin) means 'feathers'; 'gras bilong sol-wara' (salt water) is 'seaweed'; and 'gras nogut' (no-good grass) is 'weeds'.

The Lord's Prayer in Tok Pisin is a thing of beauty:

> Papa bilong mipela Yu stap long heven.
> Nem bilong yu i mas i stap holi.
> Kingdom bilong yu i mas i kam.

Ponglish, by contrast, is a combination tongue in its infancy. It is unlikely to expand widely enough, or live long enough, to grow up into creole and provide a complete rendering of The Lord's Prayer. But it joins a large family of hardy hybrids, including Spanglish (Spanish-English), Hinglish (Hindi/Punjabi/Urdu-English) and Chinglish (Chinese-English).

These languages are born when a new tongue meets English, falls in love and makes a baby.

Potty-talk, the discreet art of the loophemism

MY GRANDFATHER, A FORMER naval commander, used to announce that he intended to 'go and pump ship'. My grandmother, however, was more likely to enquire if anyone needed to 'spend a penny', or disappear to 'powder her nose'. My great uncle, on the other hand, liked to scandalise his relatives by declaring loudly that he needed to 'point Percy at the porcelain'.

Euphemisms for excretion – or 'loophemisms' – are one of the most fertile areas of the English language. By the latest count, there are no fewer than 103 separate ways of saying the unsayable.

Englishmen and women will tie themselves in linguistic knots to avoid calling a toilet a toilet, or lavatory, or loo. There are more synonyms for this room than any other, ranging from blunt slang to fastidious genteelisms: WC, khazi, bog, thunder box, little house, chapel of ease, the usual offices, privy, rest room, the amenities, jakes and thousands more.

Love of a good loophemism is (or was) a peculiarly British trait. No other language has such a rich stock of these phrases, for the lavatorial euphemism combines two profound national characteristics: a delight in word-play, and the ingrained belief that going to the loo is embarrassing and therefore extremely funny.

There was a time when every family, and even individuals within a single family, would have a different way of saying the same thing.

Writers compete to mince words in this arena.

John Betjeman would announce: 'I need to go and stand up' (or 'sit down').

In Anthony Powell's *Journals*, guests are asked: 'Do you want to put your hat straight?' In *Time Must Have a Stop* (1946) Aldous Huxley refers to 'a place where even the King goes on foot – *enfin*, the toilet chamber'. This is one of the few examples of a lavatorial euphemism that crosses language boundaries to make a universal socio-political point.

The French also refer to the room *où le roi va seul* and Russians announce they are going 'where even the Tsar goes on foot'.

One strand of loophemism involves invoking some activity that one could not possibly be doing. 'Excuse me while I go and turn the vicar's bike around/see a man about a dog/look at the garden/water the horse.'

Another subset subtly implies the activity itself. 'I need to drop the kids off at the pool/go and see a friend off to the coast/empty the teapot to make room for another cup.'

Others do the same job more graphically: 'I am just going to bleed the lizard/squeeze the peach/wring out my socks/shake hands with my best friend', and so on.

Tracing the roots of lavatorial language is difficult, since such euphemisms tend to be flushed away almost as quickly as they are produced.

The phrase to 'go and pick a daisy' may refer to the floral patterns on Victorian chamber pots.

To 'go for a quick burst on the banjo' apparently refers to the Japanese word for loo: *benjo*.

The term to 'go north', much in vogue in the 1950s, may be traced to Noel Coward, who sang of it in a lavatorial context in 'The Stately Homes of England'. The origin of 'spending a penny' is more obscure. I have long believed this phrase to be the legacy of a professional magician named Jasper Maskelyne. During the Second World War Maskelyne ran the Magic Gang, a motley group of conjurors and stage performers whose task it was to bamboozle the enemy by sleight of hand; before the war he invented the first coin-operated toilet door.

Nigel Rees, author of *A Man About a Dog: Euphemisms and Other Examples of Verbal Squeamishness*, points out that we may have been spending a penny at least a century earlier.

Toilets were provided at the Great Exhibition in Hyde Park in 1851, costing one penny, and the first permanent public toilet opened in London four years later. Oddly, this euphemism has survived immune from inflation. According to the website measuringworth.com, the cost of 'spending a penny' should have risen to about 34p.

But while some loophemisms are evergreen, most seem oddly dated. During the war there was a boom in such locutions: a wartime wee was described as going to 'check the blackout', 'go and see the man I joined up with' or even 'go and telephone Hitler' – the latter phrase was particularly popular among members of the French Resistance.

Today, the parlour game of coining loophemisms may be dying out. No one powders their nose today, or puts their hat straight, let alone makes use of the coy little boy's/girl's room. Perhaps we no longer feel any need to skirt around the unmentionable, or squirt great clouds of verbal air-freshener through the smallest room in the house. Or perhaps we have just run out of ideas for one of the most euphemised activities in the world.

As George says in *Who's Afraid of Virginia Woolf?*, when asked by Honey where she may 'put powder on her nose': 'Martha, won't you show her where we keep the . . . euphemism?'

Speaking perfect Bush

WHEN GEORGE W. BUSH left office, the war finally came to an end. For years the President had struggled, locked in mortal combat, determined to crush and destroy an enemy that his father confronted before him. At times, Bush seemed weighed down by the conflict, but he never gave up the fight. This war was personal.

I refer, of course, to George W. Bush's single-handed and brutal battle with the English language.

No leader of modern times (with the possible exception of John Prescott) has attacked the language with such sustained violence. No other politician can match Bush's ability to mangle syntax and sense into surreal shapes. Even quite simple sentences found themselves remoulded into Byzantine complexity in the passage from Bush's brain to his mouth.

Malapropisms, neologisms, spoonerisms, mispronunciations and other verbal exotica poured out of the President in torrents. Rogue nouns would suddenly wander into his sentences and refuse to leave. Verbs, prepositions, tenses were locked in permanent conflict.

Jacob Weisberg, editor of *Slate* magazine, began collecting these 'Bushisms' at the start of the Bush administration, and has since published no fewer than six volumes of the President's verbal gaffes, selling more than half a million copies and almost as many calendars.

Covering Bush's campaign in 2000 was often an exercise in approximate translation. I was privileged to be present in Iowa when Bush told an audience: 'It's a world of madmen and uncertainty and potential mental losses.' I still have no idea what he meant, but the word has entered my family's lexicon: a 'mential loss' is what happens whenever anyone says something particularly idiotic, or mislays the car keys.

Bush's refashioning of the language might be incomprehensible, but it also had a sort of accidental, internal poetry. An enterprising schoolteacher, Dirk Schulze, welded together some of Bush's more famously peculiar phrases to create an entire poem:

Rarely is the question asked:
Is our children learning?
Will the Highways of the Internet become more few?
How many hands have I shaked?

Occasionally, Bush can get stuck in his own circular grammar, producing a mellifluous if meaningless rap: 'When I was
coming up, it was a dangerous world, and you knew exactly
who they were. It was us versus them, and it was clear who
them was. Today, we are not so sure who the they are, but
we know they're there.'

This is reminiscent of Donald Rumsfeld, the acknowledged master of inadvertent existential poetry:

As we know, there are known knowns.
There are things we know we know.
We also know there are known unknowns.

Opinion has long been divided over whether Bush's inarticulacy is natural or partly feigned, the mark of an honest
Texan with no time for fancy talk, or evidence of mental
(and possibly mential) confusion.

Sometimes Bush's linguistic slips brought out a hidden
truth. He once declared that racial quotas tended to 'vulcan-
ise society'. He meant to say 'Balkanise', of course, but the
malapropism probably more nearly captured what he meant:
vulcanisation (after Vulcan, the Roman god of fire) is the
process whereby rubber is cured with sulphur or other chem-
icals to create an artificial substance that is harder, denser
and insoluble. A society divided by race is truly vulcanised.

Weisberg himself admits that 'Bushisms give a misimpression of Bush; and the misimpression is they make him sound
like he's dumb.' Bush is careless of the way he speaks, he

reaches for long words and then falls over them, but this is very far from a sign of stupidity. In Weisberg's words: 'He has some particular kinds of intelligence that serve him very well. He has a strong interpersonal intelligence in that he reads people very quickly and very well.' Many Americans came to relish his unique way with words.

Bush became adept at mocking his own inarticulacy. One never knew where the language might take him, and nor did he. I remember after one particularly baffling extemporised speech, when Bush passed the press corps he simply grinned and asked: 'Bumble through OK?'

In part, Bush's language is inherited, for his father was prone to the same linguistic chaos. The former President startled a group of foreign tourists in 1992 by attempting to begin a conversation with the words 'Hey, hey, nihaoma. Hey, yeah, yeah. Heil, heil-a kind of Hitler salute.' 'Nihaoma' is Mandarin for 'How are you?' The rest is untranslatable.

In the end, Bush's numerous assaults on the English language did no harm, which cannot be said of his other battles.

At a rally in Oregon recently, President Bush declared: 'I hope you leave here and walk out and say: "What did he say?"'

Of the epitaphs on the Bush era, 'What did he say?' will be among the kindest.

A FIB: the ultimate form of geek poetry

IT IS MUCH EASIER to tell a fib than to write one. A fib is a new sort of poetry, born of the internet, and the latest evidence of the way that the language is evolving in cyberspace in the oddest ways.

The fib is a six-line, twenty-syllable poem in which the number of syllables in each line is the sum of the syllables in the two preceding lines. This corresponds to the Fibonacci sequence, one of the most elegant patterns in mathematics, in which each successive number is the sum of the two previous numbers: 1,1, 2, 3, 5, 8.

Here is a fib written by Gregory K. Pincus, a screenwriter, part-time librarian and aspiring children's author, which he posted on his blog in 2006.

One
Small,
Precise,
Poetic,
Spiralling mixture:
Maths plus poetry yields the Fib.

(Theoretically a fib could be continued infinitely, but that would be impractical: the twentieth line of a fib would have to contain 6,765 syllables.)

Composing fibs is an enjoyable parlour game, a way to force words into a pattern, but at their best fibs can be rather beautiful, a cross between a haiku and an equation, at once free and regulated.

The Fibonacci sequence was introduced to Western mathematics in 1202 by Leonardo of Pisa, known as Fibonacci. Pincus was not the first to adapt the sequence to art. Béla Bartók used Fibonacci numbers in his music, and the sequence makes an appearance (written in invisible ink on the floor of the Louvre) in Dan Brown's *The Da Vinci Code*. It even appears in nature: the nautilus, a tropical marine creature, has a multi-chambered spiral shell that follows the curve of the Fibonacci sequence as it grows.

But Pincus was the first to give the fib a name, a place in cyberspace, and thus a platform that has spawned an entirely new wave of poetry. Within weeks of Pincus's first post, fibs had begun to pour on to his website, other websites linked in, the *New York Times* picked up the idea and thousands of fibs began appearing all over the web, on hundreds of websites. Within two months of inventing the fib, Mr Pincus had secured a two-book publishing deal, and a cult following.

'What's striking about this story,' writes Mark Abley in *The Prodigal Tongue*, his fascinating account of developing English, 'is not just the quality of responses, nor even their quantity, so much as the speed at which a new literary form burgeoned across cyberspace.'

And like everything else on the internet, mathematical poetry has acquired a life of its own.

First cousin to the fib is the cadae, which relies on the concept of pi, or p, the ratio of a circle's circumference to its diameter. (The word itself corresponds, alphabetically, to the first five digits of p, 3.14159. C=3, A=1, D=4 etc.) Where fibs number syllables, the cadae is an arrangement of words with letter-counts corresponding to the sequence of p: three in the first word, one in the next and so on.

Michael Keith has written an entire 'Cadaeic cadenza' called 'Near a Raven', a tribute to 'The Raven' (1844). Not so much Edgar Allan Poe as Edgar Allan Pi, it begins:

Poe. E (3.1)
Near a Raven (415)
Midnights so dreary, tired and weary. (926535)
Silently pondering volumes as extolling all by-now obsolete lore. (897932384)

This continues for eighteen verses, taking the process to 660 decimal places. It is mathematically perfect, poetically baffling and almost exquisitely pointless.

Perhaps of more use is the mnemonic sentence composed by Sir James Jeans, an English astrophysicist, to enable students to remember p to twenty-four digits by the letters in each word: 'How I want a drink, alcoholic of course, after the heavy chapters involving quantum mechanics' (i.e. 314159265358979).

Some have hailed the fib as the ultimate form of geek poetry, a creative process in which number-crunching combines with word-crunching for people with too much time on their hands. No one could predict that the sonnet would take off as it did after it was introduced into English in the early sixteenth century. Fibs may just be the sonnets of the internet age. So here goes:

> I
> Think
> Fibbing
> Can't be bad
> Until, of course, the
> Process drives us all barking mad.

Cigarettes are good for your love life, and your career

EVER SINCE THE SMOKING ban in enclosed public places came into force last July, there has been a marked upsurge in smirting, proving that the great British public can adapt and adopt new words in the most unlikely circumstances.

'Smirting' happens when two people, smoking outside, fall to flirting, and discover that they have more in common than simply nicotine. In Ireland, where the term originated after the ban in 2004, there is even evidence of non-smokers joining the smoky throng outside because the atmosphere there is more flirtatious.

Perhaps the sense of sharing a semi-illicit activity adds to the sexual frisson. Rain even seems to encourage smirting, since smokers must huddle closer together.

'Smirting' is a portmanteau word, formed by packing parts of two words together to create another, combining the sense of each. 'Smirting' is a first cousin of 'smog' (smoke + fog). The notion of a portmanteau word is comparatively new. In Lewis Carroll's *Through the Looking Glass* (1871), Humpty Dumpty explains to Alice: '"slithy" means "lithe and slimy" . . . You see it's like a portmanteau – there are two meanings packed up into one word'; later the doomed egg adds: '"Mimsy" is "flimsy and miserable" (there's another portmanteau . . . for you).'

A portmanteau was a suitcase that hinged in the middle like a book, allowing one to carry clothes in one side and anything else in the other. The word is itself a portmanteau, formed by combining *porter*, the French for 'to carry', with *manteau*, meaning 'coat', 'cloak' or 'mantle'.

Before Carroll, the offspring of word marriages were rare, yet a number sneaked into the language anyway: 'dumb-found', a combination of 'dumb' and 'confound', and 'twirl', a portmanteau of 'twist' and 'swirl'. In 1896, *Punch* invented 'brunch', combining 'breakfast' and 'lunch'.

Yet today the portmanteau is probably the most fertile vehicle for neologisms. Entire countries have been formed by packing two place names together: 'Tanzania', for example, was formed in 1964, linguistically speaking, by combining 'Tanganyika' and 'Zanzibar'. Many people seem to regard 'Oxbridge' as a place, rather than an idea.

This is only a guesstimate (guess + estimate), but the internet (international + network) has produced thousands of new portmanteau words: 'blog' ('web' and 'log'), 'webinar' (a web-based seminar), 'Wikipedia' and so on.

Portmanteau words offer excellent opportunities for insults. 'Celebutard' is a rare blend of three words, 'celebrity', 'debutant' and 'retard', and more or less precisely describes Paris Hilton. 'Bliar' was a fortuitous combination that did incalculable damage to Tony Blair.

Combining the names in a famous couple can be a way of implying that they are a brand, indistinguishable as individuals: Billary (Bill and Hillary Clinton); Brangelina (Brad Pitt and Angelina Jolie). Some marrying couples, to avoid the social connotations of double-barrelling or to retain nominal independence, combine their names into a portmanteau: Miss Smith and Mr Jones became Mr and Mrs Smones or, less melodiously, the Jiths.

This trend began on 18 May 1992, in New York, when Valerie Silverman married Michael Flaherty and they became Mr and Mrs Flaherman. The combined surname solution would not work for everyone. If, say, I had married someone with the name Baldwin, then we might have ended up as the Baldtyres. Imagine if Mr Dickens married Miss Whitehead. Whitens is not a particularly attractive surname, but it is a lot better than the alternative.

The Watergate affair gave birth to the laziest and longest-running family of blend words, not so much portmanteaux as identical cheap matching luggage. The suffix '-gate' is routinely attached as journalistic shorthand to anything that might be even vaguely scandalous. Squidgygate, Monicagate, Whitewatergate and Nipplegate – Janet Jackson's celebrated self-exposure at the 2004 Super Bowl, which may be the stupidest gate-word ever coined but which left us with a handy and lasting euphemism in the form of 'wardrobe malfunction'.

The best portmanteaux are those that reflect a new way of thinking and behaving. 'Viagravation', for example, meaning 'problems caused in a relationship by altered sexual expectations' and 'sacrilicious', which precisely captures the pleasure of being rude about someone else's religious beliefs, and was coined by that master-etymologist, Homer Simpson.

The term 'smirting' fulfils this requirement, but the new habit, and accompanying new word, may not end there. Because senior executives now have to smoke outside along with everyone else, they apparently get to know the other smokers in the office better than non-smoking workers, and are thus more likely to promote them. Smoking may be bad for your health, but it might be good for your career. What is the correct term for this new social interaction? Smokomotion? Increasing your cancearning potential? Working nicovertime? Being a brownlung?

To tell the whole truthiness, and nothing but

MRS MORTIMER'S ODYSSEY WAS truly remarkable. Between 1849 and 1854, she published three volumes of travel writing, covering Europe, Asia, Africa and the Americas, each larded with her own special brand of disdain. The Portuguese were 'the clumsiest people in Europe'; the Welsh were 'not very clean'; the Zulus were 'a miserable race'.

Favell Lee Mortimer held her Victorian readers spell-bound with her colourful descriptions of foreign lands and their benighted inhabitants.

But what made Mrs Mortimer's attitude to foreign countries even more extraordinary was that she had never been to any of them. Mrs Mortimer wrote her entire travelogue from her drawing room in England. Apart from a child-hood trip to Paris and Brussels, she never set foot outside this country and had no wish to – already convinced, as she was, that abroad was full of all those clumsy, unhygienic and unhappy foreigners.

Mrs Mortimer's spiritual heir is the former Lonely Planet writer Thomas Kohnstamm, who cheerfully admitted that he had written a section of the Colombia guide without having visited the country. Bogus travel writing has a long and inglorious history, but in another way Kohnstamm is representative of a wider and more modern malaise: writers reviewing books they have not read, politicians claiming to have braved dangers they never faced, novelists depicting places they have not seen, memoirists describing a past that never happened, journalists making up stories about people that never existed and, most pernicious of all, writers simply cutting and pasting words they have not written.

In most cases this is not active deception, but rather a strange cultural blurring of truth and fiction, the confusion of first-hand knowledge with second-hand electronic cut-tings, the elision of personal experience with a reality bor-rowed or imagined from elsewhere.

This is the victory of information over experience. In Wiki-world, where so much semi-reliable information is available at the push of a button, there is no need to see something first-hand in order to be able to describe it with conviction and authority. A comparison of Paris guidebooks reveals entire chunks of identical text for some tourist spots: why actually visit somewhere to find out what it is like when one can merely paste together a version of reality?

Hillary Clinton's embarrassed writhings after it was revealed that she had not actually come under sniper fire in Bosnia in 1996 are emblematic of this strange melding of fact and imagination. In her own mind Mrs Clinton did not lie, or even exaggerate, but rather 'misspoke'. Appropriating the broader reality of a situation for political gain was nothing more than a 'minor blip'.

At all levels of the culture, the ability to spin a good yarn is valued more highly than its veracity. Novelists, of course, can make up whatever they like, but I could not help feeling oddly cheated to discover that Stef Penney, the prize-winning author of *The Tenderness of Wolves*, had set that novel entirely in Canada without ever seeing the place.

Far more damaging is the spate of misery memoirs depicting various degrading aspects of human behaviour – drug addiction, alcoholism, abuse, poverty – that are really novels, or at best novelised reality.

Even more worryingly, it seems that most readers do not really care whether the horror is true or not: voyeurs would rather not know that the whole thing is merely an act, a simulacrum of reality.

The plagiarism of words is a familiar crime, but the plagiarising of experience is something more subtle, and far harder to detect. 'I never read a book before reviewing it,' declared Sidney Smith. 'It prejudices a man so.' There is now an entire literary subculture devoted to the art of not-reading books, but pretending to have done so. In his recent book *How to Talk about Books You Haven't Read*, the professor of French literature Pierre Bayard offered a complete guide for literary charlatans.

OK, I admit that I have not read all of Professor Bayard's book, but what I did read was both ironic, in that slightly baffling French way, and deeply depressing, since it accepted as axiomatic that no one would ever want to read a challenging book for pleasure when a six-word crib, or a quick skim, will do the trick.

There is even a new word for this sort of fakery: 'truthiness'. Coined by the American television comedian Stephen Colbert, truthiness describes anything that a person claims to know intuitively without regard to actual experience, evidence or the facts. In Colbert's words: 'We're not talking about truth, we're talking about something that seems like truth – the truth we want to exist.' When Mrs Clinton remembered dodging the bullets in Bosnia, she was indulging in truthiness, adopting an experience she wanted to be true.

Whenever a politician claims to be speaking 'from the heart', he or she is likely to be expressing truthiness more than truth. The row over James Frey's partly invented memoir *A Million Little Pieces* was an object lesson in truthiness, and the danger of melding fact and fiction.

When Thomas Kohnstamm wrote about the sights of Colombia without seeing them, his descriptions were not exactly untrue, merely exercises in truthiness. Does it need to be said that there is no substitute for reading the book, or describing the beauties of Colombia from first-hand? A nonfiction memoir that tells the truth, rather than a truth the author has wished into words, packs an emotional punch that is the equal of the greatest fiction.

Mrs Mortimer's crime was not just to be an armchair travel writer who imagined a world she never visited; it was not just that she saw that imaginary world through a thick veil of ignorance and prejudice. Mrs Mortimer's problem was that by relying on truthiness, she managed to get her view of the world consistently, vividly and hilariously wrong.

The Atwood sisters headed Heavenward with a mushroom warning attached

OF LAST WORDS, NONE is more final than an epitaph: a definitive moment of self-congratulation, a conclusive opportunity to commend oneself to the Almighty or simply a chance to settle old scores in stone.

Epitaphs have fallen out of fashion over the past half-century – which is a pity, for the English epitaph is often a thing of beauty and sly wit. The late Robin Cook is the only modern personality I can think of with a memorable epitaph: 'I may not have succeeded in halting the war, but I did secure the right of Parliament to decide on war.' In its self-justification, precision with words and slightly rebarbative tone of superiority, it perfectly reflects the man.

Epitaphs are not supposed to be true. The epitaph is a single pithy statement, either by or about the lately departed. There are few words more carefully crafted and carved out of the language: the epitaph writer has a very small page, and only a few words to play with.

'That's all, Folks!' reads the inscription on the headstone of Mel Blanc, the voice of Bugs Bunny. Spike Milligan's grave memorably insists: 'I told you I was ill.' Distinct from the one-liners are the exhortatory epitaphs: 'Here lies the body of Jonathan Swift ... where savage indignation can tear his heart no more. Go, traveller, and if you can, imitate one who with his utmost strength protected liberty.' W. B. Yeats considered Swift's 'the greatest epitaph in history'.

My favourite epitaphs are those that tell a story. In most instances the events behind the headstone can never be fully known, but the few words leave the taste of a mystery part-obscured.

Take, for example, the gravestone of Donald Robertson at Hillswick in the Shetland Islands, who died on 4 June 1847. 'A peaceable, quiet man, and to all appearances a sincere Christian . . . his death was caused by the stupidity of Laurence Tulloch, who sold him nitre instead of Epsom salts, by which he was killed in the space of five hours after taking a dose of it.' Why do I feel that there is more to this story than Tulloch's chemical confusion? Perhaps it is the phrase 'to all appearances'. If I were investigating Robertson's death, I would start by interviewing whoever paid for his gravestone, which fingers Tulloch but is unable to resist a small moral jab at the deceased.

An epitaph can offer an entire play in a few words, like that of Ellen Shannon in Nova Scotia, 'Who was fatally burned March 21, 1879, by the explosion of a lamp filled with R.E. Danforth's Non-Explosive Burning Fluid'. I can find no other reference to Danforth's Fluid. Shannon's gravestone appears to be the only place it was ever written down: in attempting to damn Danforth's Non-Explosive Burning Fluid from beyond the grave, Ellen Shannon gave this fatally misleading product eternal life.

All epitaphs are, in a way, warnings, but some read like health and safety announcements. Elizabeth Picket of Stoke Newington, her headstone proclaims, died in 1781 at the age of twenty-three, 'in consequence of her clothes taking fire'. The stone warns: 'Reader if you ever should witness such an affecting scene, recollect that the only method to extinguish the flame is to stifle it by an immediate covering.'

The grave of the three Atwood sisters offers similarly grave counsel. The sisters 'were poisoned by eating

funguous vegetables mistaken for champignons' in 1808:
'Let it be a solemn warning that in our most grateful enjoy-
ments even in our necessary food may lurk deadly poison.'
There is something rather touching about the sisters heading
Heavenward with a severe mushroom warning attached.

While most epitaphs speak of piety and uxorious love,
a few echo with resentment, recrimination and adultery.
Charles Ward's grave of 1770 carried an addendum: 'This
stone was not erected by SUSAN his wife. She erected a
stone to JOHN SLATER her second husband, forgetting the
affection of CHARLES WARD her first husband.' So there.

The widow of John Barnes, in a Vancouver cemetery, did
put up a stone for her late husband, which reads like a 'situation vacant' notice: 'Sacred to the memory of my husband,
John Barnes, who died January 3, 1803. His comely young
widow, aged 23, has many qualifications of a good wife, and
yearns to be comforted.' But the greatest untold story in an
epitaph is that on a casket in Madeley, Shropshire, which
simply reads: 'Mary Tooth, died November 15th 1843, Aged
65 years The Beloved Companion, Faithful friend and zealous Successor of the late Mrs Fletcher of blessed memory.'
Did Mary Tooth succeed her friend in the affections of Mr
Fletcher? Exactly how zealous was she? And what unspoken
warfare existed between these two bosom friends? Mary
Tooth's grave is silent, but her epitaph speaks volumes.

Eat your words

IT IS SWEET TO reflect, as you savour a bar of chocolate,
that you are also consuming a little of the ancient Aztec language, Nahuatl. The Aztecs called the juice from the pods

of the cacao tree *xocoatl*, which meant 'bitter water'. The Spaniards first adopted and then adapted this pretty word, and the English misheard it from Spanish, as 'chocolate'. The Aztecs may have gone, but their language lives on, in Quality Street, Mars and Easter eggs.

Food is surely the single most important conveyer of words between and among languages. Early travellers traded in exotic goods, but also in words. Just as our palates were changed and expanded with foreign tastes, so the English language has been constantly enriched by new and strange food words, which were themselves gradually absorbed into everyday speech.

Chocolate was only one element of the linguistic banquet laid on by the Aztecs. They gave us guacamole, chilli and tomato, the supposedly aphrodisiac qualities of which persuaded hopeful Italians to dub it the 'golden apple', *pomodoro*. Some Nahuatl words were quite indigestible. *Tlilxochitl*, for example, was a prized delicacy meaning 'black flower'. The Spanish simply couldn't get their tongues around it, so Willem Piso, a Spanish doctor serving under the Governor of Brazil, renamed it 'vanilla' (meaning 'little sheath').

'Avocado' comes from the Nahuatl term for 'testicle', on account of its shape. This piece of information may explain the collapse of the Aztec empire. It is amazing they could even walk.

Fewer than one quarter of words in English reflect its Germanic origin: the rest have been plundered (a Swedish word) from other tongues, and frequently via the kitchen table. Words travel in much the same way as trade and tastes in food, so different cultures have adapted and served different food words in different ways.

Food words invade with the invaders. 'Wine', 'pepper', 'butter', 'radish' all came to English from the Roman invasion. 'Cheese' is related to the Latin *caseus*. The Norman Conquest brought a banquet of table words, as sophisticated French cookery colonised simpler Saxon fare. It is only a slight exaggeration to say that the Normans invented English cooking words: Saxon animals (sheep, pig, cow) became Norman terms when cooked and seasoned: 'mutton', 'pork' and 'beef'. More exotic words followed: 'gravy', 'mustard', 'liquorice'.

Food words were exported from wherever the empire spread. And when no word was easily available for import, its very foreignness became its description. 'Walnut', for example, comes from Old English 'walhnutu', which means 'foreign nut', since the first walnuts seen in Britain came from Italy.

'Sugar' was introduced to Western Europe by Berbers about 1,000 years ago, from the Arabic *sukkar*. The roots of 'apricot' can be dug back, via Spanish, to the *al-burquq*, a fruit introduced to Andalusia by the Arabs. 'Marzipan' may take its name from a Burmese city, and 'orange' grew from the Sanskrit word for the citrus tree, *naranj*. When a weird-looking vegetable from the Mediterranean appeared in Britain in the early sixteenth century, English tongues simply adopted its Arabic name, *al-kharshuf*, and mangled it into English: 'artichoke'.

'Squash' was adapted from a word in the Native American language Narragansett, *askutasquash*, meaning 'vegetable eaten while green'. 'Kedgeree' comes from the Hindi *khichiri*. The word 'miso' first appears in English in the logbooks of William Adams, the Elizabethan trader and adventurer.

Spices blazed their own etymological trail. 'Coriander', slightly unnervingly, comes from the Greek word for bedbug, *koris*: apparently coriander smells of crushed bedbugs. 'Potato' is a Spanish corruption of the Carib *batata*, a solid, round, tuberous word that somehow fits.

Some words match the food they describe, and some do not. The word 'margarine' was invented by Hippolyte Mège-Mouriès in 1869 and was adapted from the far more poetic Persian term *murwarid*, meaning 'pearls', a reference to the fatty droplets that formed marge. 'Its name is far lovelier than its taste,' reflects Henry Hitchens, author of *The Secret Life of Words*, a fascinating exploration of the rich borrowings, exchanges and couplings of the language. 'If only we could disassociate the two.'

While English was almost omniverous, a few food words have been too big to swallow. Early visitors to Hawaii were thrilled to find a fish called a *humuhumunukunukupuaa*, but as a food, and a word, it never caught on. Some words, like some foods, are best consumed where they originate.

How H.G. Wells put a
man on the moon

DOODLING ON HIS NOTEPAD in 1981, the science fiction writer William Gibson was trying to think of a name for an invisible electronic communications network he had dreamt up for a new short story, 'Burning Chrome'. 'Dataspace'? No, he crossed that out. ' Infospace'? No, too nerdy. Then he hit on the perfect word, scientific-sounding but also alliterative and oddly poetic: 'cyberspace'. Later, he reflected: 'It seemed like an effective buzzword. It seemed evocative and essentially meaningless.'

It would be another decade before the internet transformed the world, but a novelist's imagination had already given shape and meaning to something that science had yet to invent. The naming of cyberspace is just one example of the way fiction has informed scientific fact, which in turn enriches the fiction of science in a strange, endlessly self-replicating process that is unique to the genre. Science fiction writing is too often dismissed as childish, badly written and unrealistic (it is often all three); science writing tends to be drab and dry. But science fiction, at its best, is proof of the art and poetry that lie at the heart of great science, and the way science can underpin the finest literature.

The late Arthur C. Clarke embodied the symbiosis between scientific expertise and the novelist's imagination. Like all great science fiction writers, he wrote of futures and technologies on the outer edge of possibility that almost magically lured the truth towards them.

His science was scrupulous and rigorous. His was not science fantasy, nor the creation of invented worlds to cast a light on this one. He imagined humans in a not-so-distant future in which science – genuine science – has changed the world. His imagineering was usually optimistic, and astonishingly accurate.

Clarke's capacity for prophecy was extraordinary precisely because his imagination was so wide, and his scientific expertise so deep. In 1945, more than a decade before the first orbital rocket flight, he predicted communications satellites in fixed orbits high above the Earth. (He was dissuaded from patenting this idea by a lawyer, who insisted it was too outlandish to be taken seriously: Clarke later wrote a book on the subject, with the subtitle: *How I Lost a Billion Dollars in My Spare Time.*) He explained how man would land on the Moon, and when *2001: A Space Odyssey* imagined a Moon base. Nasa now envisages a permanent Moon colony as a staging post on the journey to Mars.

Clarke knew that the greatest technological achievements lay not simply in the appliance of the laws of physics, but in the more subtle and unpredictable ways of the imagination. The dream precedes the reality: 'I'm sure we would not have had men on the Moon if it had not been for H.G. Wells and Jules Verne,' he once said.

The greatest science fiction writers sometimes got it spectacularly wrong (one that sticks in the mind is the inspired though sadly never-attempted idea of keeping hundreds of cats in an insulator with a device for stroking them to create static electricity). Or very nearly right but not quite. H.G. Wells correctly predicted, as early as 1907, that there would be a fierce aerial conflict with Germany (*The War in the Air*), but he got the technology wrong: the fighting flying machines in his novel flap their wings.

Fiction writers have also imagined and inspired future reality, often unintentionally. Douglas Adams thought up an electronic, hand-held book with all of galactic knowledge in it. He named this impossible invention *The Hitchhiker's Guide to the Galaxy*; we call it a BlackBerry.

Orwell's 'versificator' in *1984*, which generates pap music to keep the proletariat docile, prefigured the computer software used to churn out pop music today. Verne predicted the submarine and the rocket ship, deploying the most reliable science he could muster. Igor Sikorsky was inspired in 1939 by Verne's *Robur the Conqueror* (1886), to build the first helicopter, a device with propellers that has 'made conquest of the air'. The pioneer of parallel supercomputing, Daniel Hills, decided to study artificial intelligence after reading the works of Isaac Asimov and Robert Heinlein.

Sci-fi has crept, almost unnoticed and usually unacknowledged, from popular culture into popular technology. Your mobile telephone with the flip-down mouthpiece owes a debt to *Star Trek*, as do automatic sliding doors in supermarkets.

But perhaps the most important legacy of Verne, Clarke and other science fiction pioneers is the simple idea that fiction can inspire fact; that making up vivid stories from science inspires more and better science. Many scientists openly acknowledge the inspiration of fiction. Astronauts read space novels to expand their own dreams, to influence and inspire real life, as all great literature must.

Science fiction is important less for its prophetic ability to offer blueprints for machines as yet unmade than for its capacity to instil wonder and adventure in the pursuit of earthly science. 'Anything a man can imagine, another man can create,' wrote Verne.

Science and literature are too often seen as polar opposites. Good science fiction represents an extraordinary fusion of the two into a single narrative, a way of imagining the impossible based on the scientifically plausible. Technology is the point where human imagination and science intersect: this was the mysterious world explored by Clarke, and his most enduring invention.

A quarter of a century ago William Gibson conjured up a word that was, by his own account, meaningless, a portentous-sounding term for something that did not yet exist. That might stand as the best definition of great science fiction: the art of inventing words for science to aspire to.

Roget, in other words

LET US NOW PRAISE, admire, commend, extol, honour, eulogise, congratulate and applaud Peter Mark Roget, the patron saint of synonyms.

But let us first tackle the 150-year-old debate over whether Roget's *Thesaurus*, which first appeared in May 1852, is the most useful book ever written or, conversely, a blight on the language that has enabled countless lazy writers to bulk up their prose with words they barely understand and immediately forget.

A thesaurus may be both these things. At its worst, it is a crutch, for crossword enthusiasts, students desperate to imply a little learning in an essay crisis, headline writers, nervous after-dinner speakers and, yes, journalists. At its best, a thesaurus can jog out of the memory a word that would otherwise remain lost.

Critics sniffed at Roget's *Thesaurus* from the start. 'Its practical utility, we think, is overrated,' declared *Harper's Magazine*. *The London Critic* agreed, insisting that the vast compilation of words and their close relations was 'not likely to be so practically useful as the care, and toil, and thought bestowed upon it might have deserved'. How wrong they were: Roget's *Thesaurus* has sold upwards of thirty-five million copies; every edition sells more than the last.

Roget is known for this one book, written as a diversion and published late in life, but in a way his entire life was itself a homage to words, their richness, strangeness and therapeutic power.

Roget was born in London's Soho to a French Huguenot father and Swiss mother. The early death of his father and a beloved grandfather left Roget on the edge of a lifelong depression, which he salved with words: he gathered, nurtured and hoarded them. He grew into an astonishing polymath and an obsessive list maker. Taking his cue from the great taxonomist Carl Linnaeus, who codified and classified plants and animals, Roget set about organising words as a way, perhaps, of holding back the chaos he feared in his own personality, and the mental illness that ran in his family.

Roget is remembered for his book of words, but he was interested in everything. A doctor by training, and an intellectual magpie by inclination, his work on the persistence of vision (the way an image briefly lasts on the retina) would lead, eventually, to the invention of cinema. He studied Dante, water purification, dinosaur bones, phrenology and insects. He worked, lucky man, at the Pneumatic Institution for Inhalation Gas Therapy, where Coleridge came to breathe nitrous oxide. He helped to create the slide rule and London's sewerage system. He invented the first travel chess set.

The words also poured out of him: 300,000 for the *Encyclopaedia Britannica*, including the entries for 'Ant' and 'Bee'; his 250,000-word *Bridgewater Treatise* was an attempt to systematise the animate world into four branches of physiology. At the same time, he gathered words, their synonyms, their siblings, their cousins, correlatives and opposites in a vast family tree of vocabulary. He did this for half a century, starting when he was twenty-one, in private, for his own personal pleasure and self-improvement. 'Conceiving that such a compilation might help to supply my own deficiencies . . . I often found this little collection, scanty and imperfect though it was, of much use to me in literary composition.' He was seventy-three years old when he finally decided to publish the fruits of this hobby.

Roget had no time for writers who 'indulge in the habit of arbitrarily fabricating new words and newfangled phraseology . . . in the illegal mint of their own fancy'. Yet his thesaurus (a word he invented) is today at least twenty times as long as the one he published, thanks to the never-ending evolution of words and phrases.

The word gatherer made no claim to be a great writer. He was merely fascinated by the interconnectedness of words, and brilliantly realised that the more words available, the broader the possibilities of language. Some people are lucky enough to be able to find the *mot juste* without ever needing to consult those parallel words. For the rest of us, who find that the right word is sometimes lurking just out of reach, there is Roget and his thesaurus.

Of course, some use the thesaurus as a cheap supermarket, simply whipping off the shelves the first halfway decent substitute word they see. One can usually spot the thesaurus-abusers, for they tend to reverse George Orwell's rules in *Politics and the English Language*: using two words where one will do, (one syllable bad, many syllables good), and deploying a £5 word when an honest and serviceable penny word is to hand.

But, well used, Roget is a synonym for lucidity. At its best, his *Thesaurus* is a reminder of what words can do, a testament to the rich density of the language itself.

There is something refreshingly honest about Roget, a man who knew so much about so much, yet whose greatest contribution to literature was the understanding that no one can hold an entire dictionary in his head. Roget's *Thesaurus* should be used as a memory refresher, to keep the language for ever young.

That, perhaps, is what Peter Pan means in J.M. Barrie's classic, when he remarks of Captain Hook: 'The man is not wholly evil – he has a Thesaurus in his cabin.'

Spookspeak, or talking espionage

WHEN 'MISS X' OF MI6 took the stand, invisibly, during the inquest into the death of Diana, Princess of Wales, she offered a small peek into the arcane world of spookspeak, the strange, fertile and semi-secret language of spying. Miss X revealed that to assist the earlier investigation into the crash, she had temporarily been granted 'God's access' to the files of the Secret Intelligence Service (SIS): the term apparently refers to the topmost degree of security clearance, a level usually reserved for the three most senior officials of the service.

The term 'God's access' has never before been deployed in public. Before this week, it did not even exist on the internet. But it is most certainly part of the lexicon now: 'Carruthers, if we are going to get to the bottom of this parliamentary expenses fiddling, we are going to need God's access to all MPs' expenses claims.' Like all small, self-contained tribes, the intelligence community has always communicated in its own patois, a language For Your Ears Only. Euphemisms thrive in this world of disguises, half-truths and deception: sleepers and cleanskins, moles and bagmen, dead drops, honeytraps and wet jobs. Some of the language seems to have evolved organically and internally because so little of what happens in espionage can be described openly: just as agents and operations are designated by codewords, so the language of spying is itself an elaborate code, in which nothing may be described as what it is. A bodyguard is a 'babysitter', a false passport is a 'shoe', forged by a 'cobbler' and so on.

Such words serve a dual purpose: to clarify matters for those who speak the language – the 'Friends' – and to confuse or mislead those who do not.

The East German Stasi deployed an estimated 400,000 agents and informants, and developed a secret language so complex and verbose that anyone trying to sift through the files of the secret police requires the *Dictionary for State*

Security: 500 pages long, with fifty-one separate subheadings and containing almost 1,000 special jargon terms.

Many of the terms we associate with spying have been borrowed or adapted from literature. John le Carré is the master of spy language, having forged a lexicon so rich and memorable that genuine spies have adopted it: 'lamplighters' (watchers, safe-house men), 'pavement artists' (shadowers), and above all, 'moles', the spies lurking within the 'Circus'.

Aldrich Ames, the American CIA agent convicted in 1994 of spying for the Soviets and Russians, has frankly acknowledged the linguistic debt owed to le Carré. '"Mole" is the best example of jargon created by literary or journalistic use,' Ames told the *New York Times* (in a letter from prison). 'Whether or not SIS ever used it, it gradually entered use in the American community from John le Carré's novels.' There is a natural link between the language of fiction and that of spying. As Graham Greene (who joined MI6 in 1941) demonstrates so memorably in *Our Man in Havana*, the spy is already part novelist, turning his imagination into truth. As a naval intelligence officer, Ian Fleming referred to his various schemes to baffle and confuse the enemy as 'plots'; transferring those plots to fiction after the war, to create the most memorable fictional spy of all, was a natural progression. The real language of espionage and the invented language of literary spying are now so entwined that they cannot be untangled.

While spies guard their secrets, they share their vocabularies with remarkable openness. The literary language of spying was even adopted on the other side of the Iron Curtain, where some of le Carré's inventions are said to have entered KGB parlance. At the same time, Soviet spies developed their own secret language, rich with euphemism: 'illness' is Russian spy slang for someone under arrest; 'nursemaid' is the term for the security officer accompanying delegations abroad to prevent defections; a 'pig' is the term for traitor.

The term 'wet job' or 'wet work' is often used to refer to an intelligence operation that will involve bloodshed or killing. According to Ames, 'wet job' is 'a literal translation of GRU/ NKVD (former Soviet intelligence agencies) jargon for "killing" – assassination or elimination of people by murder'.

My own favourite intelligence term is 'walking the cat back'. This refers to the laborious process of examining past events in the light of present knowledge to establish exactly what happened. The image of someone trying to get a cat to retrace its steps, backwards, precisely captures the problem of reconstructing the slippery essence of espionage.

Spy language is so vivid perhaps because the real business of intelligence, in the testimony of Miss X, 'can sometimes be very boring'. In her evidence to the Diana inquest – itself a vast exercise in 'walking the cat back' – Miss X described a parallel world of paperwork in another, less colourful spy language: 'pink memos', 'white minutes', cards and indices.

God's access, it seems, can lead a secret agent into the Devil's own filing system.

Isms create schisms

'ISMS' CAN BE LETHAL. More people were killed by isms in the last century than any other suffix. Nazism, Stalinism, racism, imperialism, nationalism, totalitarianism and now Islamic fundamentalism, the labels of human bigotry, have all provoked savagery on a grand scale. 'Ologies' are not much better. Theology, ideology, even biology have all, at times, fomented conflict and violence.

The language – particularly academic language – is rife with 'isms' and 'ologies'. It is impossible to approach the formal study of art without hacking through thickets of isms: impressionism, realism, serialism, surrealism. Such words offer a convenient shorthand for pulling together very different strands of thought or behaviour. Often they obscure and oversimplify as much as they reveal and clarify.

People resort to isms to try to explain themselves and their beliefs, or, just as often, to define or denigrate the beliefs of others. From great ideas to small eccentricities, we have developed, and continue to evolve, an elaborate taxonomy of behaviours. We need them, but they can also be dangerous and deliberately misleading.

The range of human thought is so wide, it seems, that the only way to grasp its intricacies is to chop it into comprehensible lumps. Some of the larger lumps define entire swaths of history, but the smaller isms are often the most fascinating. Most people seem to crave an ism, and if an appropriate one does not exist, they invent one. George Eliot, for example, considered herself a 'meliorist', adhering to the philosophy that the world is, in general, improving. 'I will not answer to the name of optimist, but if you like to invent meliorist, I will not say you call me out of my name,' she wrote.

The formation of isms seems to follow idiosyncratic rules – or none. Thatcherism and Blairism are definable concepts, but Majorism and Brownism are not. Reaganism is a respectable political term: but a Bushism is a joke at the expense of the world's greatest living neologist, or inventor of new words.

Since ideas are complex, coining isms inevitably leads to sesquipedalianism (the use of words that are a foot-and-a-half long). The most famous is 'antidisestablishmentarianism': a term coined to describe those who opposed

Gladstone's efforts to 'disestablish' the Church of Ireland's official status as the state religion, so exempting Irish Catholics from having to tithe to two churches.

It is remarkable how many historical figures once important enough to merit their own isms are now all but forgotten. Who now follows Owenism, the Utopian beliefs of the early nineteenth-century reformer Robert Owen? Swedenborgism, named after the Swedish mystic Emanuel Swedenborg (1688–1772), once influenced thinkers and writers as diverse as Samuel Taylor Coleridge, Henry James and Helen Keller, but is now an intellectual relic.

Muggletonianism sounds like something from Harry Potter, but is a seventeenth-century English religious sect named after Ludowick Muggleton, who preached that the Apocalypse was imminent. The end was not as nigh as he thought, and Muggletonians proved more durable than Swedenborgians. One reason for their longevity, I suspect, was that they held their prayer meetings in taverns. The last Muggletonian, Philip Noakes, died in 1979, in Kent.

Some isms live on in modern parlance, while others wither. 'Jingoism' is still in widespread (and perhaps increasing) use, having been invented 130 years ago when Britain's threat to enter the Russo-Turkish War was backed up by a popular music-hall ditty:

> We don't want to fight, yet by jingo if we do, We've got the ships, we've got the men, And we've got the money too!

If some isms define the great (and terrible) intellectual movements of history, others lead us down intriguing blind alleys. Take the Collyer brothers, Homer and Langley, who lived in a large mansion on Fifth Avenue and could not throw anything away. In 1947, police broke in to find

Homer's body behind tottering piles of junk; after removing 136 tons of other things, including ten grand pianos, newspapers dating back four decades, a car and an X-ray machine, they found what remained of Langley. He had been crushed to death years earlier by his own book collection. I have suffered for years from Collyer Brothers Syndrome, Collyerism or disposaphobia, I just never knew what it was called. But otherwise I have always been averse to both isms and ologies – which I suppose makes me some sort of ismist.

Lost in translation

I RECENTLY VISITED THE Great Wall of China and found myself lost in awe. I was overpowered with admiration, stunned by the sheer ingenuity of the mistranslated noticeboard at its foot. Someone had gone to a lot of trouble to render the rules into English; each word had been analysed with extraordinary care – and each was very slightly wrong.

It began: 'Please don't carve arbitrarily on the Great Wall. Protect one brick and one stone conscientiously.' Then the signwriter offered a couple of suggestions: 'In order to keep fit no spitting' and 'Please pay attention to your safety in the rain and snow weather.' Before this rousing coda: 'Please walk carefully on abrupt slope and dangerous way: Don't run and pushes to pash violently and the laugh and frolic.'

Mistranslated English is one of the great pleasures of travelling abroad. It is, I suppose, one of the privileges of a lingua franca that English speakers have more opportunities than anyone else to see their tongue twisted. I am sure that our efforts to translate for the benefit of visitors are just as inadvertently amusing.

Mistranslations often seem to have a sort of internal poetry, conveying far more meaning than an accurate version, and sometimes offer a small glimpse into the mind of the translator. I can't help feeling that the warning not to 'pash violently and the laugh and frolic' was written by some curmudgeonly old Communist convinced that Westerners do nothing but pash violently and frolic all day.

A little further along the wall I was introduced to some of the local fauna: 'Black bear, eating meat catalog, bear branch.' Then the warning: 'Bear is a direct bowel animal so if eat sundry good easy to cause bowel block, especially plastic bag and bottle of mineral water can cause death.' I found that rather moving.

Mistranslated menus offer particularly rich fare, from the 'fried nun' found on many an Indian menu and 'hamburgers' the world over, to more elaborate preparations such as 'three cute prawns suntanning on the rice'.

There is such competition between restaurants, and such a hunger for the supposed sophistication that English affords, that linguistic over-egging is practically standard. 'Fragrant bone in garlic in strange flavour' is, of course, a precise description, if hardly enticing. But English can be just too specific, such as with the Chinese offering of 'Dumpling stuffed with the ovary and digestive glands of a crab'.

It only takes one word to go awry for the product to take on a very different complexion, such as the Japanese advert that wonders: 'Why does coffee taste so good when you're naked with your family?' On the other hand, 'Believed ham of the country' sounds so much more delicious than the merely 'authentic' or 'traditional' stuff.

I vividly remember a tailor's shop sign in India that boldly declared: 'Our best is none too good', and a French wine list promising: 'Our wines leave you nothing to hope for.' Then

there is the Cypriot restaurant that recommends of its speci-
ality dish: 'Try it, and try to forget it.'

Mistranslations may be divided into two categories.
In some, one can glimpse what the translator is driving
at, however dimly: the 'Beach of irregular bottoms' sign
in Spain, for example, or 'Beware of your luggage', and
the sign outside a cathedral in Cancún, Mexico, that says:
'Please keep loud, wild babes out of the sanctuary.' (I have
been to Cancún, and the place for loud, wild babes is in
the beachfront bars.) I particularly like the sign at Jeddah
airport: 'You are required to declare all sorts of private
things.'

Then there is the variety that simply makes no sense at
all, no matter how hard one squints, such as this sign on an
inflatable slide in Jeddah: 'Thereto each participant taken
circumspection and the carefulness the aquitable.'

The best mistranslations aspire to a degree of philosophical grandeur that would be impossible in both the language
of the translator and 'correct' English. Take, for example,
the creator of the Indian Highway Code, who reaches for
a truth more important than mere law-abiding motoring
when he (for it is surely a he) writes: 'We should not drive in
the drinking mood and with the worries of the mind. At the
time of driving, we should not accompany by ladies. If we
do it so, it will create accident.'

But before we get too smug about distorted English, it is
worth remembering that native English speakers are just as
capable as falling into the elephant traps of the language
as anyone else. For just one example, recall the famous sign
in a small Cornish hotel: 'Will any guest wishing to take
a bath please make arrangements to have one with Mrs
Harvey.'

Etymythology:
the word-legends we love

HENRY VIII DID NOT knight a lump of steak to create 'Sir Loin'; Thomas Crapper (1836–1910), despite his worthy work popularising the flush lavatory, was born several hundred years after the word 'crap' was coined; 'kangaroo' is not the Aboriginal for 'I don't understand what you are saying', supposedly the response when Captain Cook asked an Australian native to name the curious leaping creature he first saw in Queensland in 1770. (*Gangurru* means 'grey kangaroo' in the Guugu Yimithirr tongue.) And 'Welsh rarebit' derives from the word 'rabbit', even though it contains no rabbit, and doesn't come from Wales.

All of which is rather disappointing, since the false but widely accepted story of a word's origin is often so much more colourful and interesting than the truth.

Sometimes false etymologies are deliberately forged to serve a political or social purpose, but mostly they seem to emerge spontaneously, providing a psychologically or emotionally satisfying explanation for the birth of a word, irrespective of reality.

As a rule of thumb, the more elaborate and widely accepted the explanation, the more likely it is to be wrong.

Take 'rule of thumb'. For decades, it was widely believed to refer to the practice of wife-beating. One standard women's studies textbook in the US states unequivocally 'the popular expression "rule of thumb" originated from English common law, which allowed a husband to beat his wife with a whip or stick no bigger in diameter than his thumb ... (it) essentially allowed a man to beat his wife without interference from the courts'.

A pretty nasty little phrase, then, to be deployed with extreme caution and sensitivity. Except that 'rule of thumb' has no such origin: it has never appeared in any statute book, and does not originate in legalised domestic violence. The first joint of the thumb is approximately an inch in length, so the rule of thumb allowed joiners to make rough measurements (the use of 'hand' to measure the height of a horse is similar). It may also derive from the beer trade, as brewers traditionally tested the temperature of a batch of beer by sticking a thumb in.

Through no fault of its own, this innocent phrase became a semiotic battleground, with feminists using a false etymology as a stick to beat male chauvinists, and chauvinists debunking the word's false origins as a way of getting back at feminists.

The Nazis claimed, falsely, that the word 'Slav' was related to 'slave', providing a built-in etymological excuse for oppressing and enslaving Slavic peoples.

Enemies of the Dominican order (founded by Saint Dominic in the thirteenth century) falsely claimed that their name derived from *domini canes*, 'God's dogs'. Even melted cheese has been deployed for oneupmanship: 'Welsh rabbit' (which evolved, for no clear reason, into 'rarebit') was a cheap and meatless meal, dating back to when Welshness was a byword for extreme poverty. Cheese on toast became known by an ironic term, as a dig at the Welsh.

Most false or folk etymologies are not so overtly political, seeming to evolve from pure pleasure in a good story and an agreeable explanation. The myth of sirloin, for example, may date back to a pun made by the poet John Taylor in 1630, when he referred to a character who would 'presently enter combat with a worthy knight called Sir Loyne of

Beefe'. The joke was so good that it has run and run, and the act of knighting a lump of meat has been attributed, with authority but entirely without basis, to at least three kings: Henry VIII, James I and Charles II. The truth is less tasty: the word derives from the French *sur*, 'on top' or 'above', to describe the top cut of the loin.

'Marmalade' was apocryphally used by Mary Queen of Scots to treat headaches.

Whenever she tucked into a jammy confection of sliced citrus fruit, her French-speaking servants would supposedly observe: '*Marie est malade*' (Mary is ill), corrupted into 'marmalade'. A great story, but sadly only that: *marmelo* is Portuguese for quince, the original fruit used to make the stuff.

The human tendency to create and believe false origins for words is as old as language itself, a way to demystify and control the word, to stamp it with additional, local meaning. 'OK', for example, can be held to be German (from *Oberst Kommandant*, meaning 'Colonel in command') or Finnish (from *oikea*, meaning 'correct') or Scots (from *och aye*), or West African (from *o ke*, in Mandingo, meaning 'certainly'.) OK was probably coined in Boston as shorthand for 'orl korrect', but the word is now so universal that any and all may claim the word by dressing it up with a relevant backstory.

In some ways, false etymologies – etymythologies, as they are sometimes known – are like family anecdotes. They may not literally be true; indeed, they may not be true at all; yet they contain a deeper kind of truth. The true origins of words is the archaeology of human culture; what we choose to believe about the birth of words can be just as revealing.

Thinking outside the box has now jumped its shark

EVERY SO OFTEN, ONE must dare to do the unthinkable, commit a cruelty for the greater good and seize an opportunity whatever the pain: in short, one must 'shoot the puppy'.

'Shooting the puppy' is the sort of graphic phrase that seems to emerge, spontaneously, from the workplace. It has been traced back to the 1960s TV producer Chuck Barris, who imagined that the ultimate entertainment might involve seeing how much money would persuade someone to shoot a puppy live on air. 'Shooting the puppy' has come to denote a thing that only the toughest executive dares to do.

Such jargon blooms and withers with astonishing speed. A few years ago, everyone was 'thinking outside the box', 'running it up the flagpole' and exhorting others to 'wake up and smell the coffee'. Today they are more likely to talk of carrying out a 'muppet shuffle' (sacking or reassigning junior workers), searching for the 'boggle factor' (the must-have element in a retail product) or 'blamestorming', that familiar ritual in which everyone tries to pin responsibility on everyone else.

A few years ago, when a project went wrong, it had almost inevitably gone 'pear-shaped'; today it is more likely to be 'tanking' or 'circling the drain'. ('Pear-shaped' may originate from the shape of a disintegrating balloon, a pregnant or obese woman, or what happens when a glass bubble is overblown.) Often these picturesque coinages are used by professionals to lend superficial fizz to a meeting, to demonstrate a grip on cutting-edge parlance or simply to baffle everyone else. I know a venture capitalist whose favoured technique when meeting foreign business associates is to use a Britishism such as 'let's not get our knickers in a twist', in the certainty that it will utterly confuse and probably intimidate them.

New jargon often involves animal imagery. 'Kicking a dead whale up the beach' is a task that is boring and unpleasant but necessary, as in 'I have been trying to get Whitworth in accounts to do the new spreadsheets for weeks, but it's like kicking a dead whale up a beach.' 'Jumping the shark' is the moment when a project has reached a tipping point and is going downhill. The 'pig in the python' is marketing speak for a historical bump in consumer spending caused by the baby-boom generation.

'Whose ox gets gored?' is a way of asking who would suffer from a course of action. 'It's like herding cats' is a way of complaining when others won't do what you want them to do when you want them to do it.

We have all experienced a 'salmon day', though we may not know it as such. It has been spent toiling upstream, through waterfalls and cataracts, only to be killed, gutted and eaten. A similar experience is 'boiling the ocean', used to describe a task that is time-consuming, boring, ultimately impossible and entirely pointless.

Euphemism, another word for lie

'SUB-PRIME' SURELY DESERVES A prize as unquestioned euphemism of the decade. For months, as America's 'subprime mortgages' rocked financial markets across the globe, commentators deployed the word with the eagerness that people always show for a word that doesn't say what it really means.

If something is sub-prime, that means it is less than good: in other words dodgy, or just plain bad. There are plenty of words for bad: my online thesaurus lists eighty-three. But to say that US homeowners have taken out bad mortgages is too bald, too truthful. In finance, as in politics, war, sex, human waste and occasionally journalism, euphemism is a refuge from reality or – to put it more euphemistically – a way to economise with the truth.

Sub-prime is a prime example of litotes – a figure of speech in which one disguises a statement by expressing it as a negative of its opposite. 'She is not bad looking' is a less vivid way of saying that she is attractive. Someone 'not all there' is bonkers. Litotes has a long and distinguished literary pedigree: 'O, Oedipus, Unhappy Oedipus,' was Sophocles's way of saying that, having killed his father and married his mother, Oedipus was feeling distinctly sub-prime.

Minnesotans, a polite people predominantly of solid Scandinavian stock and not given to overstatement, are particularly reliant on this form of words. 'The Vikings played not too bad tonight' is the equivalent, in Minnesota-speak, to a lavish hymn of praise.

The English have a unique talent for understated circumlocution. Shirley Williams, commenting on the SDP leader David Owen: 'It does not follow that what the leader has said is the same and identical with the policy of the party. It would be excellent if he (were) prepared to listen to other points of view and possibly even consider whether there is room for some improvement on his part as well as on the part of the rest of us.'

Strip out the euphemism, and Shirley is saying that David is off message, over-critical, blind to his own faults and deaf to good advice, i.e. hers.

Euphemism is not only alive and well, but expanding, and in no area more rapidly than in warfare. The word 'war' itself tends to be clouded over in favour of 'conflict', 'engagement', 'armed confrontation', 'intervention' and so on. The War Office became the Ministry of Defence in 1964, but remains firmly in the war business.

The Reagan administration achieved a brilliant feat of verbal camouflage by describing the airborne assault on Grenada in 1983 as a 'pre-dawn vertical incursion'. Once a war is over, it often ceases to be a war at all, becoming instead 'the late unpleasantness'. Even people cease to be human in time of war: they are 'soft-skinned targets' if the enemy, and 'collateral damage' if not. The term 'friendly fire' never fails to evoke a shudder, with its inbuilt self-exculpation. Military types tend to get enraged when their carefully polished euphemisms miss the target. In the Cambodian war, one Colonel Opfer lambasted the media for failing to adopt the official euphemism: 'You always write it's bombing, bombing, bombing. It's not bombing. It's air support.'

The words used to describe the effects of war on soldiers have also evolved, in chronological order, from 'shell shock' to 'battle fatigue' to 'operational exhaustion' to 'post-traumatic stress disorder', a phrase so clinical that it loses almost all impact. 'Shell shock' at least described cause and effect.

'Euphemism' derives from the Greek for 'to speak well'. A eupheme replaced a word that could not be spoken according to religious taboo, the opposite of 'blaspheme'. Euphemisms form a code for topics too embarrassing, unpleasant or impolite to be stated directly. In many ways, they are a reflection of linguistic ingenuity. But too often they disguise the indefensible, or sweeten the unpalatable.

Businessmen have long relied on litotes to escape the stark reality of the bottom line. In 1987, the Irish businessman

Tony O'Reilly referred to a 'disimproved revenue position'.

Rather than fire workers, a company 'downsizes', 'rationalises' or 'implements a skills mix adjustment'. Rather than admit to losing money, the accountants will report 'negative cash flow', 'net profit revenue deficiencies', or the mind-bending 'negative contributions to profits'. Businessmen talk about 'preserving optionality' – finance-speak for 'doing nothing'.

If low-grade US mortgage lenders had found a more honest word to describe their loans, thousands of borrowers might have paused. But by the time they realised the meaning of the word, it was too late – and the effects of combining euphemism with optimism have been more sub-prime than anyone could have imagined.

Hell is other people

'JEEZ,' SAID THE GRIZZLED cowboy as my wife, my children and I galloped over the Montana prairie on a ranching holiday, shouting 'Yeee-Haaa!' in English accents. 'You all must be the Limey Posse.'

The remark was not, I think, intended to flatter, but I have long assumed that the term 'Limey' is a back-handed compliment, referring, as it does, to the sensible British naval practice of eating citrus fruits such as limes to ward off scurvy during the long transatlantic crossing. We owe the word to the British naval surgeon James Lind (1716–94), who worked out that Dutch sailors suffered less from vitamin deficiency than his own sailors because of their consumption of boiled cabbage. From 1795, lemons or limes were a mandatory part of the diet on British ships.

A less flattering etymology, however, holds that 'Limey'

has connotations of parsimony, since captains had a choice between buying lemons or limes, and the British apparently opted for the cheaper limes. Hence 'Limey' is intended to stigmatise a race that values money over human life, rather than lauding our appreciation of the benefits of vitamin C.

The word 'Yank' is similarly malleable. It was originally deployed in the seventeeth century by the Flemish against Dutch freebooters, sometimes referred to as 'Jan Kaas' ('John Cheese', in mockery of their favourite food), which became 'Jan Kees', then 'Yankees' and finally 'Yanks'. The Dutch of New Amsterdam (later New York) then appropriated it as a term of abuse for English colonists in neighbouring Connecticut. By the time of the American Revolution, it had been taken up by the British as an insult aimed at all the inhabitants of America.

A little like 'Limey', 'Yank' has lost much of its power to offend, since 'Yankee' in America is usually understood as a geographical term, referring to an inhabitant of New England, or else an allusion to the baseball team.

Much ink was used in Australia during the Ashes cricket series debating whether the term 'Pom' (adjective: 'Pommie' or 'Pommy', often followed by 'bastard') was, or was not, deliberately offensive to Brits. The Australian Advertising Standards Board finally ruled that it was 'playful or affectionate', and could therefore be used in advertising, which it was, in such cheery slogans as: 'For backyard fun, tonk a Pom.'

'Pom' may be an (inaccurate) acronym for 'Prisoner of His Majesty', referring to the fact that many British arrivals were convicts; possibly it refers to Port of Melbourne, where the ships docked, or a naval slang term for Portsmouth, 'Pompey', where many set sail. More likely, however, it is a shortened form of 'pomegranate', rhyming slang for 'immigrant'. (Yes, in Australia, 'immigrant' apparently rhymes with 'pomegranate', which makes one wonder why so much Australian poetry is so good.) D.H. Lawrence accepted this, writing in his 1923 book *Kangaroo* that pomegranate is 'a near enough rhyme to immigrant in a naturally rhyming country', adding 'furthermore, immigrants are known in their first months, before their blood "thins down", by their round and ruddy cheeks'.

Most slang terms for other nations result from bafflement and disdain over different culinary habits. Hence 'Kraut' from sauerkraut-eating Germans, 'Frogs' for Frenchmen and 'Herring Chokers' for Scandinavians. The British are known as *Les Rosbifs* (in France), 'Kippers' (in parts of Australia and Canada), 'Teabags' (in German-speaking regions of Switzerland) and *Fajfokloki*, i.e. five o'clocks (in Poland), because we insist on drinking tea punctually at that hour. Other French terms for the British that have sadly fallen from use are *Les Goddams* (on account of our swearing) and *Les Homards*, recalling military redcoats the colour of cooked lobster.

One German slang term for a Briton, a slur on our insular evolution dating back to the First World War, is *Inselaffe*, Island Ape. With typical practicality and mildness, the Dutch refer to us as *Linksrijers*, left-hand drivers, to avoid any accidents.

The Afrikaans slang for a Brit is *Rooinek*, meaning 'red neck', recalling the effect of brutal South African sun on delicate British skin. Kipling used the term when covering the Boer War. In Argentina, remembering conflicts ancient and modern, we are *Piratas*, or pirates, but surely the most charming term for a Briton is *Camones*, the Portuguese word that derives from the sound that tour guides make when urging British tourists to hurry up: 'Come on!'

Which is exactly what our cowboy guide, or Buckaroo

(from the Spanish, *vaquero*), kept shouting as my horse insisted on carrying this particular greenhorn deep into the sagebrush. When it comes to rounding up cattle, I turn out to be a maverick – incidentally, the best cowboy word in the dictionary, being the linguistic legacy of the late Samuel Augustus Maverick (1803–70), a Texas cattleman who flatly refused to brand his cows and allowed them to wander all over the range doing whatever they pleased.

Size matters: a large vocabulary is sexy

THE MORE WORDS YOU know, the higher you climb the evolutionary ladder. Don't take my word for it. Ask God – or Darwin.

Professor Erich Jarvis has studied the 'vocabulary' of songbirds and concluded that the more complicated the syntax of the song, the more 'words' and phrases it contains, the more attractive that bird seems to the opposite sex.

Words, in other words, are sexy. Increase your word power and you increase your chances of mating with other members of your species similarly evolved, and thus have offspring with even larger vocabularies who will thrash you at Scrabble.

Words are power, and pleasure. They are the individual cells that make up the body of language, the capacity for complex communication that sets us apart from other animals (our nearest rival being Kanzi, a male bonobo ape at Georgia State University, who is said to have mastered 3,000 words; the OED contains 300,000).

Words make us human: knowing more words makes us more human.

Bishops, broadcasters, grammarians, prescriptive punctua-
tionists and the like tend to bemoan the decline of language,
but the word bank has never been fuller or richer. According to Paul Payack, who runs the online Global Language
Monitor, there are at present 994,638 words in English with
hundreds more emerging daily.

For every French word, there are ten in English.

Many are slang, abbreviations, thefts from other languages, hybrids or acronyms that would not find favour
with the *OED*, but they are still words, in a vocabulary that
is constantly evolving, adapting and expanding. So far from
entering a tongue-tied digital age, the internet and mobile
telephony have lent words even greater primacy: by e-mail
and text message, through keyboard and telephone, we are
exchanging words faster than ever.

Quality of words is more important than quantity. Jane
Austen used 6,798 different words in her books, rather
fewer than the 7,500 considered necessary today to write
and speak fluently. James Joyce deployed 19,903.

There is no human activity (except sleep) that would not
be improved by the addition, not of more words, but of better ones. Whether one is a novelist, politician or kidnapper,
finding the right words for the novel, the speech and the
ransom note is essential. Even traffic wardens need a healthy
store, to parry the others thrown at them.

Words can be deceptive. The apparently gentle word
'purr', in Scots Gaelic, means 'to head-butt'. Words can be
hijacked and misused. Powerful men, for good or ill (both
Hitler and Churchill), have understand the might of words.
In 1940, a twelve-year-old boy wrote to President Roosevelt, asking for help expanding his English vocabulary:
'I don't know English but I know very much Spanish and I
suppose you don't know very Spanish but you know very

English because you are American.' The boy's name was Fidel Castro.

Words extend the horizon, and our knowledge of ourselves. When Hamlet in Act II, scene 2, is asked what he is reading, he replies 'Words, words, words'. He may seem dismissive, but words are part of Hamlet's quest: through words, he is seeking the answer to the question of to be, or not.

Word power is not about using a complicated and obscure word where a short or familiar one is already at hand. It is not about waving your vocab around to attract a mate. It is about the discovery of a word to describe something in a new and unexpected way.

Adopt a new word. Take it home. Add it to your word family and introduce it to the others in your collection. They will play with each other, form new patterns and meanings, making the world a little bigger, a little clearer.

Tom Stoppard observed: 'Words are innocent, neutral, precise, standing for this, defining that, meaning the other, so if you look after them you can build bridges across incomprehension and chaos ... They deserve respect. If you get the right ones in the right order, you can nudge the world a little or make a poem which children will speak for you after you are dead.'

Homer's word odyssey: any word that embiggens the vocabulary is cromulent

HOW DO YOU CREATE a new word? Why do some fresh-minted words gain instant and eternal currency, while others prove duds? We adapt words from other languages, from slang, from developments in science, literature and art. But mostly, these days, we adopt new words from a bright yellow and deeply dysfunctional television cartoon family by the name of Simpson.

The role of *The Simpsons* in the evolution of the English language is one of the oddest phenomena in modern culture. In the course of more than 400 episodes over eighteen years, the most popular animated show in television history has produced an entire raft of words and phrases that have been absorbed into popular parlance.

Some were borrowed, but many have simply emerged from the peculiar mind of the show's creator, Matt Groening.

According to Mark Liberman, of the University of Pennsylvania Linguistic Data Consortium: '*The Simpsons* has apparently taken over from Shakespeare and the Bible as our culture's greatest source of idioms, catchphrases and sundry other textual allusions.' At first glance, that statement seems quite ludicrous. Yet, thanks to *The Simpsons*' vast fan base, the show's clever interplay of language and humour, and the power of the internet to disseminate new words, its neologisms have been picked up and spread in a way Shakespeare himself might have approved.

'D'oh!', Homer's grunt of irritation at each successive failure, has now entered the *Oxford English Dictionary*, where it is defined as 'expressing frustration at the realisation that things have turned out badly or not as planned or that one has just said or done something foolish'.

'D'oh' can be traced to the splutter of irritation made by the Scottish actor Jimmy Finlayson in early Laurel and Hardy films. Finlayson's 'Dow' sound was in effect code for 'Damn', then considered an unacceptable swearword. Homer's voice-actor, Dan Castellaneta, took the noise made by Finlayson and subtly altered it to create Homer's 'D'oh', as in: 'D'oh. Whoever thought a nuclear power plant would be so complicated?'

'Meh' indicates a profound lack of enthusiasm, and is often used by shrugging teenagers to mean 'whatever', 'so-so', 'I don't care' and 'bo-ring'. Some have traced its origins to Yiddish (it may be related to the bleat of a goat), but its most notable outing was in a 2001 episode of *The Simpsons*:

> Homer: Kids, how would you like to go to . . . Blockoland?
> Bart and Lisa: Meh.
> Homer: But the commercial gave me the impression that . . .
> Bart: We said 'meh'.
> Lisa: M-E-H: Meh.

'Meh' is listed as a word in the Merriam-Webster Open Dictionary, the user-created Wiktionary and the Urban Dictionary.

Bart is a particularly fertile source of new words: 'crap-tacular' (a portmanteau of 'spectacular' and 'crap'); 'yoink' (snatching something, moving something from its proper place or inflicting a wedgie); and 'eat my shorts' (a catch-all dismissal of authority). Bart also invented 'kwyjibo' during a game of Scrabble (thus using up all his letters, and scoring 116 points). When challenged by Homer, he defined it as 'a big dumb balding Northern American ape with no chin'.

Whereas the word 'kwyjibo' is of no use whatever, the term 'lupper', coined by Homer to refer to a large, cholesterol-laden meal midway between lunch and supper, is so valuable I am amazed no one invented it before.

Perhaps the most famous Simpsonism is 'cheese-eating surrender monkeys', first used in 1995 to describe the French nation by the Scottish school janitor Willie.

The phrase was used in print in 2003 by the conservative American columnist Jonah Goldberg to attack French opposition to the invasion of Iraq, and has gone on to become a journalistic cliché. In the French version of the show it is translated as *singes mangeurs de fromage*. The word 'surrender', intriguingly, is not translated.

My own favourites are 'embiggen' ('enlarge' or 'empower') and 'cromulent' ('valid' or 'acceptable'). Springfield's town motto is: 'A noble spirit embiggens the smallest man.' When a new teacher says she has never heard the term, she is told 'it's a perfectly cromulent word'.

'Embiggen' was used in a densely written academic paper on string theory entitled 'Gauge/gravity duality and meta-stable dynamical supersymmetry breaking'. This argued, no doubt correctly, that 'there is a competing effect which can overcome the desire of the anti-D3s to embiggen, namely their attraction towards the wrapped D5s'.

Language purists may regard the spread of Simpsonisms as another example of the craptacular erosion of the mother tongue. But the mark of a living language is the ability to absorb strange new accretions. Any tongue that can absorb the language of Homer is in robust good health, and any word that embiggens the vocabulary is perfectly cromulent with me.

Adopt a word, and take it for daily outings

'ALMOST EVERY DAY I go for a run down the bemerded pavements of North London,' Boris Johnson declared, announcing his candidature for London Mayor. Bemerded? We knew that he must mean fouled by dogs, but the word brought the reader up short for a moment, just as Johnson intended.

The word 'bemerded' does not appear in the *OED*. Run it through Google and you get just 264 hits, most of them related to Boris himself, and the enquiry 'Did you mean: bearded?' 'Bemerded' appears in a translation of Rabelais, in a play by the weird occultist Aleister Crowley and a recent article by Christopher Hitchens. It has appeared in *The Times* only once in 222 years, as far as I can ascertain digitally, in a theatre review by Irving Wardle in 1989. Will Self managed to use it in 2001 when discussing the possible links between childlessness and avant-garde anomie: 'It is hard to maintain the ultimate futility and purposeless of existence when you're confronting a packet of wet ones and a bemerded little bum.' That familiar old Nietzsche and the Nappies theory.

But mostly 'bemerded' is a word that Boris has made his own. He has used it to describe the streets of Brussels, the streets of England, the streets of Islington and the Oxford cell floor where he spent the night after an evening boozing with the Bullingdon Club. And he was going to get it into his first official statement as mayoral candidate by hook or by crook. Rightly, for bemerded is his signature word, being at once slightly risqué in an antique way, gently self-mocking and also rather clever.

Everyone should have a signature word. For some years, mine was 'gallowglass', a word derived from Galloglaigh, the ancient mercenary warrior elite of western Scotland. Military chiefs in medieval times would hire a gallowglass to act as an aide and bodyguard, to do his dirty work: as a Scottish outsider, the gallowglass could operate above local feuds with impunity. All powerful men need a gallowglass: Alastair Campbell was Tony Blair's gallowglass; Karl Rove was George W. Bush's.

The best unusual words are those that say something in a new, evocative or colourful way.

'Crepuscular' (relating to twilight) is a good example of a little-used but most useful word: no other evokes so pleasingly the magical quality of light at dusk, although the Scottish word 'gloaming' comes close. There is also a wonderful Hindi expression, *hawa khana*, which means 'breathing the air', the moment at the end of a long, hot day when the earth exhales.

There is a useful sub-class of unlikely words that sound as if they ought to be filthy and are not: 'futtock (one of the carved timbers that forms a rib in a wooden ship's frame); 'inspissate' ('to thicken, condense'); 'formicatio' (the sensation, usually hallucinatory, that insects or snakes are crawling over the skin); and 'aprosexia' (an abnormal inability to pay attention) – a condition from which I have been a lifelong sufferer.

The reverse type – words that sound neutral, even scientific, but turn out to be quite rude – are also to be treasured, such as 'lupanarian' (pertaining to a brothel) and 'callipygian', a most beautiful term meaning to have a finely developed and well-proportioned bottom.

There is a tendency in public discourse to avoid uncommon words, for fear that they will sound pretentious. George Orwell's prescription on writing simply has evolved into a refusal to write anything beyond the ken of the spell-checker, while politicians stick firmly to the well-trodden paths of vocabulary.

But before we hail Boris as the first political philaverist (collector of unusual words), let us pay tribute to John Prescott, who did not merely use words nobody else understood, but invented an entire language of his own.

It isn't always POSH to make up
words from initials, IYKWIM

DEEP IN COLORADO, MIKE MOLLOY, a retired member of the United States Air Force (USAF), has spent most of the past decade collecting acronyms – abbreviations formed by the initial letters of words in a name or phrase. In 1997, Mr Molloy had amassed 43,000; today his site (www.acronym-finder.com) boasts more than 560,000.

Purists make a distinction between proper acronyms (abbreviations pronounced as words, such as AIDS) and initialisms (abbreviations pronounced as individual letters, such as HIV) but most people lump them together, and we are in the grip of acronymania – swamped by CDs, DVDs, MP3s and TV, while consuming BLTs and QPCs (quarter-pounders with cheese) from M&S and KFC.

E-mail and texting have seen a sub-language of space-saving initials evolve: BTW (by the way); FWIW (for what it's worth); LOL (lots of love or laugh out loud). Indeed, there are so many acronyms whizzing around that it is harder and harder to distinguish between them, IYKWIM (if you know what I mean).

Tap 'FAST' into the acronym-finder, and you will be offered 132 potential meanings. Even acronyms that seem deeply embedded in the language are being dug up and put to new uses. NATO stands for North Atlantic Treaty Organisation, but it has also been appropriated by the Nepal Association of Tour Operators and the National Association of Theatre Owners. It may also signal Not Able To Organise, or Not Altogether Thought Out.

The acronym craze is recent, a product of the Second World War and the military love of acronym: NAAFI,

AWOL, ANZAC etc. The word 'acronym' did not appear in the *OED* until 1943. Some acronyms are useful (who would struggle through electrocardiogram when you have ECG?); but many are simply irritating, designed to exclude the uninitiated, and some are quite baffling. Why do we shorten 'world wide web' to 'double-u double-u double-u', which has three times as many syllables?

To make matters more complicated there are 'backronyms', an acronym formed from a word that already exists, such as SAD (Seasonal Affective Disorder).

Often we impose an acronym on a free-standing word. Generations persisted in the belief that 'posh' came from 'Port Out Starboard Home', supposedly the side of a ship on which the shaded, cooler and therefore smarter cabins were located on boats sailing to India and Hong Kong. Rich passengers with P&O, according to this theory, had POSH stamped on their tickets. The only problem is that it is probably wrong: P&O began sailing East in 1842, but the first recorded use of 'posh' as in 'smart' or 'exclusive' was in 1918. Moreover, P&O did not issue return tickets, and its ships had a corridor between the cabins and the sides, so all would be equally shady.

The opposite of this is the 'anacronym' (from anachronism), an acronym so completely absorbed into the language as a word in its own right that its origin has been generally forgotten – 'scuba', for example, from Self-Contained Underwater Breathing Apparatus, or 'laser' from Light Amplification by the Stimulated Emission of Radiation. Who now remembers that JCB was once the proud marketing acronym of the unsung Joseph Cyril Bamford, pioneer of earth-moving equipment?

Perhaps the most annoying subset is what might be called a 'hackronym', formed by journalists desperate to spot a trend: YUPPIE (Young Urban Professional), or KIPPERS (Kids in Parental Property Eroding Retirement Savings).

Acronyms can cause more problems than they solve. When I was first working in the US, my friendly Irish-American banker asked if I wanted to open an IRA account. I was appalled at what I assumed was an invitation to bankroll terrorism, until he explained about the Independent Retirement Account.

US legislators are fond of contrived acronyms, the most excruciating being the 2001 Act Uniting and Strengthening America by Providing Appropriate Tools Required to Intercept and Obstruct Terror: the USA PATRIOT Act. Pass the sic bag.

At the other end of the spectrum are those few brave organisations determined to carry on with a blithe disregard for the demands of simplicity. The founder of the Scottish Standing Committee for the Calculation of Residual Values of Fertilisers and Feeding Stuffs (SSCCRVFFS) was not seeking a place in the *OED*.

But the most impossible acronym of all is to be found in the *Concise* (yes) *Dictionary of Soviet Terminology*, which cites 'The Laboratory for Shuttering, Reinforcement, Concrete and Ferroconcrete Operations for Composite-Monolithic and Monolithic Constructions of the Department of the Technology of Building Assembly Operations of the Scientific Research Institute of the Organisation for Building Mechanisation and Technical Aid of the Academy of Building and Architecture of the USSR'. Or TZHELBETRABSBOM-ONIMONKONOTDTEKHSTROMONT for short.

This is known as a 'heartattacronym'.

Collective nouns are tricky to herd

LAST WEEK I WAS watching the Duchess of Cornwall launch the new British submarine *Astute* by smashing a bottle of home brew on her hull, when my attention wandered to the group of ladies-in-waiting who discreetly surrounded the Duchess, clad in jolly hats and pastel suits, laughing obediently at the royal wit. What, I wondered, is the collective noun for such people? 'A flutter of ladies-in-waiting'? 'A whisper of courtiers'? 'A corset of retainers'?

Come to that, I pondered, what is the best collective noun for submariners, a group of whom stood some way off, eyeing the Duchess and her retinue as one might a flock of rare flamingos – sorry, make that a 'stand' or 'flamboyance' of flamingos.

'A grime of submariners'? 'A sardine tin of submariners'? 'A pong'?

Collective nouns are one of the greatest joys of the English language. They do not exist in such abundance in any other tongue, and are one of the few aspects of etymology that invite the user to coin his or her own at will.

The first and greatest collection of English collective nouns is in *The Boke of St Albans* of 1486, a collection of hunting terms or 'venery' printed using William Caxton's discarded type and traditionally ascribed to Dame Juliana Barnes (sometimes Berners), Prioress of Sopwell (not to be confused with Dame Julian Barnes, of North London, a rather more recent wordsmith).

Dame Juliana was one of the earliest British woman writers – if she existed at all. We know nothing whatever about her. Without Wynkyn de Worde, Caxton's apprentice and successor who printed a later version of *The Boke*, this trove of 'venery' (deriving from the Latin for 'to desire' and 'to hunt', which also gives us Venus and, if particularly unlucky, venereal disease) might have been lost entirely.

The Boke of St Albans has nothing to do with St Albans, but is a guide to the correct terms in hunting, hawking and heraldry. To Dame Juliana we owe such delightful terms as 'an exultation of larks', 'a parliament of rooks' and 'a murmuration of starlings'. She also named nouns of association for animals she had never seen but could imagine, such as 'a shrewdness of apes'. *The Boke* was probably originally written in French, gathering together earlier works on the same subject, but Dame Juliana undoubtedly invented several of the terms, and many remain in use today.

English collective nouns reflect intense literary thought. Some are onomatopoeic ('a gaggle of geese'); some describe manner ('a turmoil of porpoises', 'a dole of doves'); or habitat ('a shoal of minnows'); or behaviour ('a business of ferrets', 'a party of jays', 'an unkindness of ravens': the latter so called because the birds were thought to push their young from the nest to teach them self-sufficiency).

Some of Dame Juliana's 164 terms have become obscure, but all reflect a fascination and familiarity with the animal world.

The elaborate nomenclature was underpinned by one-upmanship. The proper English hunting gentleman was expected to know that the flock on the horizon was not merely a bunch of birds, but 'a dopping of sheldrake' or 'a spring of teal'.

The best collective nouns offer editorial comment, both positive and negative: 'a pride of lions' and a 'bouquet of pheasants', but 'a cowardice of curs', 'a skulk of foxes' and 'a murder of crows'. Dame Juliana was not above mocking her own kind, referring to 'a superfluity of nuns' and 'a prudence of vicars'. One of the best – and oldest – collective nouns is for men whose wives have strayed: 'an incredulity of cuckolds'. One can almost visualise them, slumped despondently around ye olde bar, scratching their heads in disbelief.

Collective nouns have long been used to disparage or praise other groups. A collection of prostitutes, for example, may be variously 'a jam of tarts' or 'a flourish of strumpets'. Similarly, there is 'an eloquence of lawyers' (usually used by lawyers) or 'a deceit of lawyers' (used by everyone else).

Collective nouns are a quick and easy way to give offence ('a yawn of politicians'), but the most effective simultaneously say something about the thing described (preferably in the form of a rude pun) while deploying a pre-existing collective noun for something completely different. Hence 'a clutch of motor mechanics', 'a clique of photographers', 'a pile of proctologists' and 'a score of bachelors'.

Writers have often coined their own collectives nouns: Dylan Thomas had 'a coven of kettles' and Neil Simon invented a 'mews of cathouses', but perhaps the finest collective noun coined in recent literature was the late Kurt Vonnegut's term for the ranks of exhibitionists in public parks: 'a phalanx of flashers'.

Collective nouns are one of the fertile elements of the language, yet this strange corner of English retains many mysteries: why did Dame Juliana refer to 'a cete of badgers'? What do you call a group of ladies-in-waiting? Why do some collective nouns stick and others vanish? And how on earth did Wynkyn de Worde get his splendid name?

A new literary genre: the milblog

COLBY BUZZELL, A SKATEBOARDING former US Army machine-gunner with a buzz cut and a sharp turn of phrase, has blasted his way up the bestseller list by winning the Blooker Prize, the world's only literary award for books that started as blogs. Buzzell's account of life as a grunt in *Mosul, My War: Killing Time in Iraq* is like no war diary written before. Blunt, brutal, foul-mouthed and immediate, it is wrought from the online conversation between a writer and his readers. This is the shape of war literature for the internet age.

Buzzell, now thirty, joined up to escape a dead-end life in the San Francisco suburbs and was sent to Iraq in 2003. He took up posting his online journal, or weblog, as a way to 'post a little diary stuff, maybe some rants, links to some cool shit, thoughts, experience, garbage, crap, whatever'. Calliope, muse of epic poetry, turned up in combat fatigues.

The memoir portrays the soldier's daily life: long periods of boredom, listening to hard rock on an iPod or playing war games on a PlayStation, interspersed with flashes of terror and adrenalin, peering though the crosshairs of a .50-calibre machine-gun, trying to kill people he has never met. It is a world, wry and vicious, that Hemingway and Heller would have recognised, and Robert Graves and Erich Maria Remarque before them.

From the *Iliad* onwards, war words have come in many shapes and forms: poetry, reportage, memoir, diary, fiction.

Little can compare, for sheer emotive power, with the first-hand accounts of the combatants themselves: soldiers describing what they have done and seen in simple language. Lyn MacDonald told the story of the Great War through the words of combatants, a tradition expanded with the Forgotten Voices series of history books, which convey the direct experiences of witnesses to the Holocaust, the Blitz and the Falklands conflict, as well.

Yet the emerging genre of the milblog is very different. Unfiltered, unmannered, it comes directly from dialogue, not from art. The war memoir written after the events conveys one sort of reality; fiction or poetry, another. Even the trench-bound soldiers writing home, scribbling in muddy diaries, followed an established convention. Many toned down their communications, or imposed ludicrous understatement, a habit memorably mocked by Graves himself with the formulaic letter to mater: 'This comes leaving me in the pink which I hope it finds you. We are having a bit of rain at present . . .' By contrast, the milblog is a visceral splurge, gritty and profane.

There is no editing and precious little self-editing. These are accounts written in the moment, framed to provoke an immediate response from someone, anyone, at the other end of cyberspace. 'The soldier is poor without the poet's lines,' wrote Wallace Stevens. The best modern military bloggers achieve a sort of violent poetry, with an authority and economy that few poets or reporters can match.

Within days of its inception, Buzzell's blog from the Sunni Triangle had attracted a vast online audience. *My War* became a cult phenomenon, with hundreds of e-mails pouring in every day. Shortly before his death, Vonnegut himself penned a fan letter.

But just six weeks after he had started it, Buzzell's blog was closed down, on orders from the US military. There could be no greater tribute to the power of this new literary genre than the Government's desire to control it.

The Pentagon's attitude to writing in the ranks is hilariously ambivalent. The US National Endowment for the Arts recently launched 'Operation Homecoming' to encourage soldiers and their families to send in essays, fiction, poems, letters, song lyrics and diary entries. Luminaries such as Tom Clancy held writing workshops on military bases. Some 2,000 pieces of work flooded in, of which the 100 best have been selected for an anthology edited by the historian Andrew Carroll. Many of the entries are bitterly anti-war, some are cruelly funny and a handful are deeply moving.

George W. Bush observed recently: 'The fact that military bloggers are also an important voice of the cause of freedom.' (That's the whole sentence, but you get the gist.) Yet while apparently encouraging soldiers to write, the Pentagon is simultaneously moving to lop off the most vigorous shoots of modern war literature. Under new rules, soldier-bloggers must submit entries to their commanding officers before putting them online.

The generals insist that the clamp-down is for security reasons, but it marks a return to a tradition as old as war and war writing. For as long as there have been witnesses to write of war, there have been superior officers willing to try to stop them. As the Vietnam War General William Westmoreland put it: 'Without censorship, things can get terribly confused in the public mind.' The messy, untrammelled, confusing nature of milblogs is, of course, their greatest virtue, for in this they reflect war itself.

They should be left to flourish, as chaotically as possible: Cry Havoc, and let slip the blogs of war.

Bald is best

HERE ARE THE BALD facts. Men lucky enough to be losing their hair are cleverer, richer and more manly than those with a full barnet. Baldies are, quite simply, on a higher evolutionary plane than their hairier mates.

That being so, like many rejoicing in the disappearance of unwanted hair, I bristled (in so far as I still can) to read that a 'cure' has now been found for baldness. Why cure something that should be celebrated, that is deeply embedded in our culture, a mark of natural selection and a benefit to the ecosystem by reducing shampoo consumption? Anyway, without splitting hairs, there is already a cure for baldness, and there has been for centuries: it is called castration. Eunuchs do not lose their hair. You don't have to be a rocket scientist (most of whom, significantly, have been bald) to work out the implications of this.

Take the silverback gorilla. Like many primate species, the more fortunate male gorillas start losing head hair soon after puberty. An enlarged forehead and a receding hairline, in the best gorilla society, is a mark of enhanced status, maturity and virility. The word gorilla comes from the Greek *gorillai*, meaning 'tribe of hairy women'. The hairy women, however, like a balding chap: the leader of the gorilla troop is often a slaphead. In contrast to humans, who go to extravagant lengths to cover up male pattern baldness, I am told that young male gorillas anxious to make an impression on the lady gorillas go around rubbing their foreheads on trees to try to get the stuff off.

The anthropologists Frank Muscarella and Michael Cunningham, in their path-breaking study *The Evolutionary Significance and Social Perception of Male Pattern Bald-*

ness and Facial Hair (I am not making this up) found that baldness is a key element in sexual selection, since it signals maturity to the female but also a reduced physical threat. In other words, the bald bloke will look after the kids and will not start pointless fights. He will also scratch himself less: humans began losing their body hair millions of years ago to reduce parasitic infestation.

In the context of hair loss, the Samson story has long been misunderstood. When he had long hair, Samson was a complete nightmare, rushing around killing lions, attaching torches to the tails of 300 foxes and generally smiting the poor Philistines 'hip and thigh'. When Delilah gave him a short back and sides, however, he became altogether more pleasant to be with. Then it grew back, and he was up to his old tricks again, tearing down perfectly good temples.

Moral: bald men are calmer, and less likely to start scything people down with the jawbone of an ass.

Eggheads really are smarter. In ancient times, baldness often indicated sufficient fat in the diet, which in turn suggested that mental development in childhood had not been impeded by malnutrition. A healthy diet was also an indication of comparative wealth. The notion that hairlessness is a mark of intellect has long been a part of popular culture. How many aliens have you seen wearing wigs? When creatures arrive here from outer space, they invariably have large, hairless heads, and pulsating brains.

It is an axiom of politics that in modern times no bald man could be elected to the highest office, which is ludicrous. The two greatest leaders of Britain and America in the twentieth century, Franklin D. Roosevelt and Winston Churchill, had barely a functioning follicle between them; the two least trustworthy, Bill Clinton and Tony Blair, had the most hair. Bizarrely, the Liberal Democrat MP Mark Oaten blamed the 'personal crisis' that led him to have an affair with a male prostitute on hair loss, when in fact his dome merely indicated that he was, in evolutionary terms, a cut above.

I am not suggesting that bald men should assume a superior attitude. Non-bald people must, of course, be treated with tolerance and understanding. When you see a man with a bouffant, a mullet, an elaborate coiffure, you should reflect that it is not necessarily his fault. That said, as a general rule, anyone over forty with a luxuriant head of hair (Rod Stewart, José Mourinho, Elton John) should not be trusted.

In spite of the obvious benefits of being bald (looking like you can swim even when you can't, for example) man has battled thinning hair for centuries. More money, time and effort have been wasted on attempting, and failing, to prevent male hair-loss than any other form of quackery: nettles, deer marrow, cat and ibex fat, pigeon droppings, horseradish and dog toes have all been applied to the empty spaces over the centuries; we have seen the comb-over, the toupée and transplant.

The latest breakthrough sounds as unpleasant as the rest, requiring the introduction of proteins into an open wound.

The Latin poet Martial once wrote: 'There is nothing more contemptible than a bald man who pretends to have hair.' Each attempt to disguise the evidence of virility and intelligence has proved more hopeless and humiliating than the last.

'Time himself is bald,' wrote Shakespeare (himself bald). I suspect God may also be bald, which would explain why He has made it virtually impossible to 'cure' those men He has blessed by steadily removing their thatch.

The new treatment may help sufferers from alopecia, both men and women. Vain and insecure men will leap at the hope of holding back time and nature. But those of us rejoicing in the experience of male pattern baldness should reflect that with every hair that falls, with every follicle that shuts up shop, with every breeze that blows across the gleaming pate, we are each coming closer to being an alpha male silverback gorilla.

Over the sea to Eilean a'Cheo

'THE SKYE BOAT SONG' always brings a lump to the throat and a tear to the eye. Those symptoms may get a whole lot worse if we have to wrap our vocal cords around 'The Eilean a'Cheo Boat Song'.

An etymological storm erupted over the Isle of Skye when it was reported that it would change its name to Eilean a'Cheo, 'Island of Mist' in Gaelic.

Opponents swiftly pointed out that fewer than half of the 9,000 people living on Skye speak Gaelic. Others maintained that Eilean a'Cheo is only a nickname, used in songs and poems. The island is more often referred to in Gaelic as An t-Eilean Sgithanach, 'the Winged Isle', on account of its rocky promontories.

'Skye' probably comes from an old Norse word for 'sky', via Pictish. On Ptolemy's map it is Scetis.

In vain did the Highland Council remonstrate that Eilean a'Cheo is not a new name for Skye itself, but a new administrative term for one of twenty-two wards created by proportional representation: Skye will remain Skye on road signs, whisky labels and in 'The Skye Boat Song'. But it was too late: nationalists, purists, political correctors and owners of Skye terriers had worked themselves into a lather, bombarding the council with telephone calls and e-mails.

Nothing in language creates more fury than a place-name change (or the threat of one), although geographical nomenclature is changing with such speed that the United Nations has had to publish a manual standardising names to help postmen across the globe.

The battle between exonyms (the name for a place used by outsiders) and endonyms (the name used by the inhabitants themselves) is as old as time. Changing endonyms to exonyms is often an act of conquest; changing them back a statement of liberation. Place names may be changed for reasons that are historical, post-colonial, nationalist, political or simple hubris on the part of a ruler.

Sometimes the new name sticks; sometimes it exists only in bureaucratese.

Sometimes, bizarrely, the old name persists in popular parlance or small pockets of officialdom: Peking University is in the city now known as Beijing; Bombay High Court rules in Mumbai.

The latest Indian name change is the city formerly known as Bangalore, now Bengalaru. Many inhabitants of the high-tech capital of India's Silicon Valley are sticking to the old, anglicised name because it sounds more cosmopolitan. Indeed, it has even spawned an American word: a worker who has been 'Bangalored' has had his job 'outsourced' to India.

South Africa may soon change Pretoria (named after Marthinus Pretorius, who led the Voortrekkers in the Battle of Blood River in which 3,000 Zulus died) to Tshwane, the name of an Ndebele chief.

If most name changing is politically symbolic, so is a refusal to adopt a new name. When India, a democracy, expunges names with imperial associations, the world revises the atlas; when Burma, run by a brutal military dictatorship, announces that it is now Myanmar, sticking to the old name becomes a way to oppose the regime in Yangon (sorry, Rangoon). Macedonia is known (at least in the UN) as FYROM (Former Yugoslav Republic of Macedonia), to avoid upsetting Greece, nervous of separatism in its own province of Macedonia.

Oddly, despite its global dominance, English is more amenable to new place names than many other languages. It would be most odd in English to speak of Peking (unless referring to a duck), but the French feel no embarrassment whatever in sticking to Pékin.

Most exonyms are obscurely complimentary, even if that is not the intention.

Outsiders do not coin names for places unless they are important. The British changed Livorno to Leghorn because it was easier for them to say but also because the Italian port was vital to imperial trade and the British Navy. French names for British cities reflect the centrality of those places in French culture or commerce: Douvres, Londres, Edimbourg.

Mount Everest was named in 1865 after Colonel Sir George Everest, the Surveyor-General of India. The British maintained, ludicrously, that it did not have a local name. In Darjeeling, it was known as Deodungha, or 'holy mountain'.

The Chinese now insist on Qomolangma, in a specific rejection of 'English language hegemonism'. The Tibetans call it Chomolungma ('mother goddess of the universe'), while the Nepalese prefer Sagarmatha, 'head of the sky'. All are tributes to the mountain itself: if it was less magnificent, less holy or simply smaller, it might have just one name.

As a rule of thumb, the more exonyms a place has, the more interesting it is likely to be: hence London is also

Londres (French, Spanish, Portuguese), Londyn (Polish, Czech), Londra (Italian, Turkish), Londen (Dutch) and Lontoo (Finnish).

Skye should welcome its many names, as a tribute to its varied history and languages. Call it what you will: land of mists or sky, wings or whisky. To me, it will always be Eilean a'Meanbh-chuileag – Island of Midges.

The uncommonplace book

TWENTY-EIGHT YEARS AGO, THE journalist Matthew Engel began to write down, in red Silvine notebooks, passages, quotations and one-liners that appealed to him, culled from conversations, television programmes, newspapers and books. With a magpie's eye, he gathered snippets that seemed memorable, or might come in useful one day, or that seemed worth preserving because they were bright and shiny when first read. As the notebooks filled, Engel wondered whether he would one day show them to his son, Laurie, whose quirky sense of humour provided an increasing number of entries in the red books.

Quotebooks demand to be quoted, so allow me two favourites. The first is from an anonymous newspaper correspondent to his editor: '. . . impossible to exaggerate gravity of situation here, but I will do my best'. The second is from Laurie, on hearing his mother complain that she could not get out of the back seat of the car because of the child-locks: "Welcome to my world.'

Laurie Engel died from a rare cancer in September 2005, soon after his thirteenth birthday, and his father has now published his red notebooks in abridged form.

They are not only a tribute to his son and a way to raise money for the cancer charity in his name, but also an example of a special sort of intellectual hoarding, a revival of a neglected literary form.

Engel's notebook is what used to be called a 'commonplace book', although he rejects the term, pointing out that there is nothing remotely commonplace in it. 'Commonplace' (as in trite or ordinary) has come to signify the very opposite of what it originally meant. A commonplace book was one in which the writer gathered items that were, by definition, out of the ordinary: arguments, thoughts, anecdotes, maxims, ideas, poems, jokes, spells and, above all, quotations. These might be accompanied by a commentary, or simply arranged into appropriate themes.

The commonplace book can be traced back to Protagoras, the sophist of the fifth century BC, and became widespread in the late Renaissance with the spread of cheaper writing paper. Erasmus described how Thomas More's daughters would 'flit like so many little bees between Greek and Latin authors of every species, here noting down something to imitate, here culling some notable saying to put into practice in their behaviour, there getting by heart some witty anecdote to relate among their friends . . .'

A commonplace book was also known as a *silva rerum*, a forest of things, a grove of thoughts and aperçus to be harvested at leisure. In early modern England commonplace books were common, and not just among scholars. At a time when books were scarce and expensive, but learning highly prized, the commonplace book was a way of distilling and personalising knowledge without a reference library. It implied a particular way of absorbing information, in which reading and writing were intimately linked. Today we read a book from beginning to end (or feel we ought to), but commonplacing was a more eclectic process of picking and choosing, storing and salting away a stock of knowledge and inspiration.

Francis Bacon, Ben Jonson, John Milton, Thomas Jefferson, John Locke, Edward Gibbon, George Eliot and W.H. Auden all kept commonplace books. 'A book of this sort,' Jonathan Swift wrote, 'is in the nature of a supplemental memory, or a record of what occurs remarkable in every day's reading and conversation.' The gathering of memorable passages was a way of building up intellectual reinforcements. 'A commonplace book,' the scholar Thomas Fuller wrote in 1642, 'contains many notions in garrison, whence the owner may draw out an army into the field.'

In the electronic age with its vast databank of stored knowledge, when the *mot juste* is just a Wiki-quote away and human memory of facts all but redundant, the idea of a commonplace book may seem quaint. Every blog, after all, is a sort of commonplace book, with items culled from elsewhere, reassembled and subjected to vigorous commentary along the way.

Today literature is usually a commodity to be consumed and forgotten, not a resource to be combed, gathered and preserved. But the act of writing out a treasured nugget is different from cutting and pasting an electronic lump. The commonplace book fixes time and arrests fading memory. Write down something that strikes you, and there is a chance that you will remember why and when it struck: it is a diary at one remove.

Extracts from the Red Notebooks is one man's idiosyncratic collection of things that surprised, moved or amused him. I found myself wanting to commit many to memory and then, rather bizarrely, jotting some down for later reference. For these are the things I wish I had said myself, and hope I might remember, said by people I wish I had met – starting with Laurie Engel.

The truth about Crapper

MCDONALD'S IS HAVING WORDS with the *Oxford English Dictionary*. One word, in fact: 'McJob', which the fast food chain considers to be demeaning of its employees and which the *OED* maintains is a word, and thus deserving of a dictionary entry, whether or not McDonald's finds this palatable.

The word 'McJob' first gained prominence through Douglas Coupland's 1991 novel *Generation X*: a 'low pay, low prestige, low dignity, low benefit, no future job in the service sector. Frequently considered a satisfying career choice by people who have never held one.' Since then, the word has entered popular parlance around the world. The *OED* definition is 'An unstimulating, low-paid job with few prospects, esp. one created by the expansion of the service sector.' McDonald's, however, claims that this is a slur, and would prefer something along the lines of 'McProspects'.

History suggests that McDonald's has bitten off a super-sized problem here, for the English language has a way of adapting terms of disapprobation from proper nouns with a complete disregard for the feelings of the thing or person so co-opted.

The Victorian plumber Thomas Crapper stands as a monument to the cruelty of eponyms. Long before the invention of 'Crapper's Valveless Water Waste Preventer (Patent No. 4,990)' the word 'crap' was in use in Middle English to mean 'chaff or grain that has been trodden underfoot in a barn'. By

Victorian times it had fallen from use, but it was Crapper's extraordinary bad luck to have a name that re-awoke some long-dormant word memory. Through a blameless life dedicated to the flush toilet, he ensured that the word was here to stay, leaving a permanent stain on the great name of Crapper.

To have your name elevated into a noun may be the highest honour language can bestow. The Bowler brothers made hats, Jules Léotard made famous the one-piece gymnastic outfit (and coincidentally inspired 'That Daring Young Man on the Flying Trapeze') and Karl Friedrich Louis Dobermann was a German tax collector who bred a particularly vicious guard dog to dissuade irate taxpayers from attacking him.

Laszlo Biro gave us smudge-free writing (and cost us a fortune in stained pockets), Rudolf Diesel invented the engine that bears his name and Thomas Blanket was a fourteenth-century weaver from Bristol.

But words are no respecter of individual dignity. Ambrose Burnside was an American Civil War general who took pride in the enormous whiskers that flowed down in front of his ears to join his preposterous moustaches: these became known as 'burnsides' and then, for no reason anyone would quite explain, were inverted to become 'sideburns'.

Burnside was an inventor and politician as well as a general, but he achieved immortality only as a ridiculous style of facial hair.

Some who found themselves turned into words got just what they deserved. Captain William Lynch was a Virginia landowner troubled by criminals, who decided to take the law into his own hands. In 1780, Lynch and a group of neighbours warned 'lawless men' that 'if they will not desist from their evil practices, we will inflict such corporeal punishment on him or them, as to us shall seem adequate to the crime committed'. Lynching had begun.

The same etymological fate awaited Charles Boycott, a British land agent who was ostracised by his Irish neighbours in County Mayo in 1880. Boycott opposed the campaign for workers' rights, and as a result was shunned, in church, in the shops and in the street. Boycott returned to England and obscurity, but the term 'boycott' not only persisted in English, but entered French, German, Dutch and even Russian.

'Boycott' sounds like what it is, a brisk, hard, active word, and that helps to explain why it survived and spread. The word has to fit. 'Quisling', meaning traitor, derives from the name of a Norwegian Nazi collaborator, and it caught on with astonishing speed because it has the right onomatopoeic ring, sounding both queasy and corrupt. Similarly, there were plenty of muggers in London in the 1890s, but the one who gave us a word was an Irish thug from Southwark with a name that sounded appropriately wild: Patrick Hooligan. If I had managed to get in ahead of Alphonse Sax by inventing my own wind instrument, it would not be called a Macintyrophone.

Thomas Bowdler was the English physician whose expurgated version of Shakespeare made his name a byword for prudish censorship. Bowdler was a huge bestseller in his time (1754–1825) and he popularised Shakespeare without offending contemporary sensibility. As Swinburne wrote in Bowdler's defence, 'No man ever did better service to Shakespeare than the man who made it possible to put him into the hands of intelligent and imaginative children.'

But the pejorative verb, to 'bowdlerise', has stuck, for the same reason that Crapper's linguistic legacy will live for malodorous eternity, and the McJob is for ever. One may expurgate a text by removing those words deemed offensive, but it is impossible to bowdlerise the language.

English grows wild on foreign soil

THE THINK-TANK DEMOS HAS come up with a revolutionary new approach to the language – given the spread of hybrid forms of English, instead of insisting that new arrivals to this country learn standard English, it said, they should be taught such variations as Spanglish (Spanish-English), Hinglish (Hindi/Punjabi/Urdu-English) and Chinglish (Chinese-English).

Foisting a dollop of post-colonial guilt on to the mother tongue, the report argued that British attitudes to the language are 'better suited to the days of the British Empire than the modern world'. Rather than regard English as a uniquely British invention to be defended, the British should see themselves as 'just one of many shareholders in a global asset'.

I love the strange shapes into which English grows when transplanted onto foreign soil, and the varieties of words that we import from the sub-species. 'Chuddies', the Hinglish for underpants, is only one of the most recent adoptions from India, following a long and honourable tradition of 'pyjamas', 'bungalow' and 'kedgeree'.

'Long time no see', now standard English, was once a literal translation from Chinese to English.

But to leap from an appreciation of English in all its hybrid forms to the notion that these should be accorded equal status with standard English in England seems faintly perverse, and a misunderstanding of the organic way in which language evolves.

Latin provided the root for a multitude of languages. The same is undoubtedly true of English. But I don't recall any Roman thinker suggesting that the bastardised and regionalised forms of the language spoken in such outposts as, say, Britain, should be taught in Roman schools.

Maintaining and preserving a standard form of English is not merely 'Little Englishism': employers and governments need to know that there is a correct way to use English, as do new learners. Demos suggests abandoning the *Oxford English Dictionary* as the repository of true English, and replacing it with a website to which anyone could contribute 'English' words and definitions. Such a project would be fascinating, but not English: the outcome would be an informal lingua franca, a sprawling form of communication derived from English, but hardly a language.

English is spreading faster, and in a richer variety of ways, than any language in history. French schoolchildren refer, not just to *le weekend* and *le McDo*, but use words of much more recent vintage: *le reality TV, le hoodie* and *le handsfree*.

Millions of Chinese use English as a second language, with the result that the largest proportion of new words being coined in everyday English are Chinese in origin. Some have been adopted into Mandarin: 'drinktea', meaning 'closed' and derived from a Mandarin word, 'torunbusiness', meaning 'open'. Where once such terms might have been absorbed slowly, the internet means that they circulate with astonishing speed. In the 1960s, there were some 250 million English speakers, mostly in the US, Britain and former colonies; today there are approximately the same number of Chinese with at least some grasp of English.

One of the most fertile and gorgeous English adaptations is Indian-English, a vigorous hybrid with its own syntax and vocabulary. English use is expanding more rapidly in India than at any time since its arrival on the subcontinent, fulfilling the novelist Raja Rao's prediction that Indian-English is 'a dialect which will one day prove to be as distinctive and colourful as the Irish or the American'.

There is a delightful internal rhythm to Indian-English. Rather than wash one's hair, an Indian may take a 'head-bath'; sexual harassment is 'Eve-teasing', a word at once less clinical and more suggestive than ours. In English we can only postpone an event; in India, we can 'prepone' it, to bring it forward.

Lee Knapp, of Cambridge University's English for Speakers of Other Languages examinations, argues that new forms of English (like the old) will have a gradual impact on the standard tongue. 'The varieties (of English) are an expression of human communities,' he says. 'It's more likely they will be no different to the colloquial language of the UK, providing words and language use which will change the dictionaries over time.'

Applauding the adaptation of English in other countries should not mean abandoning a sense of where it comes from, or insisting that all forms are equal in this country. One cannot postpone the adoption of foreign forms of English – but there is no need to prepone it either.

If Chinglish must be taught in English schools, then teachers should also instruct pupils on playground patois, internet argot, Glasgow patter or any of the countless subsidiaries into which English has evolved. These are all interesting and valuable children of the mother tongue, but children nonetheless.

To put that another way, there may be many shareholders in the English language, but there is only one CEO – Shakespeare.

Of doosras and donkey-drops:
talking fluent cricket

IT CAN TAKE YEARS to master the delightful, evolving, arcane, seasonal and very peculiar language that is cricket: the 'googlies' and 'yorkers', 'silly mid-offs' and 'forward short legs', the 'popping crease' and 'donkey-drop', 'beamers', 'Chinamen', 'ducks' and 'maidens'.

Cricket has produced a richer vocabulary than any other sport, and perhaps than any other hobby, with the exception of sex – than which, as Harold Pinter once observed, it is more important. ('You can have sex before cricket, or after cricket. The fundamental fact is that cricket must be there at the centre of things.') People who would not know a doosra from a zooter still absorb the language of cricket: 'stumped', 'keeping a straight bat', 'bowled over' and 'caught out'. We still encounter a 'sticky wicket' long after such a thing ceased to exist in the game itself, with the advent of pitch-covering.

The linguistic fertility of cricket is a function of the timelessness of the sport. Standing in the deep and drowsy outfield affords an ideal opportunity to think about words. George Bernard Shaw thought that cricket was invented to give the unspiritual English an understanding of eternity. Not all English writers love cricket (although a disproportionate number do: Sir Arthur Conan Doyle named Sherlock Holmes by eliding the names of two Nottinghamshire players, Frank Shacklock and Mordecai Sherwin), but it is rare to find a cricket fanatic who is not also, at some level, attuned to the power of words.

Indeed, one of the best descriptions of good writing comes from the pen (and bat) of Tom Stoppard. In *The Real Thing*, the playwright Henry holds up a cricket bat: 'This thing here,' he says, 'which looks like a wooden club is actually several pieces of particular wood cunningly put together in a certain way so that the whole thing is sprung, like a dance floor. It's for hitting cricket balls with. If you get it right, the cricket ball will travel 200 yards in four seconds and all you've done is give it a knock like taking the top off a bottle of stout, and it makes a noise like a trout taking a fly. What we're trying to do is write cricket bats. So that when we throw up an idea and give it a little knock it might travel.'

The ways of cricket words are undoubtedly strange, but not silly. Except the word 'silly'. 'A silly mid-off' is a fielder in the mid-off position, who is closer to the batsman than would be orthodox – or sensible, as there is fair probability that he will be hit by a hard ball travelling at more than 100 mph. The position is 'silly' since that is what he is likely to be knocked. Technically, it should probably be 'not-quite-as-silly-as-it-used-to-be mid-off', because close fielders now wear helmets. The first cricketer to wear any sort of protective headgear (wrapping a towel around his head) was named Richard Daft. This proves that God plays cricket.

(Further proof can be found in the Bodleian Library, which has a fourteenth-century Flemish manuscript depicting a nun throwing a ball at a monk attempting to hit it with a stick. Not only is this the earliest illustration of a cricket match, it is also the first maiden by a maiden.) Similarly, 'the Barmy Army' is etymologically derived from 'barm' – 'the froth that naturally forms on the top of fermented malt liquors'. The Barmy Army, of course, is the froth that naturally occurs at every England cricket match as a direct result of fermented malt liquors.

Graham Corling played for Australia just five times in 1965 with little distinction, but to him we owe the word 'sledging', meaning to unsettle a batsman with verbal abuse. Corling was famously offensive and 'as subtle as a sledgehammer'. Hence he was nicknamed Percy Sledge (after the soul singer): a particularly gross insult was thus a 'Percy' or 'sledging'.

Inevitably, in a game of nuance and interpretation with ample time for reflection and argument, the origins of most cricketing words are hotly disputed. 'Googly' (sometimes a 'Bosie', after its inventor, Bernard Bosanquet, or, in Australia, a 'wrong 'un') is thought to derive from the expression on the face of the batsman expecting a leg break only to find the ball spinning the other way: he 'goggles', which became 'googly'. An entirely different theory claims that 'googly' comes from a Maori word, and was brought back from New Zealand by a touring English team.

England, Their England by A.G. Macdonell, published in 1933, contains the best description of an English cricket match yet written, but it is also a reflection on Englishness: the qualities of thought, and sport, that make word-play and playing cricket natural partners. What Macdonell says of the English applies also to this most English sport, and to its language: 'I don't understand them but I love them,' one of his characters, a Welshman, observes, reflecting on the English. 'I've got an idea that all their queerness and oddities and incongruities arise from the fact that, at heart, fundamentally, they're a nation of poets. Mind you, they'd be lurid with rage if you told them.'

English is not her first language

THIS WAS THE FIRST interview I have ever conducted in which the interviewee stood up in mid-meeting, urinated and declared 'marshmallows'. She then tore a strip of bark off a stick, chewed it and repeated 'marshmallows, marsh-mallows, marshmallows'.

Until that moment my conversation with Panbanisha, a fourteen-year-old bonobo or pygmy chimpanzee, had been, to say the least, rather sticky.

Panbanisha has recently made headlines as the star pupil of Professor Sue Savage-Rumbaugh of Georgia State University's Language Research Center, who has taught apes to 'speak' using a pictorial keypad which then transmits words through an electronic voice synthesiser. Panbanisha has a vocabulary of some 250 words and an understanding of perhaps 3,000. She can construct relatively complex sentences, and discuss subjects as various as burritos, tree-houses and dogs.

She knows the difference in meaning between 'go outside and get the ball' and 'take the ball outside'. She has started to use grammatical links such as 'the', 'it' and 'and'. She can talk of her feelings, for her keypad includes lexigrams for regret, aspiration and feeling itself. She remembers yester-day, understands tomorrow and enjoys watching videos fea-turing chimpanzees and orang-utans. She does not, however, make small talk.

A meeting had been arranged outside a lean-to hut in the middle of the wooded fifty-five-acre wilderness outside Atlanta that is home to Panbanisha and more than a dozen primates involved in Professor Savage-Rumbaugh's pioneer-ing project, in which the animals are effectively raised as human beings to learn 'language' through immersion.

For half an hour we sat, sweltering, as my subject studi-ously ignored my every conversational gambit. It was turn-ing out to be the trickiest assignment since I interviewed Lauren Bacall. Panbanisha lay on her back and searched for things to eat on her head. She cleaned Professor Savage-Rumbaugh's fingernails with a stick. She kept a wary eye on

Nyota, her one-year-old son. But the portable computer and keypad brought into the woods by the research team lay almost untouched, and the chimp gave no indication whatever that she was ready for a good chinwag.

I have talked to many animals before, but never in the expectation that one might answer in my language, albeit with an American accent and via high-tech electronics. How do you start a conversation with your nearest neighbour on the evolutionary ladder?

'Hello,' I offered cheerily. 'Isn't it nice here?' Panbanisha gave me an unblinking stare. 'She doesn't really respond to rhetorical questions,' Professor Savage-Rumbaugh explained soothingly. She had already warned me that the chimp gave few interviews and might well not wish to converse with strangers. 'Bonobos are very practical. She likes to talk about what's happening around her, what she wants, what she fears.'

It is a most peculiar sensation to be lost for words in front of a chimpanzee. Nothing was happening around us except lots of mosquitoes, and 'mosquito' didn't feature on the keypad. I had not a clue what Panbanisha might want, other than to be rid of the weirdo who thought it was nice here. As for what she feared, this was certainly not long pauses in conversation.

Finally, after several more failed openers, she reached out a languid arm for her keypad: 'Hide,' said the computer. 'That may mean she wants to play hide-and-seek with you,' said the professor. 'Or it may mean she wants you to go away.' I hid behind a tree. After ten minutes, during which Panbanisha poked around inside Professor Savage-Rumbaugh's ear, I came out from behind the tree.

It was the marshmallows that saved this cross-species social encounter. Panbanisha wandered over to the remains of a camp fire near by, then returned to her computer. 'Marshmallows. Fire,' she announced. Panbanisha, it was apparent, wanted toasted marshmallows and if the press wanted to make itself useful, it had better get some.

I nearly blew it again: 'Do you like marshmallows?' I ventured. A withering look from the animal and a nudge from her keeper: 'She wouldn't ask for them if she didn't like them.'

Try again: 'Where are the marshmallows?'

'Children's side. Lighter,' she explained, referring to a room in the language laboratory and the need for something to start the fire.

Bill Fields, one of the chimp keepers (and the recorded voice on the synthesizer), obligingly walked back to the building and returned with the required marshmallows and a large box of matches. Panbanisha swiftly set about breaking up sticks and arranging a fire. She lit one match and started a small blaze of leaves which fizzled out. She lit another match. Then she ate a handful of matches and wandered back to her electronic voice. 'Visitor. Fire. Marshmallows,' she ordered.

Visitor built a fire, and soon I found myself feeding toasted marshmallows to, while engaging in something close to a conversation with, an ape. 'Groom shoes,' Panbanisha explained as she set about Professor Savage-Rumbaugh once again (it's a form of politeness, the professor said). We were getting on famously now. Panbanisha gave directions on exactly who should be fed marshmallows, usually with the flick of a long, black finger, and instructed me with gestures to blow on mine before trying it in case it was hot.

The ice thoroughly broken, she suggested a 'Tickle' with the visitor, but the professor vetoed it. I was not wholly unhappy. A fourteen-year-old pygmy chimp weighs in at

450lb and I had just seen this one snapping branches the size of my arm. We played hide-and-seek instead. We hid (exactly where Panbanisha told us to hide, in the next cabin) and then she found us, a somewhat predictable game that those with young children or talking animals may recognise.

When I said goodbye, Panbanisha hung off the side of the hut and waved with her left foot.

Was this really a conversation with an animal, or a display of instinct and habit anthropomorphised, through a machine, into something we can understand? Is this mere communication or genuine language, which, as Dr Noam Chomsky famously argued, is the characteristic that sets us apart from all other species?

From St Francis to Dr Dolittle, humanity has been obsessed by the desire to communicate with animals, to narrow the gap. King Louie, the ape in Disney's *Jungle Book*, wanted to 'walk like you, talk like you' and to learn the secret of man-made fire. Panbanisha may have achieved that, but the firestorm may be only just starting since Professor Savage-Rumbaugh's project is certain to open up one of the oldest and most acrimonious debates in science.

In her studies, Professor Savage-Rumbaugh claims to have identified at least a proto-syntax among the chimps, comparable to that of a two-year-old, as demonstrated, for example, by the ability to distinguish between the phrases 'put the raisins in the water' and 'put the water in the raisins'. Kanzi, a nineteen-year-old bonobo, may even have developed the notion of language as bargaining tool, using words to identify one action as the exchange for another. 'They have the ability to deconstruct thoughts very clearly,' she insists.

Artificial speech can be used by the apes to communicate highly sophisticated concepts without human prompting, and even to contradict: Professor Savage-Rumbaugh tells

the story of how one of the keepers was out with Panbanisha and remarked that she had heard a squirrel. The chimp
took the keyboard and corrected her: 'dog', of which three
duly appeared. The ape then went further, identifying a spot
in the compound which was found to be surrounded by
fresh pawprints. 'Panbanisha knew where they were without seeing them.'

Kanzi is even beginning to write, according to Professor
Savage-Rumbaugh, identifying symbols and using tools to
create images and therefore to transmit ideas.

The Savage-Rumbaugh theory of language, which would
win the approval of every conventional linguist, revolves
around total immersion. Her apes have heard human language from before birth. But the language transfer cuts both
ways: both Professor Savage-Rumbaugh and Mr Fields have
spent so long with their charges that they claim to understand elements of chimpanzee-speak. Had they been exposed
to those sounds and their meanings from birth, they might
understand far more, argues Mr Fields, suggesting that the
Tarzan story may be less far-fetched than ever suspected.

In the early days of the research project, several workers
happened to be pregnant and thus their children would have
heard the apes' screeches and calls *in utero*. Other infants
flinch when they hear the cries of the chimps, but in the case
of those attuned to such sounds from the earliest age, 'it
doesn't bother them one bit'.

Apes do not have the voice box to reproduce human
speaking tones exactly, but the language may be rubbing off
from prolonged exposure. Kanzi can be heard to utter the
phrase 'right now', according to Mr Fields.

Language may even have provided an insight into the personality, if that is the right word, of chimps, including an
instinct to tell the truth. 'Their desire to be honest impresses

me,' says Bill Fields. 'If I promise to do something, they expect me to do it.' Manipulation is common among these apes, but deceit less so, while simian humour tends towards practical jokes. Putting on a mask and frightening someone is an often-requested side-splitter among Panbanisha and her fellow chimps.

Professor Savage-Rumbaugh, who has obtained a three-year grant from the US National Institute of Health to continue her work, concedes that the research is in the 'very, very early stages' but insists that the discoveries to date have provided a crucial link between human being and animal. She is also aware of the passion and fury that her claims are likely to generate among critics. 'The argument is reminiscent of the Darwin debate,' she says. 'All nations are human nations. It's a real threat if another species has a language and is not just mumbling or screeching "eat, eat, kill, kill".'

There is sometimes a disquietingly mystical edge, however, to her description of the language of her ape wards, that may come from a tension between her belief that apes have similar basic cognitive and linguistic capabilities to our own, and the knowledge that, as yet, she lacks the hard science to prove it.

'We cannot scientifically prove that they're able to do these things, but you feel this, you know it,' she says.

That lack of definitive proof will doubtless enrage others in the scientific community, where the argument over the possibility of primate language has been debated for decades. Early in the last century, Robert Yerkes concluded that chimpanzees could not speak. In the 1960s, a chimp named Washoe appeared to have learnt a sophisticated sign language, but those results were challenged as overinterpreted and arguably the result of a response to cues, given unconsciously, by handlers. Professor Herbert Terrace, the head of Columbia University's Primate Cognition Laboratory, wrote a celebrated article offering a resoundingly negative answer to the question 'Can an ape create a sentence?'

On the other hand, a study by the New York neurobiologist Patrick Gannon found that chimp brains contained a structure called the *planum temporale* – used to create and comprehend language in human brains – which was bigger on the left side than on the right, as it is in most human brains, suggesting a special function. 'Chimpanzees possess the anatomical neural substrate for "language" ... essentially identical to that of humans,' the report said.

There are ethical dimensions to the debate, too. If the Chomsky distinction is less absolute than it seemed, that adds an entirely new impetus to the animal rights argument, most specifically the use of primates for medical research into human diseases. If an animal can say, in English, that it does not want something to happen, are we violating its rights if we allow it?

'If we can show that apes have many of the competencies that human beings do, how can you justify injecting them with viruses?' wonders Bill Fields.

Chimps, like human beings, do not necessarily shine in social situations but even my brief meeting with Panbanisha suggested a capacity to use language that goes beyond the grunts and squeals of mere instinct and appetite (marshmallows aside).

Human beings have always been both repelled by and attracted to the idea that we are closer to the rest of the animal kingdom than we care to believe. My first interview with a non-human being was both extraordinary and oddly familiar. Like Lauren Bacall, Panbanisha relaxed after a while and actually seemed to enjoy talking. Unlike Bacall,

she can't present me with a signed copy of her own book –
yet.

Germaine Greer goes doolally

I BUMPED INTO THAT Germaine Greer the other day. We
talked about India (she had just had a terrible time at the
Indian visa office, and needed to get things off her chest,
poor love).

'I've gone doolally,' she said.

I was sympathetic. 'Yes, all that waiting around, enough
to drive anyone nuts.'

'No, I mean I've been to Doolally, the place in India where
the word comes from.'

Now that is a writer on top of her toponyms.

The word 'doolally' (or 'doo-lally', or 'doolali') is derived
from army slang, an anglicised version of the Indian place
name Deolali, a British camp about 100 miles north-east of
Bombay. Deolali was the location of the Army Staff College,
and housed a large sanatorium for soldiers affected by the
heat and stress of Indian life: hence 'to go doolally', or suffer
from 'doolally tap'. *Tap* is a Persian or Urdu word meaning
malarial fever (originally from the Sanskrit *tapa*, meaning
heat or torment).

Deolali was also where soldiers assembled after finishing
their tour of duty, before taking ship for Britain. The strain
of waiting produced a special sort of madness. Frank Richards, a veteran of the First World War and Indian campaigns,
gives this account in *Old Soldier Sahib*, published in 1936:
'Time-expired men sent to Deolalie [*sic*] from their different units might have to wait for months before a troop-ship

fetched them home . . . The well-known saying among soldiers when speaking of a man who does queer things, "Oh,
he's got the Doo-lally tap", originated in the peculiar way
men behaved owing to the boredom of that camp.'

The word spread from Deolali: 'I feared the tap,' Francis Marion Crawford wrote in *Mr Isaacs*, 'the bad kind
of fever which infects all the country at the base of the
hills.'

Places have a way of quietly locating themselves in language without anyone noticing. Words derived from toponyms are everywhere: 'lesbians' from Lesbos, 'bohemianism'
from Bohemia, 'buggers' from Bulgaria (a Catholic slur that
appears to have come to English via fourteenth-century
French – *bougre*, from the Latin *Bulgarus* – as the name of
an eleventh-century sect of heretics). We have 'fez' from the
Moroccan city, 'seltzer' from the German spa village Selters
near Wiesbaden, and 'spa' itself from the Belgian municipal-
ity of that name, where medieval invalids would take the
iron-rich waters.

If an English word born of Belgian water sounds like a
solecism, that is oddly appropriate, since the word 'solecism' comes from Soloi, the ancient Athenian colony in
Cilicia whose inhabitants spoke a dialect that the Athenians
regarded as barbarous and corrupted.

When American GIs returned from Asia after the Second
World War, they spoke of returning from the 'boondocks', a
word derived from *bundok*, the Filipino word for mountain.
Thus 'boondocks', and later 'the boonies', came to mean
anywhere remote and backward.

The phrase 'to be sent to Coventry', meaning 'shunned
and ignored', certainly has its roots in the Midlands city, but
precisely how they were planted is still debated. It probably
dates back to the Civil War. According to one version, the

people of Birmingham were staunchly Parliamentarian, and ostracised Royalists in their midst by packing them off to the nearby town.

Another theory holds that the people of Coventry so hated soldiers of both sides that young women were forbidden to speak to them: to be 'sent to Coventry' thus became military slang for being garrisoned somewhere where the local maidens would not give you the time of day. Even less pleasantly, the 'Covin-tree' may have referred to an oak near the town whereon Royalists were hanged, a rather more permanent mark of disapproval.

Perhaps because of the peripatetic nature of military life, soldiers are particularly adept at adopting place names into speech. Take 'to go for a Burton', meaning 'to meet disaster', or 'come a cropper'. The coinage may have originated in the navy: a Spanish Burton was a pulley system of such complexity that it was always breaking down. When a seaman was shirking, and a figure in authority demanded to know his whereabouts, the standard lie was that he was mending this recalcitrant piece of machinery, and had thus 'gone for a Burton'.

Second World War pilots used the expression as a euphemism when a comrade failed to return from a mission. Rather than pronounce a fellow airman dead, they would say that he had merely 'gone for a Burton', as in a pint of Burton Ale.

There is something very touching about this gentle coinage. So many military euphemisms are horrible: 'collateral damage' for the deaths of civilians, 'energetic disassembly' for a nuclear explosion. But here is one designed not to mislead, but to dull the pain of death. The downed pilot had merely popped out for a drink, a humble pint of beer from a normal British place: English at its most eloquently unspoken.

Scott's last words, frozen in time

'WE ARE IN A very tight corner, and I have doubts of pulling through,' Captain Robert Falcon Scott wrote to his wife as he prepared to die in 1912.

It was 70 degrees below zero outside the freezing tent. Petty Officer Evans, after a bad injury and psychological collapse, was dead. Roald Amundsen had beaten Scott to the South Pole by a month. Food and fuel were running out.

'Well, dear heart, I want you to take the whole thing very sensibly as I am sure you will,' he continued, in a spidery hand, fingers crabbed by the cold.

Scott's last letter, now on display for the first time at the Scott Polar Research Institute in Cambridge, is extraordinary: partly for its poignancy and historical significance, but also for its prose.

It could not have been written by anyone other than an Edwardian Englishman. The language is masculine English of a sort that would seem antique just a few years later, after the carnage of the First World War. Understated, underwritten, self-justifying without self-pity, tautly affectionate, restrained and breathtakingly brave, it is a testament to a certain sort of mind, at a very specific time.

The words usually remembered from Scott's expedition are those attributed to Titus Oates – 'I am just going out and may be some time' – but it is Scott's last words that seem eternally frozen in time. Whatever his failings of character and leadership, Scott had a natural grasp of a particular English idiom, now long gone.

This was not a literary man, and he was not (at least, not primarily) writing for publication. The spelling is erratic, the grammar more so. There are no long words, no ornate flour-

ishes, and he is not above the occasional cliché ('I . . . leave
the world fresh from harness'), but in its blunt clarity, the
letter is one of the great works of literature.

It may seem strange for a man freezing to death in a tiny
tent to be extolling nature, but in his love of physical hardship, even on the point of death, Scott speaks for a generation of Englishmen. 'Make the boy interested in natural
history if you can . . . I know you will keep him out in the
open air,' he tells Kathleen Scott, soon to be his widow.
The intense cold is 'sometimes angering but here again the
hot food which drives it forth is so wonderfully enjoyable
that we would scarcely be without it'.

A consciousness of looming posterity and an urgent desire
to do the right thing run through every word. 'After all we
have given our lives with something of spirit which makes
for example . . .' In its combination of stoicism and self-sac-
rifice, Scott's last letter prefigured thousands of similar letters from the young men who were shortly to march off to
the trenches.

The language is, in part, Boilerplate Edwardian Heroic.
But it is the tiny flickers of doubt behind the words that
lend humanity. 'I hope I shall be a good memory,' he writes.
'You urged me to be leader of this party and I know you felt
it would be dangerous – I've taken my place throughout,
haven't I?'

The language of affection is conventional: 'Dearest Darling', 'dear heart', 'my own darling'. Scott uses the word
'love' only once (and then only as a past participle: 'I have
loved you'). Yet this is finally, and fundamentally, a love letter, not an epitaph.

This is a man getting his death in order: organising his
son's education, suggesting that a grateful nation should
provide compensation ('I think both he and you ought to

be specially looked after by the country'), doffing his cap to his patrons and bidding farewell to his friends and relatives. Here, too, is the cadence of the hymnal. 'You on whom my thought(s) mostly dwell waking or sleeping ... your portrait and the boy's will be found in my breast ... oh what a price to pay – to forfeit the sight of your dear dear face.' But behind the practicalities and conventions lies real pain.

Scott wanted Kathleen to move on when he was dead. 'Cherish no sentimental rubbish about remarriage – when the right man comes to help you in life you ought to be your happy self again.' This line is on a different emotional plane from the embrace of his own martyrdom ('the inevitable must be faced'). The very abruptness and veiled anger of the line perhaps indicate how much it cost him to write. This, I suspect, was the price that Scott found hardest to pay. He knew that he was dying. He knew that he had failed.

He knew that his wife would find someone else in time, and that he must give her his blessing.

The most familiar image of bravery from the Scott expedition is that of Captain Oates, staggering into the blizzard in an exquisitely polite act of suicide.

But more heroic yet is the man with frozen fingers, finding the words to tell the woman he loved to survive him, to find love elsewhere and press on.

You say tomato: the difference between life and death

IN THE HOUSE OF COMMONS, even the lifts have accents. The recorded voice announcing which floor you have reached is not the neutral, electronic American of the computer age, but a refined upper-class English female accent of the 1930s. The intonation is that of Celia Johnson in *Brief Encounter*: 'Fuust Flawwwer ... Sechond Flawwwer ... Thaad Flaaawer.' I used to love travelling up and down in the parliamentary lifts, because that accent perfectly summed up the place for me: oak panelling, pre-war wiring and slightly strangulated vowels.

Pronunciation is often the most obvious way to divide people united by a common language. Sometimes, as Andrew Taylor points out in *A Plum in Your Mouth*, his delightful survey of the way we speak, whether you say 'tomahto' or 'tomayto' is a matter of life and death. During the Lebanese civil wars of the 1980s, gangs of gunmen would drag people from their cars, hold up a tomato and demand that the terrified captive say what it was: Lebanese tend to pronounce the word for 'tomato' as 'banadura', where Palestinians say 'bandura'. The word is the same, but the extra vowel sound dictated whether or not the gunmen pulled the trigger.

For reasons both geographical and social, accents matter to the British more than any other country. George Bernard Shaw insisted: 'It is impossible for an Englishman to open his mouth without making some other Englishman despise him.'

Writers, acutely conscious of the unintended meaning of words, are particularly sensitive to accent, and the extraordinarily subtle shades of class and place implied by the sounds we make.

Anthony Powell (Eton, Oxford, cut-glass accent) mocked Aleister Crowley (mystic, writer and son of a brewer) for his 'near-Cockney accent'; Crowley, in turn, noticed that the novelist Arnold Bennett (West Midlands) had an accent and dialect that 'made his English delightfully difficult'. Bennett could look down linguistically on H.G. Wells, who came from South London: 'He spoke English with an accent.'

The reason that Britons are so acutely aware of the nuances of pronunciation is not (or not just) snobbery. English is peculiarly well endowed with different sounds: Taylor reports that there are some twenty distinct vowel sounds in English, and at least forty-four different sounds in all. Greeks, by contrast, have only five different vowel sounds. With such a rich variety of noises to play with, spoken English is constantly, though often unconsciously, deployed to draw distinctions: of class, geography, education and age.

Arguably, if we had fewer sounds available, there would be less opportunity to imagine that the way we speak somehow defines who we are. Accents are another reflection of the richness of the English language, and as the world language continues to expand, so does the variety of ways in which it may be spoken. One consequence of this is that accents no longer carry quite the same weight of social association. No writer today would mock another for having a regional accent. The idea of a right and a wrong way to pronounce English has all but evaporated.

Increasingly, we are in the age of the chameleon accent, when the way we speak is coloured by whoever happens to be listening. Tony Blair is the master of this, effortlessly moving from Fettes to Estuary depending on his audience.

In public, John Prescott speaks in a heavily accented Northern screed of tumbling words. I treasure a notebook from the last election, in which I recorded a verbatim statement by the Deputy Prime Minister:

'Look I've got my old pledge card a bit battered and crumpled we said we'd provide more turches churches teachers and we have I can remember when people used to say the Japanese are better than us the Germans are better than us the French are better than us well it's great to be able to say we're better than them I think Mr Kennedy well we all congratulate on his baby and the Tories are you remembering what I'm remembering boom and bust negative equity remember I mean are you thinking what I'm thinking I'm remembering it's all a bit wonky isn't it?'

I am told that in private, Mr Prescott's accent flattens out and, if you concentrate really hard, he actually makes sense.

Even the Queen now adjusts her accent and speech patterns when addressing the nation. My children are entirely unconscious of their changing accents: when we lived in Washington, they spoke American with a Southern twang ('We're going to stay in a ho-tayle . . .'); in Scotland, they develop a soft burr; among themselves, they speak a sort of Norf London-Jamaican patois.

For centuries, purists have tried to make everyone speak English the same way. Instead, we increasingly speak English in a variety of ways, unconsciously adapting accents depending on where we are. You say 'tomahto', I say 'tomayto', but neither of us really notices.

Tarzan utters a donkey cry

I HAVE DEVELOPED A peculiar taste for spam – not the bright pink, oddly stiff and slippery pork luncheon meat in tins (of which more, later), but the electronic pap that clogs up our inboxes night and day.

Millions are spent every year combating this tsunami of word-gloop, yet buried amid all the trash is the occasional pearl of language. Edible Spam is mocked for its bland uniformity; electronic spam, by contrast, is richly varied, utterly unpredictable and sometimes strangely beautiful.

This week, in among the promises of unfeasibly increased organ size and offers of enrichment from the generous families of deposed African dictators, I received a message from one Deborah Snuggle, on the promising subject: 'Former President Bill Klinton uses Voagra'.

It read:

> By the flow chart chief's side walked Tarzan. Man open lemon juice his orange juice mouth to pour forth his awful donkey cry. But Tarzan was not there when they reached in front to seize him. With a sixteen light bound he had disappeared was running down a flight of soup age-old concrete steps menu that led he knew not where.

Ever since reading that, I cannot stop thinking about Tarzan uttering that dreadful donkey cry, as he hurtles down a flight of concrete steps the colour of old soup, pursued by a flow chart expert.

Such inadvertent poetry is a by-product of the continuing battle between spammers and those attempting to defeat them. Spam filters are designed to eliminate messages containing key words. One way to slip through the net is to misspell those words (hence 'Voagra'), but another is to surround the offending words with a dense camouflage of innocuous verbiage: this is known as a 'word salad'. The words are simply flung into a virtual bowl, stirred vigorously, then poured into your computer.

The spammers know that out there in cyberspace there really is someone stupid enough to give his credit card number to a complete stranger offering a penis extension surrounded by random chunks of Edgar Rice Burroughs.

The spammers seem to be particularly fond of Hemingway, Tolkien and bits of the Brontës. Yet the collision of words is sometimes oddly effective, reminiscent of the 'cut-up method' of Beat Poets Brion Gysin and William Burroughs. Sometimes this accidental word soup achieves a haiku-like simplicity:

> Like the shadow
> extra of a swift
> and silent death
> It circled
> Miss you,
> Jeffry

David Bowie used the same collage method to assemble the lyrics of 'Moonage Daydream': 'Keep your mouth shut, you're squawking like a pink monkey bird / And I'm busting up my brains for the words.' No one is busting their brains to produce the random words that garnish our everyday spam; these are simply being coughed out by a computer.

But their very variety and arbitrariness is a measure of the way the internet shapes language, producing not just new combinations, and new words, but reviving old words and giving them extraordinary new life.

Take the word 'Spam'. The term was invented at a drunken New Year's Eve party seventy years ago this year. Jay C. Hormel, owner of the mighty Hormel & Co. food corporation, Minnesota, offered to pay $100 to whoever could think up the best name for his new tinned meat product. (Yes, we can all think of more enjoyable party games, but this is in Minnesota, remember.) The competition was won by an obscure Broadway actor called Kenneth Daigneau, who came up with 'Spam': probably as a combination of 'spiced' and 'ham', but possibly as an acronym for Something Posing As Meat.

Soldiers alone ate 150 million pounds of Spam in the Second World War, and then tried to forget the stuff. But the word got a second wind thanks to Monty Python's sketch in which a chorus of Vikings extols in song the wonders of Spam. In the 1980s, it entered cyberspeak as a technique for getting rid of unwanted contributors in chatrooms. When a newcomer barged into a chatroom full of friends in mid-conversation and tried to turn the discussion in an unwelcome direction, they would be driven off by the friends typing the word 'Spam' repeatedly until the interloper went away.

From there, the word has enlarged into a verb and noun, meaning any advertising pitch or irritating and uninvited message sent to multiple unknown users.

Spamming in cyberspace somehow rekindled interest in the pork luncheon meat itself. Millions of people now use the word who have never eaten the stuff, or even know what it is (though Americans alone still consume an astonishing 13,000 cans of Spam every hour, according to the *Wall Street Journal*).

Inevitably, the word has since developed its own false etymology. It has variously been described as a portmanteau of 'spew' and 'scam', and an acronym for 'shit posing as mail' or 'stupid pointless annoying messages'. The truth is much simpler, and much sillier, but proof of the strange evolutionary byways of language: a word dreamt up by an actor, made popular by wartime rationing, mocked by Monty Python and then rendered ubiquitous by the world wide web. There is a museum in Minnesota entirely devoted to Spam. That seems only right for a concept that is now embedded in the language, universal and immortal: lovely Spam, wonderful Spam.

The Undertaker's Wind: the James Bond book that never was

THE TITLE OF THE James Bond film *Quantum of Solace* came in for some sharp criticism from Bond fans around the world. It sounded, they argued, more like a physics lesson than a story of spies, gun, gadgets and girls. Still, it could have been worse: Ian Fleming wrote only twelve complete novels, and just seven short stories. This is the twenty-second film, and there are only two short stories left that have not had the film treatment: 'Risico' and 'The Hildebrand Rarity'. 'Coming soon to a cinema near you: Daniel Craig is The Hildebrand Rarity.' No, I don't think so.

Fleming took the business of titles very seriously, but sometimes got it wrong. When he was casting around for a title for *Live and Let Die*, he originally came up with *The Undertaker's Wind* – a reference, I believe, to a prevailing wind in Jamaica, and not to a mortician's flatulence.

Live and Let Die was only the second Bond novel, and the Bond craze had yet to take off: if Fleming had stuck to his original title the book might have bombed, he might never have written another, and the history of popular culture might have been very different.

The words that matter most in any book, of course, are neither at the beginning nor the end, but on the front cover. Would great books have become great books had they been called something else? In 1924, a young writer sent his latest novel to his publisher with what he considered to be a catchy and intriguing title: *Trimalchio in West Egg*. His editor loved the book and hated the title. 'Consider as quickly as you can a change,' he wrote. F.

Scott Fitzgerald duly considered *Trimalchio*, *Among the Ash Heaps and Millionaires*, *Under the Red White and Blue*, *The High-Bouncing Lover* (a good title, certainly, but perhaps not for this book), *Trimalchio's Banquet*, *On the Road to West Egg* (which would have made Jack Kerouac's life more difficult) and *Incident at West Egg*. Finally, he settled on *The Great Gatsby*, which was just as well for him, and for us.

Joseph Heller had planned to call his novel *Catch-18*. But then it emerged that Leon Uris was about to publish a war novel entitled *Mila 18*, and there was an obvious danger of confusion.

'I was heartbroken,' Heller said in an interview in 1975. 'I thought eighteen was the only number.' He toyed with *Catch-11* (rejected because of the 1960 film *Ocean's Eleven*), then *Catch-14* and finally, with extreme reluctance, Heller dragged his catch four integers higher than originally planned, and created not only a bestseller, but an enduring part of the English language.

Looking back, *Catch-18* seems pedestrian, where the gentle alliteration and duality of *Catch-22*, a novel in which everything is doubled, works as no other number could.

Margaret Mitchell wrestled with several titles for her novel, including *Not in Our Stars*, *Tote the Weary Load*, *Tomorrow is Another Day* (which sounds like a Bond film) and *Bugles Sang True*, before settling on the indisputably correct one, *Gone with the Wind*. Last year George Orwell's *1984* was voted the book that best defines the twentieth century. Would that have been the case if he had maintained the title *The Last Man in Europe*?

Sometimes, the world might have been a better place if an author had stuck to his or her original idea. If Hitler had been allowed to call *Mein Kampf* (My Struggle) by its original long-winded name, *Four-and-a-Half Years of Struggle Against Lies, Stupidity and Cowardice*, then perhaps its poison might have spread less easily.

Bleak House is a wonderful title, but I also like the one Charles Dickens came up with first: *Tom-All-Alone's Factory that Got Into Chancery and Never Got Out*. *Martin Chuzzlewit* was almost *Martin Chuzzletoe*, or even *Martin Sweetledew*.

Intriguingly, T.S. Eliot's original draft of *The Wasteland*, before Ezra Pound set to work on it, was called *He Do the Police in Different Voices*, taken from a passage in Dickens's *Our Mutual Friend* in which a young man is praised by Betty for his dramatic reading.

Raymond Chandler was a master of the apt and pithy book title, but some of his best were rejected: *All Guns are Loaded* never saw the printer's ink, and nor did *Lament but No Tears*. 'I'm trying to think up a good title for you to want to change,' Chandler wrote grumpily to his editor, Alfred A. Knopf.

The Dickensian-style deliberately over-explanatory title has recently become all the rage, with titles such as *The Curious Incident of the Dog in the Night-time*, and *A Short History of Tractors in Ukrainian*. But I am of the view – and history seems to bear this out – that in book titles, less is more.

You don't have to be a brilliant publisher, let alone Raymond Chandler, to know that only one of the following four titles was destined to be a bestseller: *The Summer of the Shark*, *The Terror of the Monster*, *The Jaws of the Leviathan* and plain old *Jaws*.

We're all speaking Geek

FIFTEEN YEARS AFTER THE birth of the world wide web, the lines of battle are clear. On one side the still young culture of the internet – anarchic, playful, joyfully (and sometimes wilfully) inaccurate, global and uncontrollable; on the other, a paper-based set of priorities – precise, polite, often national in perspective and increasingly paranoid. The latter seeks to manage, limit and define the culture; the former delights in its resistance to regulation.

The battle rages in the conflict between the *Encyclopaedia Britannica* and Wikipedia, the sprawling internet encyclopaedia, the canon versus the loose cannon. This week it erupted in the nursery, when the child-rearing guru Gina Ford threw a tantrum and launched her bizarre attempt to shut down the Mumsnet website because some of the mums had been rude about her.

But in no area of the culture is the collision more intense than over the English language, for the web has changed English more radically than any invention since paper, and much faster. According to Paul Payack, who runs the Global Language Monitor, there are currently 988,974 words in the English language, with thousands more emerging every month. By his calculation, English will soon adopt its one millionth word. To put that statistic another way, for every French word, there are now ten in English.

That claim has enraged traditional lexicographers. The twenty-volume *OED* has 301,100 entries, and purists point out that Mr Payack has little in the way of method and few criteria to define what really constitutes a word. But that, of course, is the point.

He found the remaining 687,874 words by scouring the internet. Every digital English dictionary was combed, before adding in the emerging words, the hybrids, Chinglish (Chinese-English), the slang, the linguistic odds and sods, and even Hollywords, terms created by the film industry. If a word is used in English, it was acceptable.

The nearest rival to English in sheer fecundity is Chinese, and with 1.3 billion Chinese now being officially urged to learn English, the result is nomogamosis (it is on the list: 'A state of marital harmony; a condition in which spouses are well matched') and many, many offspring, some of them rather sweet. 'Drinktea', for example, is a sign on a shop door meaning 'closed', but also derives from the Mandarin for 'resting'.

The so-called tipping point may have come in the mid-1990s at the same time as the invention of the first effective web browser, for ever since the web has served as a seedbed for language, for the cross-fertilisation and rapid evolution of words.

So far from debasing the language, the rapid expansion of English on the web may be enriching the mother tongue. Like Latin, it has developed different forms that bear little relation to one another: a speaker of Hinglish (Hindi-English) would have little to say to a Chinglish speaker. But while the root of Latin took centuries to grow its linguistic branches, modern non-standard English is evolving at fabulous speed. The language of the internet itself, the cyberisms that were once the preserve of a few web boffins, has simultaneously expanded into a new argot of words and idioms: Ancient or Classic Geek has given way to Modern Geek.

The web has revived the possibilities of word-coinage in a way not seen since Shakespearean times, when the language was gradually assuming its modern structure but was not yet codified into dictionaries (the first comprehensive English dictionary appeared in 1730). Then, as now, the lack of control, and the rapid absorption of new terms and ideas through exploration, colonisation and science, enabled a great flowering of words. Of the 24,000 words used by Shakespeare, perhaps 1,700 were his own inventions: 'besmirch', 'anchovy', 'shudder', 'impede'.

Thanks to the internet, we are witnessing the second great age of the neologism, a fantastic outpouring of words and phrases to describe new ideas or reshape old ideas in novel forms of language. Today, a word does not need the slow spread of verbal usage or literature to gain acceptance. If a word works, the internet can breathe instant life into it.

You do not have to be Shakespeare to forge words. George W. Bush is constantly evolving new words, but no one should 'misunderestimate' the ability of lesser wordsmiths to do likewise. So many words that ought to exist inexplicably do not.

There should be a term for that momentary flash of embarrassment when a mobile phone rings and you wonder if it is yours; and for the vague disappointment you feel when you think you are about to sneeze, take a deep breath and then don't. (National Public Radio in the US recently held a competition to name this proto-sneeze and came up with 'sniff-hanger'.)

Why is there a word for déjà vu, but nothing to describe the opposite experience, far more common, of knowing something perfectly well but being quite unable to remember it?

Last year *The Times* reported the existence, in the Bantu language Tshiluba, of the long-needed word *ilunga*, meaning 'a person who is ready to forgive any abuse for the first time, to tolerate it a second time, but never a third time'.

Subsequent investigations suggested that the word may not exist in Tshiluba, but it exists now in English, as thousands of entries on the web attest, and the language is better for it.

Rather than fight the word loans and word borrowings, the strange hybrids and new coinages, we should welcome them. New words expand our world. They can even change it. If *ilunga* is the thrice-repeated offence that cannot be forgiven, then its opposite is an Arabic word, *taraadin*, meaning 'I win, you win', the face-saving way to end an argument. As bombs fall on southern Lebanon and missiles on northern Israel, the world could profit from learning a new language, in which *ilunga* is solved by *taraadin*.

Of human bondage

LEE THOMPSON LEFT HIS pebble-dashed semi in Foster Road, Darlington, and went to his local butcher's to buy some bacon. Nothing strange about that, except that Mr Thompson had brought with him a woman, on a chain, with collar and wrist cuffs. The butcher refused to serve him until the lady was off the leash: in Darlington, they don't serve bacon to bondage enthusiasts.

Mr Thompson, it transpired, is the self-styled 'master of the Darlington Kaotions', an offshoot of the Goreans, a cult inspired by the science fiction novels of John Norman that has an estimated 25,000 members in Britain. First published in the 1960s, *The Chronicles of Gor* tells of mighty warriors on a distant planet, where society is strictly divided by caste and women are kept as slaves. Surprise surprise, the girl slaves really like being slaves, and do anything their masters desire, including cooking, cleaning and, of course, sex on demand.

Here is an extract: 'I took Constance by the arm, and threw her to his feet. It was a simple act of Gorean courtesy.

'Constance looked at me wildly. "Please him," I said.

'"Yes, Master," she whispered.'

John Norman, the nom de plume of Dr John Lange, an American university lecturer, has sold millions of copies worldwide, and inspired a devoted following keen to live out his sexist science fiction fantasy. The Gorean website tells us: 'Goreans believe quite naturally that men were born free, and women, born to be their slaves . . .'

Mr Thompson first read *The Tarnsman of Gor* when he was thirteen. He is now thirty-one, and says that he has been master to eight slave women so far. The turnover is quite high because, apparently, 'it's hard work for everyone. Girls leave when they've had enough.' As Mr Thompson discovered, being a Gorean does not make it easy to bring home the bacon.

The Chronicles represents a particularly excessive species of cult reading. These are not Trekkies, dressing up as Mr Spock for a weekend to chatter in Klingon, but people who believe they have found a special truth in one corner of fiction and have become, in a manner of speaking, shackled to it.

The act of reading allows the reader, briefly, to identify with someone else, to leave their own world and enter another. Some go further, and believe they have seen in fiction a reflection of who they truly are. A very few lose themselves entirely in the words.

The novelist Toby Litt recently discussed the distorted grip of the cult book on the Penguin readers' group website. 'Cult books are overvalued by the minority because undervalued by the majority,' he wrote. 'In some ways they're books that take over people's lives; in the most extreme cases, they invest so much in them that there's a feedback loop going on and they start to see that book in their own lives.'

The Kaotions, adults safely chained up behind the lace curtains of Darlington, are merely funny, but in some hands cult fiction can be actively dangerous. Mark Chapman shot John Lennon and then went back to reading J.D. Salinger's *Catcher in the Rye*. 'I am indeed the "catcher in the rye" of this generation,' he told police. John Hinckley, Ronald Reagan's would-be assassin, and Arthur Bremer, who shot Governor George Wallace, also claimed to have found inspiration in the book's alienated hero. *The Rough Guide to Cult Fiction* defines a cult book or author as one which inspires 'lengthy and irrational devotion probably, although not necessarily, by an ardent minority'. Cult readers tend to identify not just with the fictional characters but also the author, particularly if a writer's problems mirror their own. 'If the true cult book should be out of print for ten years, the truly cult author ought to have written one seminal novel, behaved abominably in public and then have died tragically young or, better still, vanished.'

Some books inspire an almost mystical fervour in readers. Then again, many religious texts, starting with the Bible, have a substantial admixture of fiction.

L. Ron Hubbard, the founder of Scientology, wrote thirty-one books related to his new religion, but more than 200 science fiction novels. 'The only demand I make of my reader,' James Joyce once joked, 'is that he should devote his whole life to reading my works.' Today Joyce would be astonished, and I suspect somewhat alarmed, at the level of devotion inspired by his novels.

Yet cult books also flourish in opposition to oppression. Samizdat editions were copied and distributed in Soviet bloc countries to evade the censors. Anyone who had a copy would make more copies, by hand or typewriter, to be passed from one reader to another on tatty carbon paper, objects of special veneration, the home-made, secret bestseller.

Many books inspire; some books can captivate. But in the hands of particularly impressionable readers, the result can be a sort of enslavement.

There is dismay in Darlington at the discovery of a sci fi-based sex cult. 'This country's going down the pan,' one neighbour said. But then, one man's perversion is another man's literary classic. The book-based Kaotian sect is really just a reading group that took things to extremes, allowing obsessive fans to escape, briefly, to a fantasy world where being offered a sex slave is a simple act of courtesy, like inviting the neighbours over for a cup of tea.

Back on Gor, 'The tarnsman returns home from his capture flight, a girl bound naked across the saddle ... Swords are often drawn on Gor over women, and particularly over lovely slaves. Women are prizes. It is no wonder that men fight over them with ferocity.'

When you think about it, the world of Gor is not so very different from Darlington on a Saturday night.

Swallow anecdotes whole

I HAVE ALWAYS BEEN wary of anecdotes. The after-dinner anecdotalist demands silence as he delivers himself of a 'funny story' that supposedly illustrates some aspect of character or modern life. One may not interrupt an anecdote: each is a small, set-piece performance, often saying more about the teller than the subject.

Towards the end of his life, it is said, Kingsley Amis tended to speak almost entirely in anecdotes, waspish little tales to sting his enemies and, not infrequently, himself. When a man is in his anecdotage, he has usually run out of conversation.

But I am now a convert to the anecdote, thanks to John Gross's *New Oxford Book of Literary Anecdotes*, a pithy and eclectic collection of tales that reveal the vanity, generosity, foolishness and wisdom of writers, but above all their eccentricity.

Collections of anecdotes are a peculiarly British phenomenon, and collections of literary anecdotes quintessentially so. It is a reflection of the status that we accord to literature that we care for the small, tall stories of a writer's life far more than any other profession. Theatrical anecdotes invariably tell of puffed-up pomp punctured; political anecdotes make their subjects seem either heroic or idiotic.

Literary anecdotes, however, can add another dimension to a character with whom the reader already feels familiar through the writing. As Gross writes: 'We value anecdotes about a writer, beyond their immediate point, because they bear the stamp of his or her personality ... anecdotes are a form of entertainment – at their best, an art form.'

The ideal literary anecdote sheds light not just on the character of the writer but also the nature of his or her writing and milieu. The stories that cluster around Oscar Wilde are legion, but the one that says most about him was written by Arthur Conan Doyle, after watching him in full flow at a dinner party: 'He had the art of seeming interested in all that we could say. He had a delicacy of feeling and tact ... he took as well as gave, but what he gave was unique.'

Discovering a writer's weaknesses through anecdote does not necessarily detract from the pleasure of reading his or her words, and sometimes the reverse. Gross retells the story of Ernest Hemingway's dinner with the American playwright Lewis Galantière, which went swimmingly until the writer, aware that his wife Hadley was as enchanted by their companion as he was, challenged Galantière to a boxing match. 'After a minute or two, during which neither man threw a single punch, Galantière straightened up and laughingly said that he had had enough.' Galantière took one glove off and replaced his glasses, at which point Hemingway thumped him in the face. The moment was telling, not just for the raw display of Hemingway machismo, but his reaction afterwards: 'He felt no contrition ... He had effectively demonstrated his masculine superiority.' The anecdote does not make one like Hemingway more – quite the opposite – but it may make one read Hemingway with deeper understanding.

Writers are drawn closer to us through their foibles, made more human by embarrassment and informality: E.M. Forster bowing, with grave myopia, to a large wedding cake, having mistaken the confection for Queen Mary; Nabokov being hailed as 'McNab' by his football team-mates who could not get their tongues around the Russian vowels of his name; Zelda Fitzgerald drunkenly calling out the fire brigade and then, when asked by the firemen where the fire was, striking her breast and shouting 'Here!'

Truth is not necessary to a good anecdote, at least not the one-dimensional truth of fact. Through telling and retelling, an anecdote achieves a status that is almost myth, something more important and lasting than mere accuracy. Dante Gabriel Rossetti, it is said, was once walking with the painter John Butler Yeats when they spotted a chaffinch in the bushes. 'Rossetti stopped and nodded towards it. "That is my wife's soul," he said sadly – and immediately the chaffinch came and perched on his shoulder.' Obviously, this never happened, but it is the perfect reflection of the overwrought pre-Raphaelite sensibility.

Gross unearths old favourites, lines you wish you had said (and you will, Oscar, you will), but he also uncovers some gems that are certainly new to me. Everyone knows William Spooner got his turds wopsy-turvy. But who knew that he also transposed ideas and actions? When someone accidentally spilled salt on the tablecloth during a dinner party, Dr Spooner carefully poured claret on to it, 'till he had produced the little purple mound which would have been the endproduct if he had spilled claret on the tablecloth and then cast a heap of salt on the pool to absorb it'.

A knowledge of English literature based solely on anecdote would encourage the conclusion (not entirely unwarranted) that writers are almost always mad, bad or sozzled, and usually all three. Yet these stories also offer revealing little vignettes, illustrating the strange ways of the writer's mind: such as the time Beryl Bainbridge fell over while tipsy, banged her head, rang her mother (who had been dead for twenty years) and discovered that she was in conversation with the speaking clock. Bainbridge then found herself wondering about the woman behind that recorded voice. Instead of consulting a psychiatrist, the writer found inspiration.

Such anecdotes are literary garnish. Not to be confused with the meat and drink of literature itself, they are the piquant canapés accompanying a writer's life: they should be savoured, swallowed whole with a willing suspension of disbelief and on no account regurgitated in after-dinner speeches.

Judge a book by its cover

IN 1943 A YOUNG Italian inmate of Mauthausen concentration camp in Austria began to collect images.

Germano Facetti collected the photographs discarded by the Nazi camp guards, mementoes of those who had died, drawings, documents, plans, small fragments of the striped prison uniform – the shards of people's lives.

He carefully stored the relics in a yellow box that had once held photographic paper. This was Facetti's collage of one of the ghastliest places devised by man, a slave labour camp, in which the prisoners were worked to death making German munitions, and died in numbers so great that the final tally has never been ascertained.

Facetti survived. He was fit and young, and he followed the advice of an older compatriot: 'Learn German, never look your enemy in the eye, and never bend your shoulders' (thus limiting the effects of the devastating cold).

Originally arrested for putting up anti-fascist posters, he tried to ensure that the bombs he made in the camp would not work by urinating on them when the guards were not looking. He was still only twenty-seven when he was finally released from Mauthausen, the last death camp to be liberated. As the Americans marched in, Facetti staggered out, with his yellow box of memories under his arm.

There is a high probability that you have a little bit of Facetti in your bookshelves, for the former resistance fighter and death camp survivor went on to become perhaps the most influential book designer of the last century. As art director of Penguin from 1962 to 1971, he changed the face of books for ever.

Facetti died in 2006 at the age of seventy-nine, but anyone who learnt to love reading in the 1960s and 1970s will know his work. He redesigned the Penguin Classics with the austere but distinguished black background: Fiction, Crime, Modern Classics, Pelican Books and the Penguin English Library were each given the distinct Facetti touch. Under the designer's eye, Penguin books – cheap, everyday paperbacks – became collectibles.

Drawing on his prodigious visual memory, Facetti designed hundreds of books himself, while commissioning other covers from designers such as Alan Fletcher and Derek Birdsall. He had an extraordinary talent for selecting the single, often very simple image that would echo in the memory long after a book had been closed: the single staring tunnel-eye that he designed for the cover of George Orwell's *1984*; David Gentleman's woodcuts for Shakespeare, and myriad others.

Facetti could even make a visual impact with no image at all. J.D. Salinger insisted that no mere picture could be used to illustrate *The Catcher in the Rye*, so the designer came up with a plain silver cover and a horizontal dividing rule.

It remains one of the most distinctive Penguin covers of all.

Facetti's reign at the Penguin design department coincided with expanding books sales in Britain, and a young, highly literate population receptive to new imagery and innovative typography. The young man who had stored images in a Nazi concentration camp knew instinctively how to render literature and history more immediate and compelling by the use of pictures. His choices were both timely (reflecting the era and atmosphere of the writing) and timeless: 'The majority of great works of art have been created with a bearing to literature,' he wrote.

Penguin became the most recognisable brand in British books, yet Facetti also knew that the bond between books and images was a special one, no mere marketing fad.

In later years he would pour scorn on the use of art and design to sell rubbish to fools: 'Cat food, stomach powders, detergent, hair restorer, striped toothpaste, aftershave lotion, beforeshave lotion, slimming diets, fattening diets, deodorants, fizzy water, cigarettes, roll-ons, pull-ons and slip-ons.'

Perhaps it was the sensory deprivation involved in life and death at Mauthausen, dreary and deadly, that rendered Facetti so responsive to colour and image. He had witnessed such chaos and ugliness, but his designs were triumphs of ordered form and heightened beauty. More than half a century after his release from the prison camp, Facetti appeared in a short film by Anthony West entitled *The Yellow Box: A Short History of Hate*. Interviewed by three students, he is filmed opening the old box, and deferentially describing the relics and their meaning, to him and to history. At the end of his life, long retired and living in his farmhouse in La Spezia, Facetti would still get up at 3 a.m., to gaze at the mementoes of Mauthausen.

Facetti was not the only camp prisoner to respond to the horror with a determined act of memory. A fellow inmate was Simon Wiesenthal, who would later become the celebrated Nazi hunter. Where Facetti gathered his small icons, Wiesenthal used his own photographic memory to record the names, faces and crimes of his Nazi tormentors. At first he wrote down details of the guilty men; later, he committed them to memory, and when the camp was finally liberated, he offered his damning mental archive to American investigators then beginning the search for Nazi war criminals.

The young Italian took his box of memories and joined the Milanese practice of the architect and planner Ludovico Belgiojoso, a fellow inmate who had helped him to survive.

Wiesenthal, the young Austrian, took his memorised indictments, and began a lifelong hunt for justice.

In their determination to preserve memory, the two former prisoners were similar, but their responses to the Nazi death machine were also very different: one was determined to extract justice, to ensure that the world did not forget; the other helped to make literature unforgettable for the postwar generation.

Intellectual (n.): clever dick,
not quite British

THE BRITISH LIKE TO dislike intellectuals. There is something a little too foreign about the intellectual, a little too self-conscious; in truth, a little too French.

I was living in France when the *Dictionnaire des intellectuels français* was published, a breeze-block tome listing every great Gallic thinker from Raymond Abellio to Emile Zola. Régis Debray, the left-wing sage, estimated that, at this moment, and every moment down the ages, France is home to at least 120,000 intellectuals, including himself. The dictionary runs to 1,300 pages.

'*Il n'est pas un intello*' is an insult in France. In Britain, it is more likely to be a compliment, for we like to maintain that we don't really have any intellectuals at all; or never did, or did in some legendary, more cultured past, but no longer do. There is considerable confusion in this country over what an intellectual actually is, but W.H. Auden probably came closest to the popular attitude:

> To the man-in-the-street, who, I'm sorry to say,
> Is a keen observer of life,
> The word 'Intellectual' suggests straight away
> A man who's untrue to his wife.

Clever Englishmen take particular delight in demeaning intellectuals. Kingsley Amis reflected that an intellectual was most likely to be 'some fearful woman who's going to talk to you about Ezra Pound and hasn't got large breasts and probably doesn't wash much'. George Orwell, the greatest British intellectual of the last century, maintained: 'The

English are not intellectual. They have a horror of abstract thought, they feel no need for any philosophy or systematic "world view".'

More pithily, he dismissed Jean-Paul Sartre as 'a bag of wind'. Great British minds think alike: intellectuals tend to be unhygienic, adulterous, small-breasted French windbags.

Yet British anti-intellectualism is as superficial as French intellectual posturing. In his excellent new book *Absent Minds: Intellectuals in Britain*, Stefan Collini, Professor of Intellectual History at Cambridge, attacks Britain's mythical self-image as a practical, no-nonsense nation that doesn't hold with Frenchified philosophising.

'British intelligentsia' still seems a contradiction in terms, yet the British intellectual may be in a healthier state today than ever before. Modern British intellectual life has neither the gloomy, preening vanity of the French variety, nor the ideological sectarianism of American public debate. It is no accident that the two most important public intellectuals in America – Andrew Sullivan and Christopher Hitchens – are both British.

For all that British intellectuals are dismissed as the 'chattering classes', their chatter is heard more widely than ever, and taken more seriously. British newspaper comment pages are a ferment of intelligent discourse compared to most other countries (although we hacks should generally be regarded as an intellectual sub-species). Avowedly intellectual publications such as *Prospect*, the *London Review of Books* and the *TLS* not only survive, but also thrive. There is still a widespread belief in the power of ideas to change the world. As Collini points out, the intellectual will continue to play a vital role in observing and shaping society, 'whether or not that particular word continues to be used to identify it'.

The lament that pop culture has swamped British intellectual life is heard constantly, and yet Britain has arguably fused the life of the mind with the world of celebrity with extraordinary success – of which Germaine Greer's appearance on *Celebrity Big Brother* was the ultimate demonstration. Salman Rushdie, a difficult writer of challenging books, is considered prime fodder for the gossip columns.

The 'information age' provides a platform for disseminating ideas that earlier intellectuals, drawn from and usually addressing a privileged elite, could never have imagined.

Yet we consign our 'eggheads' and 'boffins' to 'ivory towers' and 'groves of academe'. Politicians who show signs of excess cerebration are regarded as slightly suspicious, and derided as 'three-brains'.

There is more to this than British philistinism (though there is certainly some of that). Once again, we may blame the French. The word 'intellectual' came to Britain barely a century ago, linked to the group of thinkers surrounding Zola and supporting Alfred Dreyfus; but British ambivalence towards intellectuals dates back at least as far as the French Revolution, when dreamers and thinkers reconstructed society by deploying abstract ideas, experimental ideology and extreme violence.

The notion of a distinct and often dissident caste distributing wisdom to the masses has never taken root here, in intellectual soil rendered acidic by scepticism, empiricism and a distrust of impractical (i.e. French) constructs. That distinction is reflected in the apocryphal remark made by a French diplomat to his British counterpart: 'This is all very well in practice, but will it work in theory?' The British intellectual would never describe himself as one. This perhaps explains why a list of the 100 top British intellectuals, in

Prospect, caused such a flutter among men and women of letters: those on the list are uncertain whether to be flattered or aggrieved; and those left off it, even more so.

Orwell would have insisted on having his name expunged from any such list. Perhaps that is what defines a British intellectual, for Orwell was the defining anti-intellectual thinker. A genuine polymath, whose plain-spoken passions ranged from art to politics, Orwell raged against intellectuals for their insincerity, for imprecise language and unrealistic posturing. He understood the complacency that came with the term 'intellectual' and rejected it utterly. In response to Sartre's obscure and self-righteous pronouncements, he could not resist the very British response, in his own words, to 'give him a good boot'.

This is why there will never be a *Dictionary of British Intellectuals*. Orwell would never have agreed to join, on the pure Marxist rationale that such a club might want him as a member.

As books, online journals get blogged down

MAY YOUR BLOOD RUN cold, oh Orange Prize. Beware, great Samuel Johnson Prize. Tremble in your complacent socks, mighty Man Booker. The Blooker Prize has arrived: the first competition for books that started life as weblogs, or blogs.

The blook (blog+book) is touted as the next revolution in publishing, the moment when the online musings of unknown writers will invade mainstream literature in their hordes. The first Blooker was awarded in 2006 to Julie

Powell, a former secretary and nanny from New York, for *Julie and Julia: 365 Days, 524 Recipes, 1 Tiny Apartment Kitchen* (Little, Brown).

Ms Powell's book began as a blog, an online journal describing her efforts to cook all 524 recipes in Julia Child's 1961 classic *Mastering the Art of French Cooking*.

The blog, with its sideways comments on the author's life in New York, caught the public imagination. Hundreds, then thousands, of readers responded with comments and suggestions (and, in a few generous instances, with ingredients posted through Ms Powell's letterbox).

As tends to happen on the internet, the audience expanded in leaps and bytes.

Commercial publishers began to take an interest; the blog became a book, and has since sold 100,000 copies in the US. It is now slated to become a movie, the first film of a blog of a book – the world's first flook.

In the final chapter of this happy-ever-after tale of online literature, Ms Powell won £2,000, beating strong competition from *The Intimate Adventures of a London Call Girl* by Belle de Jour, the chronicle of a prostitute which turned its first trick online and was receiving 15,000 hits a day at the height of its popularity. Another strong contender was *Eggs, Bacon, Chips and Beans: 50 Great Cafés and the Stuff that Makes Them Great*, an artery-clogging investigation into the delights of London's greasy spoons.

The Blooker is sponsored by Lulu.com, a website that offers would-be writers the chance to put their work on the internet for download and sale 'on demand'. Bob Young, the computer entrepreneur and owner of the site, launched the Blooker as a promotional tool and immediately struck a cyber-chord: eighty-nine blooks were submitted by 'blauthors' from more than a dozen countries.

Further proof that blooks have arrived in the mainstream comes in the Samuel Johnson Prize, the British award for the year's best non-fiction: on the short list is *Baghdad Burning*, based on the blog of an anonymous Iraqi woman.

The blook, Mr Young insists, is a 'landmark in the history of books'; he predicts that in time the Blooker will overtake the Booker.

As with most things surrounding the web and its unpredictable self-replicating patterns, there is a great deal of hyperbole here, but more than a grain of truth.

The prospect of blogs evolving into books is, in some ways, alarming. There are at present thirty-two million weblogs worldwide, with more appearing at the rate of 100,000 a day. Most (and this cannot be said too often) are unrelieved tripe: barely literate musings on abstruse subjects by people who need to get out more.

Mr Young is honest about the quality of the writing on his online enterprise: 'Most of our books are really, really bad.'

There are more than 20,000 books on his website, of which three quarters have sold at least one copy – this means that one quarter of these books are so dreadful that not even the mothers of the people who wrote them can actually bring themselves to pay money for them.

But the best blogs are more than mere confessionals or the narcissistic rantings of writers insufficiently daunted by the empty page. There is a distinct literary style to the blook: edgily direct and intimate, inchoate but passionate, responsive and unfettered. Blogs are ideas explosions, rolling conversations between an individual and the rest of the world, without structure, form, chapters or endings. The epistolary style, gradually emerging in partly formed episodes, can create a real-time narrative that is genuinely engrossing. These are notebooks that have taken on a life of their own, nurtured and expanded by the reading public in an entirely new kind of literary symbiosis.

There is a subversive, anarchic feel to the best blogs, for they tend to be written by people who exist far below the radar of mainstream publishing – a London callgirl, an Iraqi woman caught up in war, a man with an astonishing appetite for greasy café food. The Booker remains resolutely highbrow; the brow of the Blooker is, by definition, as low as you can go.

There are other, more practical, reasons why the blogosphere has become fertile territory for trawling publishers. Blogs have a fan base that can be quantified before a single book is printed; the reactions of readers help to refine the writing, and bloggers have a cheap and accessible platform from which to sell their books.

Yet the number of blogs that will fit comfortably between book covers is probably quite small, precisely because of the restrictions of the format. The delight of the blog is the opportunity to tune in and see where the conversation has gone.

Formalised into book form, even the best online journals can get blogged down.

The blook may be a new hybrid literary form, but like all books (and, for that matter, all blogs) quality of writing is what marks out the few of merit from the mass of dross.

The Blooker prizewinner (who once worked as nanny for the double Booker-winner Peter Carey) may have her literary origins in cyberspace, but her feet are firmly on the ground. The blog, Ms Powell has said, 'is certainly another tool for writers out there to break their way in. But being a blogger does not make you a great writer.'

The death of the literary smoker

WRITERS HAVE PROBABLY SMOKED more enthusiastically than any other class of human being, with the possible exception of trade union officials. Novelists and poets have explored the ritual and romance, the mystery and misery, of tobacco for centuries while steadily smoking themselves to death. Great writers have often tended to be great smokers, although the greatest of all did not inhale: no Shakespeare play mentions tobacco.

But as anti-smoking culture spreads, so the evil weed is steadily being weeded out of literature. The US postal service plucked the cigarette from the hands of Thornton Wilder, the playwright. André Malraux, the philosopher and author, was seldom seen in life without a cigarette dangling from his lips, but the French Government insisted that he stub it out, airbrushing the cancer stick out of a commemorative stamp.

In a new edition of *Goodnight Moon*, the children's classic by Margaret Wise Brown, the publishers digitally altered a photograph of the illustrator, Clement Hurd, to remove a cigarette from his hand: Hurd was left making an unintended V-sign at the camera.

The crusade against smoking is changing literature itself. This week Scotland became the first part of Britain to ban smoking in public places, rekindling rumours that one of the country's favourite fictional figures might emigrate in protest. Inspector John Rebus, the chain-smoking detective created by the novelist Ian Rankin, has spent much of his literary life in bars, in an atmosphere of 'glazed smiles and cigarette smoke'.

Rebus is not the sort to be found shivering outside the pub door, sucking a smoke in the rain, and Rankin has hinted that the detective might quit Scotland altogether so that 'he can find a country where it is possible to smoke in a bar'.

Fictional characters, such as Bridget Jones, who do smoke are usually desperately trying to give up, while authors, like film-makers, are trying to cut down on cigarettes, using them only to make a point. As the novelist Alexandra Campbell wrote recently, smoking in fiction is 'often used as a short cut to convey emotions such as anxiety (and) character traits such as rebelliousness or cynicism'. Writers, she said, should 'consider their responsibilities' before allowing a character to smoke: 'Portraying cigarettes negatively is a wasted cause. It's much better not to have them there at all.'

The literary smoker is a dying breed. Even imaginary people must now be healthy.

Fictional smokers, like real ones, must hide themselves away in corners, or give up.

Smoke suffuses the literature of the past. Where would Sherlock Holmes be without his Meerschaum? Philip Marlowe's cigarettes are as integral to his character as his wisecracks. Bertie Wooster lights up straight after breakfast.

Readers of the future will look back on the nicotine-stained literature of the past with bafflement, for the process of writing is inextricably bound up with the pleasure of smoking.

Some writers simply could not do one without the other. Sir Compton Mackenzie wrote eighty-one books by the age of seventy-four, having smoked, according to his own estimate, at least half a ton of tobacco. 'The harder I work,' he declared, 'the more I need to smoke because tobacco is the handmaid of literature.'

A less likely apostle for smoking was J.M. Barrie, who wrote *My Lady Nicotine: A Study in Smoke*, fourteen years before the arrival of Peter Pan. Barrie taught generations of children to believe in fairies; he, on the other hand, believed in the magic of smoking. With the introduction of tobacco, England woke up from a long sleep, he wrote in 1896. 'Suddenly a new zest had been given to life.'

Mikhail Bakhtin may be the only writer who actually smoked what he wrote. Driven to distraction by a wartime shortage of cigarette papers, the Russian literary theorist ended up smoking the manuscript of his book on the *Bildungsroman*. Others found the joys of smoking superior to all other earthly temptations: 'A woman is only a woman,' Rudyard Kipling wrote in *The Betrothed*, 'but a good cigar is a smoke.'

Anyone who has written while smoking, and vice versa, knows how tobacco can become an addictive form of punctuation: a pause for reflection, a reward for a completed sentence, a spur to memory, a brief pocket of smoky idleness. 'The believing we do something when we do nothing is the first illusion of tobacco,' Ralph Waldo Emerson wrote.

Addicted smoker-writers tend to believe that their writing is improved by nicotine. Martin Amis once admitted: 'I'm sure if I stopped smoking I would start writing sentences like: "It was bitterly cold." Or "It was bakingly hot".'

In *Smoke: A Global History of Smoking*, Sander L. Gilman and Zhou Xun write: 'The smoking of tobacco has shaped invention and culture, capturing the imagination like nothing else in history.' Smoking has always had a mystical aura. For the Aztecs, possibly the first smokers, tobacco smoke was a goddess who protected them from witchcraft (and snakes).

Given the writerly addiction to tobacco, both as a writing aid and a literary device, giving up will not be easy, and we can expect some withdrawal symptoms as literature kicks the 7,000-year-old habit. In the words of A.P. Herbert: 'I have given up smoking again ... God! I feel fit. Homicidal, but fit. A different man. Irritable, moody, depressed, rude, nervy, perhaps; but the lungs are fine.'

As every reformed smoker can attest, literature may be healthier for giving up smoking, but it will never feel quite the same again.

English is a language o' the heid but Scots is ane o' the hairt

THE SCOTS LANGUAGE, ACCORDING to both its opponents and its practitioners, has been steadily dying for the past 400 years. In 1887, Robert Louis Stevenson predicted that 'the day draws near when this illustrious and malleable tongue shall be quite forgotten'. *The Daily Mail* reported recently that the language was sufffering from rigor mortis. Even William McIlvanney, whose novels deploy the brogue and patter so expertly, has declared that Scots is doomed.

Yet Scots, thrawn and braw, resolutely refuses to die. Indeed, the language of Robert Burns is showing signs of a resurrection, most notably in modern Scottish literature. According to the latest survey, more than 1.6 million people speak Lowland Scots (Broad Scots, Braid Scots, Doric or Lallans) in some form.

You can sponsor a Scots word for £20; the compilers of the *Concise Scots Dictionary* are appealing for Scots speakers to identify new words; there is even a Scots version of the Scottish Parliament website, including the Statement o Principles.

Scots is at present classified under European law as a 'secondary language', with Cornish and Ulster-Scots, but pressure is building to have it declared a minority language, like Scots Gaelic. Meanwhile, the political debate continues over whether Scots is really a language at all, or merely a dialect – a bastardised form of English deserving of no special protection. The issue is intensely political, inextricably bound up with issues of national pride.

Defenders of this ancient tongue recently acquired a most powerful literary ally in the form of Peter Rabbit, the world's favourite bunny, whose adventures have finally been translated into Scots: 'Aince upon a time there wis fower wee Kinnen, an thair nems wis Flopsy, Mopsy, Cotton-bun, an Peter. They bid wi thair Mither in a san-baunk, aneath the ruit o a muckle fir-tree.' Rab C. Nesbitt meets Mr McGregor.

In a new edition of his twenty-year-old study *Scots: The Mither Tongue*, Billy Kay passionately argues that Scots not only boasts a unique and expanding vocabulary, but a distinct syntax and grammar. Scots is further removed from English than Slovak is from Czech, or Norwegian is from Swedish.

Despite its regular obituaries (usually written by Englishmen) the Scots language remains one of the most expressive and muscular in the world. English may be the greatest word-well, with more than 600,000 entries in the *OED*, but Scots is almost as deep: there are half a million words in the combined *Scottish National Dictionary* and the twelve-volume *Dictionary of the Older Scottish Tongue*.

There is an agile vividness to Scots words, a lilting poetry that seems to have evolved out of the land and its weather. Consider, for example, the variety of words for different sorts of wind: 'skolder', 'guster', 'skuther', 'shushle', 'tirl' and 'gurl'. Only Scots could have produced the word 'dreich' – meaning 'dark, gloomy and dour' – but above all evoking that weather pattern, peculiar to Scotland, when the rain blots out the horizon, sometimes for weeks on end. 'Hoch-magandie' is a far better word than mere 'fornication'. Who would not rather blow their nose ('neb') into a 'snochter-dichter' than a mere handkerchief? Is there a better way to describe a nagging woman than a 'snell-gabbit besom'?

Edwin Muir was the first to point out that Scots is a language of the heart, while English is a language of the head. It was not always so. In 1398, the Scottish Parliament began publishing statutes in Scots instead of Latin, while the Scots literary tradition dates back to Barbour's fourteenth-century epic *Brus*, the narrative poem describing Robert the Bruce's wars against the English.

The two languages were ever at war. The Reformation began the erosion of Scots, for the Bible was translated only into English. Scots retreated, becoming predominantly an oral language, rejected by the educated elite. Yet it continued to flourish as a literary medium in the language of the makars, the Scottish bards, and the ballads and the revival of the eighteenth century.

Scots was the language of poetry and song, while English dominated the classroom, the courts and the Kirk. Robert Burns wrote his poetry in Scots, but his correspondence in English. In *Scots: the Language of the People*, Carl Mac-Dougal writes: 'English was seen as the language of the intellect . . . Scottish MPs at Westminster took elocution lessons, and Scots was seen as corrupt, uncouth and under-developed.' Yet it has continued to develop, in slang and song. It would be a whigmaleerie (fantasy) to suggest that Scots can regain its former power, but it retains a hearty expressiveness that can make English seem sparse and gen-teel by contrast.

As Kay observes, 'even people who do not understand the language feel its power to communicate something profound in the human condition'. To an English speaker, the individual words of a Burns poem may seem quite incomprehensible; but declaimed, or read through half-closed eyes, the cadences emerge as fresh as when they were written.

There are just three words of Scots that almost everyone in the world can say or, more accurately, sing and it is no accident that those words are indelibly associated with good fellowship and strong drink. Only a small fraction of the revellers who chorus 'Auld Lang Syne' on New Year's Eve have a clue what the words mean. But that is the enduring glory of the Scots tongue: it is spoken with the heart, not the head.

Insulting your closest neighbour

THE ENGLISH CHANNEL, THEY say, is only a few miles wide, but a thousand years deep. Britain and France like to imagine themselves as polar opposites, but no two countries have cultures so thoroughly entwined: ours is an intimate enmity, the strange minuet of *le couple infernal*. Only Japan and China could claim to have disliked one another for longer.

The Anglo-French tussle is a love–hate relationship based on mistrust and admiration, on alliance but seldom friendship, on envy and rivalry. For long periods, it has broken out in bitter warfare; mostly it rubs along with an air of uneasy distrust. This fractious bond has had a profound effect on Europe and the world.

One consequence is the extraordinarily fertile crop of Anglo-French insults. No other countries have deliberately offended one another quite so venomously over the centuries. Indeed, the trading of invective has gone on for so long that it has become ingrained in our respective cultures. British insults focus on French arrogance, deceit, inadequate personal hygiene and inability to win world wars without British help.

When the French wish to give offence, they point to a nation of shopkeepers, an unsophisticated race of brutes who cannot drink, make love or cook. Language, literature, clothing, manners, sex, sport, war and food: each has provided myriad opportunities to give, and take, offence. As Britain and France tussled over which country should host the 2012 Olympic Games, President Chirac instinctively resorted to a food fight. 'The only thing (the British) have ever given European farming is mad cow disease,' he said. 'You can't trust people who cook as badly as that.'

The statement was greeted with predictable British uproar, but M. Chirac was only speaking a language of *rosbif*-baiting and frog-bashing hallowed by time and animosity. The beef of old England was deliberately embraced as a national dish in contrast to Frenchified cuisine: fussy, and faintly effeminate. The reciprocal distaste has survived long periods of apparent friendship. In 1919, a year after Britain and France had won a bloody war as allies, the Foreign Office still insisted: 'Our relations with France never have been, are not, and probably never will be, sufficiently stable and friendly to justify the construction of a Channel tunnel.'

The French put Britain's ill humour down to poor weather. 'The vapours of the bogs of Albion,' Rigoley de Juvigny declared in 1772, 'have engendered a philosophical epidemic, which kills genius, agitates minds and produces anti-national taste.'

Britain happily responds that in the matter of humour, France is at a severe disadvantage, since the French sense of humour is obscure at best, and often impenetrable to the

Anglo-Saxon. It was not until 1932 that the word 'humour' was even admitted to the French dictionary by a reluctant Académie Française.

Great leaders of both sides have tended to blame the nation across the water for every political setback: 'England alone is responsible for all the miseries by which Europe has been assailed,' Napoleon insisted – surely deserving some kind of award in the black pot and kettle stakes. Queen Victoria opted for hauteur, although she would have rejected the word as yet another Gallic intrusion: 'I fear the French are so fickle, corrupt and ignorant, so conceited and foolish that it is hopeless to think of them being sensibly governed . . . they are incurable.'

And for every Briton laying claim to France, there is a Frenchman who sees Albion, perfidious as she may be, as a Norman outpost. Clemenceau sighed that Britain was 'a colony that turned out rather badly' (yet he remained a committed Anglophile).

Naturally, the best cross-Channel insults focus on sex. France, the country that invented sado-masochism, insists that flagellation is strictly *le vice anglais*; a French letter is, in France, *une lettre anglaise*.

Yet for all the brickbats, there is a deep undercurrent of admiration, and affection, carefully concealed. While the thinking classes sniff and splutter, ordinary folk have always delighted in the pleasures of the neighbouring culture. *Le steak-frites* – the 'alimentary sign of Frenchness', according to Roland Barthes – arrived in France with Wellington's army, and stayed. Burnley Miners' Club remains the world's largest single buyer of Benedictine, after Lancashire soldiers developed a taste for the liqueur (drunk with hot water: 'a Bene and hot') while serving in France during the First World War.

While the French and British will for ever proclaim the other to be baffling and infuriating, when they work together *la différence* not only lives, but thrives.

Wilfred Thesiger explored everywhere but himself

IN HIS LATER YEARS, when he had retired to northern Kenya, Wilfred Thesiger became a literary tourist attraction, a point of pilgrimage for British writers who aspired to a certain sort of written adventure. The explorer-writer, who died in 2003, became a living monument, the last of a Victorian breed who treated travel – demanding, independent travel – as a mystical religion. Long before his death, Thesiger's muscular accounts of his desert journeys through the Empty Quarter of Saudi Arabia and living with the Marsh Arabs of Iraq, had acquired the status of sacred texts for those of us brought up on T.E. Lawrence, Richard Burton, Eric Newby and Bruce Chatwin.

I made the pilgrimage to Thesiger's home in Maralal in 1987. He sat, like a great white African chief, under an awning, flicking away the flies with a buffalo tail and staring into the dusty distance, a group of young African men around his feet, chewing the mildly narcotic herb *qat*. He wore a floppy hat, and an expression of bored benevolence. With impeccable manners, he pretended that he had been expecting me. I doubted that I was the first sunburned Englishman to turn up to pay homage that day; I certainly was not the last.

We ate some unidentified parts of a roasted goat, and he talked about the poor quality of waiter service at the Ritz: a formal English aristocrat drinking sweet tea in the middle of the African bush. His eyes, set in a face of weathered leather, were at once empty and fierce, like those of cat. More than anything he said, I recall Thesiger's reserve, his unwillingness to say more than absolutely necessary to make his point; he seemed to husband his words, like a man eking out a precious supply of water in the desert: this was also the way Thesiger travelled – and the way he wrote.

Born in a hut in Addis Ababa in 1910, Thesiger is often described as a nomad, but his wanderings were never aimless. Of his travels in the great Arabian wilderness of Rub' al-Khali, he wrote: 'I went there to find peace in the hardship of desert travel and in the company of desert people. I set myself a goal on these journeys, and although the goal itself was unimportant, its attainment had to be worth every effort and sacrifice ... the harder the way the more worthwhile the journey.'

As Alexander Maitland shows in his masterly biography, Thesiger constantly sought the self-defining, harder path. He crossed the Empty Quarter twice, spent years living in the reed beds of Iraq, voyaged from the Hindu Kush to the High Atlas to feed his 'lifelong craving for barbaric splendour, for savagery, colour and the throb of drums'.

Some of the savagery was internal, and some of the barbarity inbred. He slaughtered as he went: scores of lions in the Sudan, a thousand wild pigs in the marshes, often shot from horseback. When two lion cubs that he had hand-reared grew too large and boisterous, he killed them. Armoured with the confidence of Eton, Oxford and the aristocratic blood that he snobbishly revered, he sneered at the natives who gave themselves civilised airs; he had no time for modernity whatever, or the opinions of others. Despite passionate emotional attachments to a series of handsome younger men, his attitude to sex, in Maitland's words, was 'perfunctory, immature and selfish'. He was beaten and molested at school. He surgically circumcised, the biographer assiduously records, 6,138 Marsh Arabs. He was cruel to his dog. This was one peculiar Englishman.

Yet from this strange and complicated mind came prose of sparkling clarity. It did not come easily, and it did not come early. He did not travel to write about it.

It was not until the 1950s that he began writing. *Arabian Sands* and *The Marsh Arabs* are his best works, marked by a style as gritty and sparse as the desert, yet tinged by a restrained English romanticism. His account of nightfall in the marshes is taut and elegiac: 'Firelight on a half-turned face, the crying of geese, duck flighting in to feed, a boy's voice singing somewhere in the dark, canoes moving in procession down a waterway, the setting sun seen crimson through the smoke of burning reed beds, narrow waterways that wound deeper into the marshes.' Some of the tension in Thesiger's writing came from his straddling two worlds.

Among his noble savages, he wore a turban; in London, he donned a bowler hat.

'Oh, East is East and West is West, and never the twain shall meet,' Rudyard Kipling wrote in that much quoted and much misunderstood poem. In Thesiger, East and West did meet, to produce a unique amalgam: the Etonian Bedu, the upper-class savage with one foot in a wind-blown tent, and the other in the Travellers' Club.

Thesiger seems to have found his only place of pure peace on the move, among the rolling sands: 'Here in the desert I had found all that I had asked; I knew that I should never find it again.' But he kept looking.

Maitland was a close friend of Thesiger and worked closely with him as a collaborator during the last decade of his life. The great virtue of his biography, however, is that it leaves a part of Thesiger's personality repressed, as it plainly was in life. Thesiger explored everywhere except himself.

Even during our one fleeting meeting on the edge of the dusty bush, I sensed that there was a part of this awkward, private Englishman that was unknown and unknowable: the empty quarter of Wilfred Thesiger.

The telegram was the soul of brevity, and wit

MARK TWAIN ONCE RECEIVED the following telegram from his publisher: NEED 2 PAGE SHORT STORY TWO DAYS. He replied: NO CAN DO 2 PAGES TWO DAYS. CAN DO 30 PAGES TWO DAYS. NEED 30 DAYS DO 2 PAGES.

Twain was making an important point about brevity, time and quality of writing: for many writers, writing at length is easier, but not always better.

No invention more clearly demonstrated the benefits of brevity than the telegram itself. E-mails promote prolixity. When one can download and despatch *War and Peace* at the push of a button, there is little incentive to be succinct.

Telegrams, by contrast, were expensive and short: every word counted.

In 1929, Western Union sent more than 200 million telegrams. In 2005, the American company sent just 21,000, and in 2006 it stopped entirely. The telegram has died, and with it a particular literary genre: concise, pithy and often splendidly rude.

Where the haiku demands seventeen syllables, the traditional telegram had to be crammed into fifteen words to avoid a higher rate. Compression required intellectual dexterity.

The American inventor Richard Buckminster Fuller somehow managed to boil down Einstein's Theory of Relativity into a 249-word telegram. Even more concisely, Victor Hugo, anxious to know about sales of his newly published *Les Misérables*, sent a telegram to his publisher which simply read: '?' The encouraging reply came back: '!' (If Hugo's publisher had been able to predict today's multi-million-pound *Les Mis* industry, he might have been moved to write: '****@$Pounds Pounds Pounds Pounds !!!') The form also developed its own truncated vocabulary, 'telegraphese', an early form of txt msg: SD for said, HV for have, TMRW for tomorrow, and the combination of words that allowed the telegram-writer to economise.

For Samuel Morse, inventor of the code, simplicity was part of the telegram's appeal. As Marvin Kitman wrote: 'Morse loved the brief, the clear, the bold, a style epitomized in his code. The Morse code was popular with the avant garde not only because it pruned the deadwood out of the language, but because it couldn't be understood by the masses.'

Journalists and writers made particularly good use of the telegram, to insult editors, hold off publishers and demand more time, or money. In 1928, F. Scott Fitzgerald cabled his publisher: MY INCOME TAX CHECK IS DUE IN NEW YORK TOMORROW MONDAY CAN YOU POSSIBLY DEPOSIT THREE HUNDRED FIFTY DOLLARS TO KEEP ME OUT OF JAIL STOP. Ernest Hemingway, outraged that his outrageous expenses when working for the International News Service had been questioned by bean-counters trying to balance the books, sent the following brief message: SUGGEST YOU UPSTICK BOOKS ASSWARDS.

Foreign correspondents were used to getting messages along the lines of: DAILY MAIL MAN SHOT. WHY YOU UNSHOT?

Evelyn Waugh, while working as a journalist covering the Italian invasion of Ethiopia, was told to follow up a rumour that an English nurse had been killed by bombing: SEND TWO HUNDRED WORDS UPBLOWN NURSE.

Waugh, believing the story to be unfounded, swiftly replied: NURSE UNUPBLOWN.

The story was unsent. Waugh was soon unemployed.

Waugh instinctively realised the comic possibilities of the telegram. In *Scoop*, he subverted the genre entirely. The accidental foreign reporter William Boot receives strange volleys of newspaper telegraphese: NEWS EXYOU UNRECEIVED. He replies in leisurely fashion: NOTHING MUCH HAS HAPPENED EXCEPT TO THE PRESIDENT WHO HAS BEEN IMPRISONED IN HIS OWN PALACE BY REVOLUTIONARY JUNTA HEADED BY SUPERIOR BLACK NAMED BENITO AND RUSSIAN JEW WHO BANISTER SAYS IS UP TO NO GOOD ... LOVELY SPRING WEATHER BUBONIC PLAGUE RAGING.

General Sir Charles Napier was as clipped as Boot is wordy. The story goes that in 1843, after annexing the Indian province of Sind, Napier despatched a one-word telegram, 'PECCAVI ...', which translates as 'I have sinned.' Some puns are just so good that they are worth invading entire countries for.

The telegram was also useful (like the text message) as a way of conveying information to somebody without having to talk or write to them. Peter Sellers once sent a telegram to his wife, while he was in an upstairs study and she was working in the kitchen: BRING ME A CUP OF COFFEE. PETER. The marriage did not last.

The pared-down style of the telegram could be used to give deliberate offence.

Sometimes the offence was inadvertent. HOW OLD CARY GRANT? a reporter once cabled to the actor. The reply came back: OLD CARY GRANT FINE. HOW YOU?

It is odd to reflect how the telegram, which seems so slow and reflective compared with instant modern communication, was once a byword for brutal modernity. E.M. Forster used the telegram as a symbol for all that was rushed and dehumanised in modern life: 'Personal relations are the important thing for ever and ever and not this outer life of telegrams and anger.'

Looking back, the telegram was a most versatile canvas, bringing good news and bad, expressive of love, despair and a delightfully wry species of humour, conveyed in a very few, well-chosen words.

In that spirit I suppose I should apologise for the length of this piece. But, to paraphrase Mark Twain, I didn't have time to write a shorter one.

To cuddle a mockingbird

ALL'S WELL THAT ENDS well. And if all doesn't end well, it should be forced to.

This is the conclusion of a new survey for World Book Day, which found that most readers would far rather read a novel that ends happily ever after. *Pride and Prejudice* was voted the happiest ending in literature, followed by *To Kill a Mockingbird* and *Jane Eyre*.

Only one in fifty readers, it seems, likes to be left tearful at the last page, so the survey also asked which unhappy endings readers would most like to change: *Tess of the D'Urbervilles* was the clear winner, with readers demanding clemency more than a century after Thomas Hardy sent his tragic heroine to her death. It was also felt that the endings of *Wuthering Heights*, 1984 and *Gone with the Wind* were all too depressing, and should be perked up.

In that spirit, therefore, I have begun rewriting great literature to bring it into line with popular sentiment. I, for one, have always found the opening line of *Anna Karenina* rather a downer. 'Happy families are all alike; every unhappy family is unhappy in its own way.'

When you read that, you just know things are going to go off the rails or, more precisely, on them. Here is something a little more upbeat: 'Happy families are just lovely; unhappy families are all the same, and tend to bang on about it.'

Madame Bovary could also do with some cheering up. How about this: Emma marries Charles, a terrifically entertaining and virile country doctor, they have eight children, someone invents Prozac, Emma buys an Aga and wins first prize for home baking at Yonville agricultural fair.

Why stop there? *Macbeth* is much too depressing. In my version the gentle, unassuming and monosyllabic thane settles down at Cawdor, where Lady Macbeth develops a profitable line in soap that leaves the hands spotless. Hamlet finds a shrink, marries Ophelia and goes into insurance. In the revised *A Farewell to Arms*, Catherine has a fat and healthy baby, and she and Henry establish a successful pacifist ski resort in the Alps.

Godot finally turns up.

And since we are making unhappy endings cheerier, for the gloomy 2 per cent there are ways of rendering happy endings a little darker, starting with *Jane Eyre*: The original 'My Edward and I, then, are happy' needs another clause: '. . . or we would be, if that bloody Bertha hadn't found the fire escape.'

Pride and Prejudice could be rendered less saccharine by introducing a scene where Darcy explains to Elizabeth that it is a truth universally acknowledged that a single man in possession of a good fortune still in want of a wife is obviously gay, so he is moving to Tangiers to live with Wickham.

Customised literature sounds barmy, but it has already started, and the sequels industry is booming. Margaret Mitchell insisted that *Gone with the Wind* ended where she ended it. But the public demanded that Rhett must be made to give a damn after all, so the Mitchell estate employed Alexandra Ripley to stage a reunion: *Scarlett*, published in 1991, recouped a $5 million advance in three months, and sold 2.2 million copies in hardback.

Even though Austen ended all her books with a definitive full stop, dozens of imitators have added sequels and prequels, new endings and new beginnings. There are sequels to *Treasure Island*, *Kim*, *Lark Rise to Candleford* and even Hegel's *Phenomenology of Spirit*. No one has yet written *The Sisters Karamazov*, but it is only a matter of time. Some of these attempts to expand on an existing work are better than the original, such as George MacDonald Fraser's Flashman canon, taking up where *Tom Brown's Schooldays* left off. Most are embarrassing pastiche, but all testify to the way great fiction continues to run on in the imagination long after the last page.

Literature is constantly being refashioned, if not actually rewritten. The whole of Austen has recently been repackaged as chick-lit, complete with pastel covers and skinny women with handbags. So-called fanfiction is booming, on websites where amateur writers continue their favourite stories: the further adventures of the Darcys, the Hobbits, Sherlock Holmes and Captain Kirk. The fanfic.net website has more than 200,000 Harry Potter stories that J.K. Rowling never wrote.

This huge wave of derivative literature is a homage to the contagious power of fiction; soon it may be generated by the push of a button. Mathematicians at Google have invented a new algorithm (how's that for a gripping opening line?) that will soon be able to produce perfect instant translation. Within a given context of prose, they say, it is possible to work out mathematically the most appropriate translation for every word.

If computers can translate English into perfect French, then they can presumably translate English into perfect Shakespeare in the same way. Thus, in some distant future realm of literature, we may be able to feed a work by, say, Stephen King into your computer and then get the same story out, but as Shakespeare would have written it, at the other end.

No writer worth the name sets out to produce happy or unhappy endings, let alone seeks to alter existing literature to produce one or the other. It is not the mere happiness or unhappiness of fiction that grips us, but the questions it asks, the people and situations it creates, the complexity of emotions it stirs. Some of the greatest endings in literature are neither uplifting nor distressing, but inquiring. *Bleak House* finishes on an unwritten question mark: 'even supposing – '.

Molly Bloom's soliloquy at the end of *Ulysses* is a climactic affirmation, 'his heart was going like mad and yes I said yes I will Yes', that echoes long after the book is closed.

I am particularly fond of the last line of *War and Peace*, which, in its very stodginess, makes the rest of the book seem even more wonderful: 'In the present case, it is as essential to surmount a consciousness of an unreal freedom and to recognise a dependence not perceived by our senses.'

We should not demand that a last line makes us either happy or sad, but thoughtful; it is this that ensures great literature lives, happily, ever after.

A nation of age-defying,
tea-bag-card-making crochet fans

THE BOOKS THAT WE borrow say more about our literary tastes than the books that we own. If your bookshelves are anything like mine, they contain several hundred acres of the printed word that will never be read, at least not by me.

There are Christmas gifts that we never wanted but cannot throw away, books we feel that we ought to read but cannot face and the obligatory copy of Stephen Hawking's *A Brief History of Time* that will never be opened because life is several aeons too short.

But library books are different. People borrow the library books that they actually want, and then actually read them. Unlike the bestseller lists, they are not an index of fashion, of reviews and book clubs, or of the effects of marketing and advertising. Library books are the works of literature that we want to read but not necessarily to own and keep.

The Public Lending Right figures for the most-borrowed books offer a strange and revealing snapshot of modern Britain. To judge from the statistics, our love affair with romantic fiction has ended; instead, we have taken up with television chefs, crochet-hooks, French people and cricketers.

For seventeen years Dame Catherine Cookson, queen of the pot-boiler romance, has reigned supreme in Britain's public libraries. In 1994, she occupied numbers 1 to 9 in the top ten most borrowed books list, with Barbara Taylor Bradford sneaking into the number 10 spot. Today, Dame Catherine does not figure in the top ten. For the third year running, the most borrowed writer in Britain is the children's author Jacqueline Wilson. J.K. Rowling, by comparison, limps in at number 74. Of the twenty most-borrowed children's titles, sixteen are by the staggeringly prolific Ms Wilson.

Casting an eye down the most-borrowed titles list, it becomes clear that there is a special category of book that people like to borrow in huge numbers, but do not wish to possess, just in case the neighbours come round. Trinny and Susannah, Kim and Aggie, Paul McKenna and Gillian McKeith all do well in this category. To borrow and read these books is one thing, but to have them in your bookshelves practically screams: I am a badly dressed, unhygienic, slightly bonkers person worried about my bodily functions.

The evergreen *Official Theory Test for Car Drivers* by the Driving Standards Agency comes in at number 19, one below Dave Pelzer's *The Lost Boy*. This seems only right, since both are written in the same style: repetitive, glutinous and heart-wrenchingly sad.

Cookery provides another window of revelation. In the country as a whole, we prefer Jamie Oliver's recipes, but this disguises wide regional culinary literary variations. Londoners are gorging on Nigella Lawson, but the Welsh prefer Hugh Fearnley-Whittingstall.

Welsh library habits deserve a study of their own. In dogs, for example, the Welsh look far afield, displaying a particular preference for Yorkshire terriers, despite the British affinity for labradors. Welsh travel reading, however, seems less adventurous. While other parts of the country read about France and Spain, and Londoners dream of Scotland, the favourite Welsh travel book is *The Rough Guide to Wales*.

Books about moving abroad are being borrowed in record numbers, but luckily we don't all want to go to the same place. The occupants of the Orkney Islands read about moving to Tuscany; in Devon they imagine buying somewhere in France; in Northumberland they think about heading for the Australian Outback. Most library users imagine moving to somewhere warmer, drier and more interesting, but not in Fife, where they still dream of relocating to Canada.

Mind you, each region has foibles. By far the most popular pet books nationwide are about tortoises; except in Scotland, where, apparently, people much prefer to read about snakes. As for hobbies, while Londoners love to crochet, in the North of England borrowers can't get enough of 'Tea Bag Folded Greetings Cards', a pastime I have never even heard of before.

The library lists also offer a rough guide to national hypochondria. Overall, the most-borrowed health book is *Defying Age: How to Think, Act and Stay Young*. It may come as no surprise to discover that the most popular medical book in the libraries of Northern Ireland is *Stress and Nervous Disorders*; in Wales readers mug up on *The Vitamins and Minerals Handbook*, while Scottish readers like to relax with a well-thumbed library copy of *How to Lower High Blood Pressure*, preferably while smoking a fag and eating a deep-fried Mars bar.

The top film, television and music biography last year was *Being Jordan* by Katie Price, whereas the top historical biography was Claire Tomalin's superb *Samuel Pepys: The Unequalled Self*. This may be a profoundly depressing statement about the contrast between great lives of the past and great lives of the present; on the other hand, I have a suspicion that Pepys and Jordan would have got on rather well.

What we read also reflects what, and how, we like to kill. *The Times*'s own Jane Shilling's *The Fox in the Cupboard* is the most popular British book in the hunting, shooting and fishing category, but in Scotland they prefer *The*

Pigeon Shooter by John Batley, and in Wales David Brian
Plummer's *Ferrets*.

When the aliens finally land in Britain, they will no doubt
head to the local library to mug up on exactly what sort
of planet they have come to. There the real Britain will be
revealed: a nation of age-defying, fox-hunting, tea-bag-card-
making, food-loving crochet fanatics most of whom, frankly,
would rather be in Tuscany; or, if Welsh, in Wales.

Old fags and cabbage stumps:
the world's most prized book

WHAT ARE THE 100 most valuable books of the twentieth
century? Not the most popular, for that is something quite
different; but the individual books that, as objects, we most
prize. The answer, as revealed by the magazine *Book and
Magazine Collector*, is surprising. Many of the most valuable books today were once deemed worthless, and published
only by the most circuitous and unpromising routes. Some
very nearly did not happen at all.

A first edition of the 1926 deluxe edition of *Winnie the
Pooh* (number 60 in the top 100) is now worth £7,500. An
almost pristine copy of *The Catcher in the Rye* (25) sold for
$24,000 last year. A first edition of *The Hobbit*, coming in
at 13, is worth more (at £25,000) than a three-volume first
edition of *The Lord of the Rings* (£15,000, and down the
list at 24).

(The birth of *The Hobbit* came about because Professor
John Ronald Reul Tolkien was marking exam papers at
Oxford one day when he found a candidate had left a page
blank. In a moment of whimsy, he wrote on the space: 'In a

hole in the ground there lived a hobbit.' Then he decided he had to find out what a hobbit was, where the hole was and so on ...) The top five most valuable volumes clearly demonstrate that the story surrounding a book is what makes it precious, not merely the story inside the covers. (The magazine survey covered only first editions with dust jackets and not the one-off editions or original manuscripts that command huge prices at auction.) The fifth most valuable book is *The Tale of Peter Rabbit* by Beatrix Potter. When she first wrote the tale, in an exercise book with forty-two illustrations, it was rejected by at least six publishers. With her post office savings, Potter herself paid for the costs of engraving and printing and had produced 250 copies, privately, in 1901. The cover was sludge-green cardboard, the cover illustration was a simple outline drawing and the pages were unnumbered. 'Obliging aunts' coughed up to buy them and make Beatrix feel better. Today each of those copies is worth £50,000.

The author would have been staggered at the mark-up on her £11 investment: 'I have never quite understood the secret of Peter's perennial charm,' she wrote.

Number 4 on the list, *The Great Gatsby*, by F. Scott Fitzgerald, had a similarly unpromising start in life. When the book appeared in 1925 it was enthusiastically reviewed, but sold poorly and barely paid off the author's advance. The novel did not achieve mass popularity until it was republished in the 1950s. First editions are now worth more than £50,000, but a fine example sold in New York in 2002 for £93,000.

T.E. Lawrence's *Seven Pillars of Wisdom* (3) is rare and valued (at least £60,000 for the 1922 edition) in large part because the author published it in a series of strange hiccups. By 1919, he had finished the introduction and books 1 to 10 of his vivid account of the Arab revolt. This introduction and the last two books were then, he claimed, either lost or stolen at Reading station. (Lawrence may well have invented this, the mother of all dog-ate-my-homework stories, to buy more time.) By 1922 the manuscript was 330,000 words long, and he had the *Oxford Times* run off eight copies (six survive) in newsprint; 100 copies of a second proof followed; then 169 copies with plates, and thirty-two without. At Lawrence's request, no further copies appeared in his lifetime, and it was not until 1935, the year of his death, that the first trade edition appeared, selling 100,000 copies in a few months.

By comparison, some 25,000 copies of *The Hound of the Baskervilles*, by Arthur Conan Doyle (2), appeared in 1902, at six shillings each. What makes it so valuable is not the book itself, but the extraordinary scarcity of the original pink dust jacket, with the memorable silhouette of a baying hound on Dartmoor.

Only three copies with dust jackets are known to have survived: the last sold at Sotheby's for £81,000.

But the single most expensive book of all time is one that D.H. Lawrence memorably described as 'nothing but old fags and cabbage stumps of quotations from the Bible and the rest, stewed in the juice of deliberate, journalistic dirty-mindedness'. Right-thinking moralists argued that the book should have been banned. Today a single, signed copy of the first edition of James Joyce's *Ulysses* is on sale for £250,000, an icon uniquely valued because of its status in literature, its rarity, its extraordinarily beautiful design and its fragility.

Five instalments of *Ulysses* appeared in Britain in *The Egoist* before the censors moved in and Joyce moved to Paris. The first edition of 1,000 copies, 740 pages long, printed in Dijon, came out in 1922. Once again, the variety of formats is a bibliophile's fantasy: numbers 1 to 100 were printed on handmade Dutch paper and signed, and are valued today at an average of £100,000; the next 150 on *Verges d'Arches* paper (£25,000) and the remaining 750 on plain paper (£10,000). There was a second printing of 2,000 copies a few months later, then a third of 500, most of which were destroyed.

Yet a book can become hugely valuable without being venerable, literary or serious. A mint first-edition copy of *Harry Potter and the Philosopher's Stone* by J.K. Rowling is already worth £15,000 (and in 28th position). A copy of the first issue of the *Dandy* comic (1937) would now fetch £12,000, being rather more valuable than a first edition of Virginia Woolf's *To the Lighthouse*, or Lawrence's *Lady Chatterley's Lover*.

In the end, the listing of the most valuable books perhaps says more about the thrill of collecting than the passion for reading: for this is not an index of taste or literary longevity, but of reverence for the rare.

James Joyce and Marcel Proust: the dinner-party pairing from hell

DINNER PARTIES SOMETIMES GO wrong. For some reason, the guests with similar interests you have seated together hate one another on sight, and a layer of permafrost settles over what should have been a warm and convivial occasion. The more elaborate the dinner party, the more elaborately they can go wrong; the larger your guests' egos, the more likely they are to dislike each other, particularly if they happen to be writers.

But for sheer, toe-curling, napkin-chewing, electrocution-level embarrassment, nothing can come close to the first and only meeting between James Joyce and Marcel Proust: the dinner-party pairing from hell.

The date was 18 May 1922. The venue was the sumptuous Majestic Hotel in Paris. The hosts were a wealthy English couple called Violet and Sydney Schiff, cosmopolitan patrons of the arts. The occasion, delightfully retold by Richard Davenport-Hines in his book *A Night at the Majestic*, was a celebration of the first performance of Igor Stravinsky's ballet *Renard*, performed by Serge Diaghilev's Ballets Russes.

Some forty people were invited, the cream of Parisian artistic society, but the guests of honour included the towering figures of early twentieth-century Modernism: Diaghilev and Stravinsky, Pablo Picasso, Proust and Joyce. Each was at the peak of his powers.

T.S. Eliot once said that the Schiffs had a talent for 'bringing very diverse people together and making them combine well'. That night they brought together Proust and Joyce, and watched them combine very badly indeed. For a start, both were late. The lobster à l'americaine (with tomatoes, cognac and white wine) had already been cleared away when an unsteady, dishevelled figure appeared among the elegant guests. 'He seemed far from well,' remarked Clive Bell, Bloomsbury art critic and the only English guest. It was Joyce, who was nervous, underdressed and drunk. He sat with his head in his hands, staring into a glass of champagne.

At half past two, Proust made his entrance, dapper in fur coat and white kidskin gloves. He had just got up.

The first exchange between Proust and Stravinsky was a taste of what was to come. Perhaps a little maladroitly, Proust attempted to engage the composer on the subject of another composer.

Proust: 'Doubtless you admire Beethoven?'

Stravinsky: 'I detest Beethoven.'

Proust: 'But, *cher maître*, surely the late sonatas and quartets ...'

Stravinsky: 'Even worse than the rest.'

Joyce began to snore loudly. Possibly, he had fallen asleep.

The critics had already set up Proust and Joyce as rivals, so the late-night rendezvous was always fraught with peril. 'M. Proust is more coherent than Mr Joyce,' Richard Aldington had written two years earlier. 'More urbane, less preoccupied with slops and viscera.' Proust's reputation was soaring, whereas Joyce felt insecure and misunderstood; his *Ulysses* had been acclaimed as a work of genius, but only by a few cognoscenti.

When Joyce woke up, Proust tried an opening gambit that is impossible not to love him for.

'Do you like truffles?'

'Yes I do,' said Joyce. And there, for the time being, the conversation languished.

What happened now depends on which of the many, probably embellished, versions you choose to believe. According to one, Proust said: 'I have never read your works, Mr Joyce,' to which came the inevitable rejoinder: 'I have never read your works, Monsieur Proust.' Joyce would later claim that he tried to engage the Frenchman in conversation about chambermaids, but Proust wanted only to discuss duchesses.

Proust: Ah, Monsieur Joyce, you know the Princess ...

Joyce: No, Monsieur.

Proust: Ah, you know the Countess ...

Joyce: No, Monsieur.

Proust: Then you know Madame ...

Joyce: No, Monsieur.

Having failed to find a point of social contact, the two great writers now competed in hypochondria, Joyce complaining of headaches, Proust lamenting the state of his stomach. The contrived nature of the meeting no doubt ensured its failure; Proust was fresh and fêted; Joyce was drunk and dour. 'The situation was impossible,' Joyce declared later. 'Proust's day was just beginning. Mine was at an end.'

But when the agonising conversation did finally end, Joyce seemed unwilling to turn in. As Proust and the Schiffs climbed into a carriage to return to Proust's home and continue their conversation, Joyce clambered in too, uninvited. He then lit up a cigarette and opened a window. Proust believed himself to be allergic to both smoke and fresh air. By this point he had also developed an allergy to Joyce.

Proust talked non-stop, and addressed not a word to Joyce, who stared at him balefully throughout the short journey.

Outside Proust's apartment, Sydney Schiff turned to Joyce and said: 'Let my taxi take you home.' It was not an offer, but an order.

So ended one of the greatest ever non-meetings of minds. Six months later Proust was dead. Years later Joyce was wistful, telling Samuel Beckett: 'If we had been allowed to meet and have a talk somewhere . . .'

As Davenport-Hines writes: 'People with great dignity are often pitchforked into absurd or fraught situations.' But even the most arctic dinner party can be thawed. Charlie Chaplin once hosted a dinner for Albert Einstein and William Randolph Hearst. This was heading for 'slow freeze-up' when Hearst's mistress, in a moment of inspiration, entwined her fingers in the physicist's famous locks and cooed: 'Why don't you get your hair cut?'

Bin Laden's paranoid gifts

OSAMA BIN LADEN FAILED to turn up for the launch party of his collected works, for the simple reason that he is probably holed up in a cave somewhere in deepest Baluchistan. Or dead. Or perhaps he was too busy recording his latest threat to the world.

Despite the uncertain whereabouts of its author, *Messages to the World: The Statements of Osama bin Laden* is a publishing milestone, a book that will probably still be read a century from now, as important as *Mein Kampf* and *Mao's Little Red Book*.

It has been a long time coming. In the wake of the 9/11 attacks, novels, poems and books of non-fiction sprouted everywhere; but it has taken more than four years for the definitive scholarly text of the words of the al-Qaeda leader to appear.

For most Western publishers, bin Laden's *bons mots* were simply too toxic to be translated into book form.

Messages is a compilation of twenty-four of bin Laden's writings, interviews, faxes and videotaped statements sent to Arabic radio and television stations since 1994; they are addressed variously to the people of Iraq, the nations of Europe and to US citizens, but they are primarily aimed at disaffected Muslims who see bin Laden as a hero. Translated by James Howarth, with an introduction by the American scholar Bruce Lawrence, they provide an extraordinary glimpse into the intellectual underpinnings of Islamic terrorism, the motivating ideology behind al-Qaeda and the personality of its peculiar leader.

Bin Laden emerges from these pages as paranoid, manipulative and, in strictly literary terms, exceptionally gifted. His writing deliberately echoes the cadences of formal Arabic: he knows his audience and he knows how to appeal to it in the language of a heroic past and a sacrificial future. These are the words of a master polemicist expressed, in Lawrence's words, with 'powerful lyricism'. Bin Laden's popularity lies not simply in the political message of al-Qaeda but in his poetry: rhetorical, mocking, nuanced and destructive.

Bin Laden's writing is about revenge. 'As the twin towers of New York collapsed, something even greater and more enormous collapsed with them: the myth of the great America and the myth of democracy.'

It is embedded in a vision of history as permanent war against the infidel, starting with the Prophet in the seventh century, continuing through the crusades of the twelfth, rekindled by colonialism in the nineteenth and twentieth centuries, and now given new relevance by the War on Terror in the twenty-first century.

His every statement is larded with heavily emotive historical references: to the 'lost' Moorish Kingdom of al-Andalus, to the fall and future restoration of the Caliphate, to the sacking of Baghdad in 1258 by Hulagu the Tartar (the precursor, we are told, to Dick Cheney) and to the oil-thirsty crusader Bush, 'blinded by black gold'.

His message is simple: to purge all Western influence from the Islamic world, to destroy the West, 'the worst civilisation witnessed in the history of mankind' and to wreak vengeance: 'Just as you bomb, so shall you be bombed . . . because you have killed, we must kill. Your innocents are not less innocent than ours.'

Like *Mein Kampf*, this is a paean to hatred. 'Every Muslim, from the moment they realise the distinction in their hearts, hates Americans, hates Jews, and hates Christians. This is a part of our belief and our religion.'

Bin Laden can bang on. The bore of Tora Bora is a one-theme writer, and yet the writing is politically astute, owing much to the spin-doctor's art, the gibe and the wisecrack: 'Who can forget your President Clinton's immoral acts committed in the official Oval Office,' he leers.

Bin Laden's statements have often been dismissed in the West as 'ranting', his historical references ignored as mere window dressing for an intellectually bankrupt creed. But read as a whole, they offer a chilling insight.

The writing is richly rhetorical, and extraordinarily robust. It is also, of course, wrong; a hopeless, murderous lie. This is an easily accessible, pop version of radical Islamic history, garnished with cherry-picked references from the Koran, while ignoring those elements of Islam that emphasise peace and mercy.

Bin Laden's is a vision of pure resentment, wounded honour and fine-sounding but false hope: 'By the grace of God the numbers of those who have conviction and have set out to wage jihad are increasing every day.'

As Lawrence points out, for all their literary virtuosity, bin Laden's statements offer no vision of what an Islamic society should be. He makes a few sideways references to the Afghan Taliban, but in reality he is a destroyer, not a builder, uninterested in how society functions. For bin Laden, what comes after jihad is irrelevant; what matters is the hereafter. As Lawrence puts it: 'His emphasis falls far more upon the glories of martyrdom than the spoils of victory.'

This is the writing of a would-be warrior, a man caught in his own self-image, the poetry of a narcissist and propagandist:

I shall lead my steed,
And hurl us both at the target,
Oh Lord if my end is nigh,
May my tomb not be draped
In green mantles.

'The ink of the scholar is worth more than the blood of a martyr.' So said the Prophet Muhammad. Bin Laden's statements, his carefully couched appeals and justifications, are an attempt to show the scholarly side of his terrorism. They are written extraordinarily well. But they are written in blood.

On the Origin of Books

IT MAY COME AS a shock to fans of *Pride and Prejudice* to learn that the behaviour of Elizabeth Bennet precisely echoes that of a female bonobo chimpanzee.

But that, broadly speaking, is the proposition advanced by a new and growing branch of literary theory known as Literary Darwinism. Jane Austen published *Pride and Prejudice* in 1813, some eighteen years before Charles Darwin set sail in *The Beagle* yet, according to Literary Darwinists, her fiction must be understood through the prism of sexual selection, which ensures the survival of the fittest – the central principle of Darwin's evolutionary theory.

According to Darwin, both the male and the female of the species compete to select mates most likely to ensure the continuance of their genetic line; over the millennia, the fittest survive. According to Literary Darwinists, this is what happens in Jane Austen's fiction.

The selection of an ideal partner is Austen's central theme, and is explicitly stated in the opening sentence of *Pride and Prejudice* as 'a truth universally acknowledged, that a single man in possession of a good fortune, must be in want of a wife'.

Austen's men compete to win the most attractive and intelligent women; the women vie to wed men of the highest status, amid courtship rituals and strutting plumage displays. A central dilemma is the struggle to distinguish between the mate who is attractive but unreliable (penniless, rakish Wickham) and the partner who is dependable breeding stock (wealthy, Alpha-male Darcy) – the cad versus the dad.

Mrs Bennet is fabulously annoying in her matchmaking but she is doing only what every bonobo mother is hardwired to do: ensuring the continuance of her genetic line by breeding her offspring with sexually eligible partners. At the book's end, Austen writes: 'Happy for all her maternal feelings was the day on which Mrs Bennet got rid of her two most deserving daughters.' In other words: an evolutionary slam-dunk.

Literary Darwinists apply their approach not just to Austen, but to the whole of literature, arguing that evolution imposes certain innate forms of behaviour on all of humanity. Joseph Carroll, in a new anthology of Literary Darwinism entitled *The Literary Animal*, argues that 'there is no work of literature anywhere in the world, at any time, by any author, that is outside the scope of Darwinian analysis'.

Homer's *Iliad* becomes, in the words of Jonathan Gottschall, another contributor to *The Literary Animal*, 'a drama of naked apes – strutting, preening, fighting, tattooing their chests and bellowing their power in fierce competition for social dominance, desirable mates and material resources'. In his essay, Ian McEwan argues: 'When one reads accounts of . . . troops of bonobo . . . one sees rehearsed all the major themes of the English nineteenth-century novel.'

Thus, when Emma Bovary commits adultery, she is merely obeying the call of her genes to find a stronger mate with whom to make better babies: it all comes down, in the end, to Madame Bovary's ovaries.

In one sense, the application of evolutionary biology to literature seems a statement of the obvious. Since evolution and natural selection describe humanity – mating, child-rearing, communal living, male-bonding for the hunt, adapting to survive, dying – it would be odd indeed if this were not reflected when humans imaginatively describe themselves.

And like all overarching theories, Literary Darwinism has its limits, since some of the greatest literature simply refuses to fit the evolutionary paradigm. For example, despite valiant efforts by Darwinists to cram *Hamlet* into the mould, it seems to me that a man who drives his ideal sexual partner nuts, fails to bump off the usurping pack leader when he has the chance, and then takes part in a bloodbath in which almost everyone dies, is not playing by the normal evolutionary rules. Even the most depressed bonobo does not wander around all day wondering whether to kill itself.

A more fertile area for Literary Darwinism is the exploration of the possible biological and evolutionary origins of literature itself. What is it, stamped into our genes by natural selection, that makes us want to read and write? What is the biological advantage conferred by literacy itself? Why do humans tell stories, when they could be doing something more obviously useful, like finding a mate, or killing a mammoth? If the invention of wheels and words can be fitted into the story of human evolution, then so can books.

There are several theories. For some Darwinists, stories are a tool of social cohesion developed about 40,000 years ago, a way to rationalise an otherwise incomprehensible world; in another interpretation, imagination and reading are a form of mental workout, an exercise in conjectural thinking to prepare us for the unexpected. According to yet another theory, writing, like art, is a form of intellectual plumage, a display of mental acuity designed to attract mates. A recent survey showed that writers tend to have more sexual partners than non-writers; the reason may be biological.

My favourite explanation for the biological point of literature is that it has no obvious point. Reading is a luxury, proof of plenty, the relaxation that comes from being a successful member of the species and thus a good mate. In short, books are sexy.

Do Darwinian evolutionary principles apply to the history of literature itself? Certainly the art of writing, that peculiar species of human activity, has been refined and adapted with each generation. The schlock bestsellers of former times have been forgotten as thoroughly as the pot-boilers of today will perish; but good books beget better books, and truly great books persevere down the ages as classics: the survival of the fittest.

The computer ate my homework

I WAS ABOUT HALFWAY through a piece of writing last week – some 2,000 words in the bag, the structure uncertain, the words unsaved, but getting there – when it disappeared. Bang. The dread banner appeared onscreen asking if I would care to send a pointless message of complaint to Bill Gates. I didn't bother. No amount of computer alchemy could bring my words back. They had vanished for ever, as surely as if they had been burnt.

Somewhere deep in the machine, a tiny electronic Savonarola had put its digital foot down and wiped out my work in progress. I felt disbelief, then anger, then a weary impotence. Then I started writing all over again.

Anyone who elects to write anything by computer is likely to have suffered the sudden, inexplicable, eradicating glitch at some point. It is a particularly brutal sort of censorship but it is not new.

In the past, writers were always losing their words: the letter that vanishes without trace, the manuscript left on a bus, the masterpiece consigned to the flames by the housemaid, the censor or the self-censor. Dylan Thomas lost the manuscript of *Under Milk Wood* three times in various pubs.

Arguably, our precious words are far safer now than in the days of pen and paper (let alone papyrus). We can copy, save, replicate and print at the push of a button. Paranoid authors, of whom I am usually one, print everything out endlessly and store continuing manuscripts in different places in case of fire.

Sometimes the loss of words can prove a blessing. T.E. Lawrence insisted that the second version of *Seven Pillars of Wisdom* was superior to the first, which he left at Reading railway station, possibly on purpose because he was unhappy with it.

In 1922, Ernest Hemingway's first wife, Hadley, travelled to Switzerland by train with a suitcase containing everything that Hemingway had written up to that date. The case was stolen. When Hemingway found out, he went up the wall; but when he started writing again, the words came crisper, faster and, perhaps, better. If it had not been for the Swiss train thief (or if the writer had been able to store his work on a floppy disk or memory stick) he might never have become Ernest Hemingway.

We can only imagine the conversation between Mr and (not surprisingly, the soon to be ex-) Mrs Hemingway. However, we do know what passed between Thomas Carlyle and John Stuart Mill after the latter accidentally allowed the only manuscript of the former's *The French Revolution: A History* to be used by a housemaid to start a fire. Carlyle found himself having to console the man who had just destroyed his book. 'Mill, whom I had to comfort and speak peace to, remained injudiciously enough till almost midnight, and my poor Dame and I had to sit talking of indifferent matters; and could not till then get our lament freely uttered.'

What a wealth of strained British politeness and suppressed rage is contained in those words. Frankly, I'm on the side of the housemaid.

Gerard Manley Hopkins burnt every word of his early poetry. To which, some critics may respond: 'Phew.' On the other hand, some works of literature that were intended to vanish, did not. If Kafka's executor, Max Brod, had followed explicit instructions to destroy all his manuscripts we would not have *The Trial* or *The Castle*.

In his delightful tribute to vanished literature, *The Book of Lost Books* (£15.99), Stuart Kelly describes 'the great books you will never read': most of Greek drama, the last six books of Spenser's *The Fairie Queen*, *The Book of Music* by Confucius, Shakespeare's *Love's Labour's Won* (if it existed).

The next time you are in Rouen, it is worth remembering that underneath your feet may lie a lost masterpiece by Gustave Flaubert. When the Prussian army was steaming into France in 1871, Flaubert buried a box of papers in the garden of his house at Croisset. A year after his death, the house was demolished and the concrete docks of Rouen built on top. As far as anyone knows, Flaubert's words are still buried there.

One of the most tantalising losses is Homer's *Margites*, which Aristotle reckoned was to comedy what the *Iliad* and the *Odyssey* were to tragedy. We get an outline of the plot from other writers. The eponymous Margites (whose name derives from the Greek for 'mad') is the ultimate comic failure. He knows how to do many things, but none of them well; he doesn't know whether he is actually related to his father or his mother; and he won't sleep with his wife because he is afraid that she will 'give a bad account of him to his mother'. Margites is Frank Spencer from *Some Mothers Do 'Ave 'Em*, circa 850 BC.

Perhaps the 2,000 words consumed by my computer last week were the best I will write. I rather doubt it, since I cannot now remember any of them. They probably deserved to die. The computer gremlin, I believe, is the direct descendant of 'the Person from Porlock', who knocked on the door while Coleridge was feverishly writing *Kubla Khan*, the poem that had come to him, fully formed, in an opium dream. The interruption made him forget the rest of the poem, which is a masterpiece in part precisely because it is unfinished. Some words are better lost or unwritten or forgotten.

Anyone who has seen their words vanish should take heart from the story of Menander, the Greek dramatist of the fourth century BC. His reputation survived the centuries, but his entire oeuvre was thought to be lost. Then, fifty years ago, his play *Dyskolos* was found. In 1959, 2,278 years after it won first prize at the Lenaian festival in Athens, the long-lost play was translated and performed by the BBC.

Everyone agreed it was terrible.

One delusional reader misread
a great book and killed a great man

WHEN POLICE ARRIVED AT the Dakota apartment building, where John Lennon was dying from multiple bullet wounds, they found his killer, Mark Chapman, sitting a few feet away, reading aloud from *The Catcher in the Rye* by J.D. Salinger. No other work of literature has been so closely linked with a single, horrible murder.

Chapman obsessively read and reread the book in 1979 and 1980; he even attempted to change his name to Holden Caulfield, the book's alienated teenage protagonist.

In the hours before the shooting, he went through a macabre re-enactment of the plot: he wandered aimlessly around New York, then checked into an expensive hotel where he 'performed' a central scene from the book, by inviting a prostitute to his hotel room. Like his fictional model, Chapman did not have sex with her but they talked until the early hours.

On the morning of the murder, he bought a paperback copy and inscribed on its title page: 'To Holden Caulfield from Holden Caulfield. This is my statement.' In later years, trying to explain his actions, Chapman declared that Lennon, once his hero, had become a 'phoney', Holden's preferred term of disapprobation for the two-faced adult world. His statement to the police, made two hours after his arrest, was unequivocal: 'This morning I went to the bookstore and bought *The Catcher in the Rye*. I'm sure the large part of me is Holden Caulfield, who is the main person in the book.' Years later he was still insisting: 'I am indeed the "Catcher in the Rye" of this generation.'

The Catcher in the Rye tells the story of a seventeen-

year-old boy who is expelled from his Pennsylvania board-
ing school and wanders New York for two days, heading
inexorably towards mental breakdown. Fifty-six years
after it was published the book remains an anthem of
teenage angst, sexual insecurity and anger at the world's
hypocrisies.

Chapman was not alone in finding a twisted inspiration
in its pages. Among those who have claimed to model themselves on Holden Caulfield are John Hinckley, who went
on to attempt the assassination of Ronald Reagan, Arthur
Bremer, who shot the Alabama Governor George Wallace,
and Robert Bardo, who murdered the television actress
Rebecca Schaeffer in 1989.

You have to search hard through Salinger's book to find
anything that might, even in the most warped mind, encourage murder. Holden has some violent fantasies, but find an
adolescent boy who does not; on page 22, he remarks of his
red cap: 'A deer hunter hat? Like hell it is. I sort of closed
one eye like I was taking aim at it. This is a people-shooting
hat. I shoot people in this hat.'

More than 70 million people have read *The Catcher
in the Rye* without resorting to violence, let alone murder. Yet the link between Chapman's obsession with this
work ('I was literally living inside of a paperback novel')
and his subsequent actions raises again the question of
whether a book, play, film or poem can be held responsible for how people choose to use it. If *The Catcher in the
Rye* has become the set text for angry adolescent boys who
hate the world, then Sylvia Plath's *The Bell Jar* enjoys a
similarly unenviable status as the book for girls who hate
themselves, and contemplate self-destruction. In the nineteenth century Goethe's *The Sorrows of Young Werther*
was blamed for a spate of suicides. One French murderer

in the 1940s claimed to have been plunged into despair and violence by reading too much Camus.

But should any work of art be made to shoulder that kind of burden? The modern equivalent of Holden Caulfield is the rap singer Eminem. Both wear their sexuality uncomfortably, swear with deadpan repetitiveness, pose constantly and offer a raw, cynical fury that talks directly to unhappy teenagers. Eminem has in spades what Ian Ousby, the British critic, called 'that quality of sensitive innocence which Holden Caulfield retained beneath his rebellious mannerisms'. Their shared, sassy toughness is skin deep, at once aggressive and vulnerable. Martin Amis once said of Salinger: 'He has listened to adolescent intonation – its exaggeration and wised-up innocence.' So has Eminem.

In 2005, an Eminem fan who beat a woman law student to death was sentenced to life in prison. Christopher Duncan, twenty-one, has the same hairstyle and tattoos as the rapper, and the murder scene was allegedly reminiscent of Eminem's 'Stan' video.

Does the self-publicising Eminem bear the blame for what a single psychotic fan did any more than the reclusive Salinger is responsible for what a delusional reader extrapolated twenty-five years ago from a book now more than half a century old? Both writer and singer, in a sense, are the victims of their success: at the extremities of their huge fan base are inevitably those who will extract from their art what psychologists call a 'fictive personality'.

Eminem and Holden Caulfield are not identical. Holden feels the pull of violence but, unlike Eminem, does not extol it. *The Catcher in the Rye* is, finally, a gentle book that has comforted infinitely more adolescents than it has inspired to violence. Salinger's vision is gentle: it is about catching innocence before it falls into a phoney world.

Anyway, I keep picturing all these little kids playing some game in this big field of rye and all . . . I'm standing on the edge of some crazy cliff. What I have to do, I have to catch everybody if they start to go over the cliff . . .

That's all I'd do all day. I'd just be the catcher in the rye.

Twenty-five years ago, one deranged individual misread a great book and killed a great man. Chapman, in the end, simply did not understand *The Catcher in the Rye*; but as Holden himself says: 'People always clap for the wrong things.'

RIP Timmy

THE MACINTYRE FAMILY IS mourning the loss of Timmy, a gerbil who lived with us for two years and was, as it happens, female. The children flatly insisted that he was a boy the day that she arrived, and I wasn't going to argue since sexing a gerbil is, I understand, a tricky business.

She is now dead. We found her stiff little corpse when we came back from a weekend away. I explained to the children that he had died of old age, but I secretly suspect foul play; the wife has recently been heard making some dark who-will-rid-me-of this-turbulent-beast remarks.

As the children wept for his soul and I laid her out, preparatory to burial, in a clean Marks & Spencer tin that had recently contained a steak and portobello mushroom pie, I felt a twinge of sadness.

Which was odd, because I really didn't like Timmy. I hadn't felt the same about her since the death of George (also female). The pair had seemed to get on well; they were the Gertrude Stein and Alice B. Toklas of the rodent world, eccentric, and hard to grasp. But then, when George died, Timmy ate quite a lot of her before we noticed anything was wrong. I was appalled.

This was also odd. I was brought up on a farm where animals died often, and were then eaten, sometimes by me. I like animals as much as the next man; indeed, I have been known to participate in animal husbandry myself, until they caught me at it. Why should I care about the demise of Timmy, the gerbil Hannibal Lecter?

The answer, of course, is that I am British, and Timmy was not an animal, but a pet.

Pets are how we learn about death, because they are the first creatures we live with and then, inevitably, outlive. (Unless, that is, you are an Earl of Devon, hereditary owners of the late lamented Timothy the Tortoise, who died last year at the age of 160. This venerable creature was present at the Siege of Sebastopol and is the subject of a detailed biography which describes Timothy as having 'the calming density of a medium-sized Le Creuset pot'.

The deaths of Blue Peter pets were occasions of national mourning. I was inconsolable when Shep passed away. But dead pets have also inspired some fine literature, for writers have been notably attached to their domestic animals, the more exotic the better: Lord Byron had a bear, Gerard de Nerval had his lobster. (Did Flaubert's parrot receive full funeral honours, or was its passing treated with Python-esque brevity: '*Ceci, camarade, c'est un ex-perroquet; il n'est plus; il a cessé d'être.*')

Thomas Hardy, however, wrote an entire funeral ode on the demise of his terrier, Wessex. He also had eight cats, a rabbit called Juno, and a private pet graveyard in the back garden, as did Queen Victoria.

Excessive pet mourning is, of course, a subject ripe for lampooning, most notably by Evelyn Waugh. In *The Loved One*, Waugh tells the story of Dennis Barlow, poet and pet mortician, who handles cremations at the pet cemetery called the 'Happier Hunting Grounds'. 'At the administration building, he carried the dog to the refrigerator. It was a capacious chamber, already occupied by two or three other small cadavers. Next to a Siamese cat stood a tin of fruit and a plate of sandwiches. Dennis took his supper into the reception-room, and, as he ate it, resumed his interrupted reading.'

What do you call th@?

WHAT SHOULD WE NAME the '@' symbol that now, thanks to e-mail, permeates everyday English usage? Other languages have come up with a delightful variety of names. According to a list compiled by Karen Steffen Chung, of National Taiwan University, in Israel the @ is known as a strudel, on account of its rolled shape. Others, however, think the curl resembles a monkey's tail, and use various versions of the word for 'monkey': *mamjun* in Serbian, *majmunsko* in Bulgarian, *aapstert* (ape's tail) in Afrikaans. The Germans see a curling pig's tail, *Schweinekringel*, the Danes see an elephant's trunk or *snabel* and the Poles see a sleeping kitten, *kotek*. The Finns have gone a step further, and invented an onomatopoeic word, *miuku mauku*: that, apparently, is what cats say in Finland. In Mongolia, a literal sort of place, the @ sign is *Buurunhii dotorh aa*, which simply means '"a" in a round circle'. The Chinese call it *xiao lao shu*, which means little mouse, and in Russia it is a dog, *sobaka*, because one of the earliest Russian computer games involved chasing an @-shaped dog around a screen.

All of this makes our 'at sign' seem distinctly pedestrian and unimaginative. We need a new word: A curlicue? A cow's lick? A Brian (as in the snail from *The Magic Roundabout*)?

I asked this important question in a column, and received hundreds of suggestions. These included 'curlicat' (combining the idea of a curled-up cat with 'at'), 'tilla' as (in At-tila, the Hun), 'twirl', 'loopyderloop', a 'cosy a', ('because it looks like an "a" tucked up in nice warm duvet'), a 'ciracle' (an 'a' inside a circle), a 'roundal' and a 'splat'. There was also strong support for 'Swiss roll' or 'miniroll', 'curlicue' and 'Brian'.

John Byrne of Dublin asked: 'Since it looks like a snail, can we call it a "smail"?'

But the most popular suggestion, combining formality with logical rigour, was 'ampersat'. Charlie Pollock writes: 'The symbol representing "and" is called an ampersand. Therefore it seems only fitting to call the @ symbol representing "at" by the name ampersat.'

Got th@?

Beware the blurb

SOME TIME AGO, I made a mildly disobliging remark in print about a forthcoming novel by Lance Price, Tony Blair's former spin-doctor.

Politicians and their acolytes seldom make good novelists, and I was not confident that Mr Price's effort would be any better. I wrote: 'Perhaps *Time and Fate* will be the corking political novel that Blair's Britain so badly needs, but somehow I am doubtful.'

Mr Price's book came out this month, and on the cover appears this ringing endorsement: 'The corking political novel that Blair's Britain so badly needs' – *The Times*. My words had been taken, spun and their meaning turned by 180 degrees.

My first reaction was fury. How could someone have so little respect for their own writing that they would be prepared to publish a deliberate misrepresentation on the cover? But then I found myself feeling a sneaking admiration for the sheer chutzpah of Mr Price and his publishers: the man is a political animal, after all, dedicated to taking black and presenting it as white. My copy came with a cheerily unapologetic note from the author, admitting this 'outrageous spin' on his part.

With careful pruning, even the worst review can be made to sound enthusiastic. The most famous, and perhaps apocryphal, example was the review of a book about Kylie Minogue in the *Sun*, which was described as 'a steaming pile of crap'. On the paperback, however, the review was simply reduced to: 'Steaming!' My first job out of university was at a publishing house, where I was responsible for blurbs and puffs. This was extremely taxing work, trawling the often execrable reviews for something positive, anything, to stick on the cover, and sending ingratiating notes to other authors in the hope of wringing a word of approval. The experience left me with a lingering mistrust of blurbs.

The word 'blurb' was invented by the American cartoonist and poet Gelett Burgess in 1907: Miss Belinda Blurb was a cartoon blonde, dishy and gushing, prepared to lavish her sycophancy on one and all. The etymology has since expanded, and 'blurb' is now defined as 'a short, highly commendatory and often extravagant publicity notice', either extracted from a review or provided by a prominent individual: hence 'to blurb' is to praise or extol, but also to flatter and inflate.

Book publicists love the single-word endorsement: 'compelling', 'searing', 'riveting'. But there is almost always a good reason why the rest of the sentence is not there. Reviewers have an amiable tendency to leave inadvertent adjectives and superlatives lying about, which can be kidnapped and turned by their captors.

A reviewer might write: 'It is quite amazing that innocent trees gave up their lives for this atrocious book'; this can quite easily be pared down to 'Quite amazing'.

Similarly, reviewers should avoid double entendres. 'This author's persistent failure to punctuate properly reduced me to tears' may end up as 'Reduced me to tears'.

Ellipses can cover a multitude of sins. 'Really ... great' might just have been born of: 'Really this is a shameful piece of work, and if the author decided to kill himself with his own blunt prose style that would be great.'

Reviewers have become wise to the rise of the blurb. If they particularly like a book, then they may intentionally frame a pithy sentence that will fit snugly on the cover of the paperback. The danger comes when reviewing a book that is good only in parts. How to praise those parts without offering a hostage to the blurb-hunters? One colleague, reviewing a book she did not like, described its better parts as 'not displeasing', a phrase that even the most desperate blurb-maker could not use.

Celebrity endorsement is hardly more trustworthy, but blurbs can make all the difference to sales. If a book carries the praise of a popular writer, most of us are more likely to buy it. If a publisher can get J.K. Rowling to describe a new book as 'Pure magic!', all other forms of advertising pale to insignificance. On the other hand, some writers see the opportunity to blurb the work of another as a way of boosting their own status. When a distinguished author commends the work of a newcomer, the effect may be mutually beneficial, carrying the gentle implications that the talented youngster is a chip off the old block, a successor, even a protégé.

The world of writing and publishing is comparatively tiny, and the reader cannot possibly know the web of quid pro quo: who shares an agent with whom, who reviewed what in the past, whether A sat on which judging panel with B to award a prize to C. This is not to say that all blurbs are simply log-rolling and mutual back-scratching, but simply that literary judgment may not be the sole motive at work. One publishing friend, each Christmas, takes malicious pleasure in joining the dots on the Christmas book round-ups: who is praising/slagging off whom, and the possible non-literary reasons.

There is nothing new about the blurb, which existed long before there was a name for it. In the nineteenth century, some prominent book reviewers were actually in the pay of publishers, running a lucrative sideline by puffing books to order. Anthony Burgess was famously fired from a newspaper for submitting a glowing review of his own book.

The blurb, then, is a strange addendum to a book: part advertising, part genuine literary assessment. Sometimes the blurb is an honest broker, a genuine reflection of taste, and sometimes it is an impostor, another example of spin.

Don't judge a book by its cover; but even more, don't judge a book by the words on the cover.

Soon the last old soldier will fade away, leaving only written words

AND STILL THEY COME, books about the First World War, marching out of the bookshops in steady ranks. The appetite for reading about the Great War has never been greater: histories, memoirs, letters, interviews, biographies, battlefield accounts and photographic collections. Other wars come and go in literature, depending on anniversaries and fashion, but this war maintains a grip on our collective imagination like no other.

This year's crop carries the distinct tinge of wistfulness. The war of 1914–18 now stands on the most distant tip of living memory. Today there are just a handful of veterans of the conflict alive. They are the last remnants of that huge, resilient army; very soon there will no one left who took part. That will not stanch interest in the war, but it will subtly change our approach, for when the last handful of old soldiers has faded away, the nature of remembrance will change, leaving only the written word and a few grainy images.

In 1996 I attended the eightieth anniversary tribute to the dead of the Somme, under the great, horrible Thiepval arch. There I met George Jameson, at 103 the oldest veteran present, and the only survivor of the regular army of 'Old Contemptibles'.

At the age of twenty-three, Jameson had ridden on horseback into a war that, eight decades later, he regarded as a crime. 'Nothing was ever settled by it. War solves nothing.' I could have spent all day talking to this bright living ember of history. One of my lasting regrets is that I did not; and now it is too late.

Max Arthur, author of *Forgotten Voices of the Great War*, has done a signal service in tracking down the last survivors and recording their accounts in *Last Post: The Final Word from Our First World War Soldiers*. Their recollections not only summon up the war but also a sepia Edwardian Britain, a place of school beatings, gaslight and baths taken in tin tubs before a coal fire.

It is the very matter-of-factness that makes these memories so moving. 'We rolled them into the shallow holes and covered a little dirt over them,' recalls Albert 'Smiler' Marshall, a private in the Essex Yeomanry. 'By the next day, there was nothing. You couldn't see anything – just plain ground again. Underneath, just a foot deep, was all that battalion. All dead.' Even with their own deaths imminent, these old men maintain a practical, honest, unsentimental approach that seems a world away from the overwrought, overwritten accounts of modern war.

To judge from the fresh battalion of war books, there is little danger of this war slipping from memory, even if the voices of its participants must soon fall silent.

The reason is simple but remarkable: the Great War was the first and last almost universally literate war. The advent of compulsory primary education in Britain meant that even the most humble private could probably read and write, and did so.

Soldiers' recollections, as collected by Max Arthur and Lyn McDonald, were often powerfully articulate. Many soldiers were not merely literate, but vigorously literary. Other forms of communication would take over in later wars, but this was a written war, a reader's war. In the trenches, often bored beyond imagining, soldiers devoured books: Kipling, Conrad and Hardy were particular favourites.

Some officers read aloud to their men, before sending them over the top. Robert Graves recalled reading Samuel Butler's *Erewhon* in his trench, for the sixth time.

Siegfried Sassoon wrote mordantly: 'I didn't want to die, not before I'd finished *Return of the Native* anyhow.'

The great literary explosion produced by the Great War, at the time and subsequently, is a resource that writers and historians will continue to mine long after the last participant is gone. For although this was not the war to end all wars, it remains the war to define all wars.

Blow, winds, and crack your cheeks!

TSUNAMI, HURRICANE, DROUGHT, EARTHQUAKE and flood. In recent years, the Earth has buckled and lashed out, piling calamity on catastrophe to the point where humanity inevitably asks whether the catalogue of disasters is natural, in the sense of random and routine, or whether these are evidence of a pattern: global warming, government failure or God's wrath.

Writers have always responded to the Earth's cruelties in this way, searching for an explanation of the forces that lie beyond human control. The biblical flood was evidence of a divine intention to cleanse the world of sin. In medieval Europe, as Norman Cohen has shown, plague and devastation prompted millennial movements, since they presaged Apocalypse and, therefore, redemption. The California earthquake of 1906 led to a sharp rise in religious fundamentalism.

In our own time, there are those who have seen Hurricane Katrina as punishment for the sins of New Orleans,

Sodom on the Mississippi. Others allocated the sin else-where, in man's alleged mismanagement of nature. In the aftermath of Katrina, Germany's environment minister declared: 'The American President has closed his eyes to the economic and human damage that natural catastro-phes such as Katrina – in other words, disasters caused by a lack of climate protection measures – can visit on his country.'

Sales of apocalyptic literature have grown hugely in recent times: the doom boom is nigh. While scientists give warning of scientific disaster – Atlantic hurricanes, a new European ice age as the Gulf Stream dies, the disintegra-tion of the Antarctic ice shelf – others foresee Apocalypse, Armageddon and Rapture, the bodily ascent to Heaven of the saved. A recent poll in *Newsweek* showed that some 55 per cent of Americans believe in the Rapture, and more than a third believe that the world will end as predicted in the Book of Revelation. The twelve novels in the Left Behind series of Christian apocalyptic fiction have sold more than 63 million copies.

Alongside the religious and scientific responses to natu-ral disaster lies another, humanist, tradition. This surveys the devastation and finds not God's vengeance but man's powerlessness and, perhaps, his courage amid the implac-able elements.

The tempest puts man in his place in the natural world, like mighty King Lear humbled by the weather:

> Blow, winds, and crack your cheeks! rage! blow!
> You cataracts and hurricanoes, spout.

The best modern example of this genre is Sebastian Junger's *The Perfect Storm*, an essay in fear telling the story of the great hurricane that struck America's Eastern Seaboard in October 1991, and the fate of the swordfish boat *Andrea Gail*, lost 500 miles from land. Junger brilliantly evokes sea weather, 'the smell of ocean so strong that it can almost be licked off the air'.

Simon Winchester has mined a rich seam of literary post-disaster reconstruction.

These authors owe a debt to Daniel Defoe. On 26 November 1703, England and Wales were struck by a devastating hurricane which ripped across the country, killing 8,000 people, hurling cows into trees, scything down forests and destroying a fifth of the royal fleet.

In *The Storm*, Defoe gathered together eyewitness accounts and scientific evidence. A factual work of reportage, *The Storm* brought out the themes that would resonate in Defoe's later writings (most notably *Robinson Crusoe*) and in modern accounts of natural calamity: collective suffering, individual resilience and the implacable might of nature.

Many saw the storm of 1703 as God's vengeance. A year earlier, the Archbishop of Dublin, William King, had declared that 'earthquakes, storms, thunder, deluges and inundations ... are sometimes sent by a just and gracious God for the punishment of mankind'.

The turning point would come a few decades later, with the Lisbon earthquake of 1755, which destroyed a third of a great European city, killed tens of thousands and undermined theological certainty.

Voltaire, most famously, reacted with a rationalist's fury, rejecting the notion that such suffering fitted some scheme of divine justice. In *Candide*, he would savage the philosopher Leibniz's placid insistence that 'all was for the best in the best of all possible worlds'.

Just as we witness the horrific images from today's earthquakes – and wonder what shapes such brutal fate – so
Voltaire railed in verse:

Women and children heaped up mountain high,
Limbs crushed under ponderous marble lie . . .
Can you impute a sinful deed
To babes who on their mothers' bosom bleed?

Fireproof books

CENSORSHIP OF ANYTHING, FOR any reason whatever, anywhere in the world, at any time in history, has always been,
and always will be, doomed to eventual failure.

Christian protesters thought they had successfully scuppered a national tour of *Jerry Springer: The Opera*, only to
find that twenty-one theatres had decided to band together
to ensure that the show must go on. People who like to
ban things never seem to realise that the more a work of
art is subjected to the outraged squeals of the censors, the
more popular it becomes. 'To forbid us anything is to make
us have a mind for it,' said Montaigne, reaching for the
absinthe (banned in France in 1915; unbanned in 2001).
The outlawing of *The Satanic Verses* in several Islamic
countries hugely boosted sales of Salman Rushdie's least
distinguished book. When the ban on *Lady Chatterley's
Lover* was lifted in 1960, it sold two million copies in a
year: on publication day, outside Foyle's, London's largest
bookshop, a queue of 400 formed before the doors opened.
Most of these were men; sadly, history does not relate how
many were also gardeners.

Books cannot be banned, and staunchly refuse to be burnt: as the Nazis discovered when they sought to eradicate 'degenerate' literature, and as anti-Nazis discover every time they try to outlaw *The Protocols of the Elders of Zion* or *Mein Kampf*.

Bash, belittle and ban the thing you hate, and it grows back even more vigorously: like bindweed, or hydra, or Anne Robinson.

Next week is Banned Books Week in the US, when the American Library Association lists all the books that, over the previous year, people have attempted to remove from the shelves of libraries, schools and universities. This makes for sobering reading: the top ten most opposed authors in the US include J.K. Rowling (for promoting witchcraft), John Steinbeck (bad language), Maya Angelou (for sexual explicitness) and Stephen King (for being scary). In the list of the 100 most frequently challenged books of the past decade, Mark Twain's *Huckleberry Finn* comes in at number 5 (use of the word 'nigger'), J.D. Salinger's *The Catcher in the Rye* at 13 (profanity, sexual references) and Alice Walker's *The Color Purple* at 18 (inappropriate language, sex). Astonishingly, Brett Easton Ellis's serial killing saga *American Psycho* (a book that possibly merits banning for adjective abuse) comes romping in at number 60.

Some of the recent attempts at censorship would be hilarious if they were not so chilling. Eureka, Illinois, removed Chaucer from its high school literature course on the grounds of sexual content. Roald Dahl's *James and the Giant Peach* was removed from some classrooms in Virginia because it promoted disobedience towards authority figures. Delightfully, *Twelfth Night* fell foul of the school board in Merrimack, New Hampshire, where the Bard stood accused of promoting an 'alternative lifestyle', with all that disgusting cross-dressing. But perhaps the most remarkable act of censorious foolishness came a few years ago when four members of the Alabama State Textbook Committee called for the rejection of Anne Frank's *The Diary of a Young Girl* on the basis that it was 'a real downer'.

The American list of opposed books reveals a society still struggling with major hang-ups about sex, race, religion and Holocaust victims who are insufficiently jolly. But it should be added that these periodic attempts to ban books have met with universal failure: indeed, every copy of *Harry Potter* consigned to the fire for blasphemy merely fans the flames of J.K. Rowling's popularity. But 'twas ever thus. In the 1930s Senator Smoot of Utah launched an anti-pornography campaign to the delight of Ogden Nash:

> Senator Smoot (Republican, Ut.)
> Is planning a ban on smut
> Oh rooti-ti-toot for Smoot of Ut.
> And his reverent occiput.
> Smite. Smoot, smite for Ut.
> Grit your molars and do your dut.
> Gird up your l--ns,
> Smite h-p and th-gh,
> We'll all be Kansas By and By.

Every book-banning says more about the censor than the book. The prosecuting counsel in the *Lady Chatterley* trial could not have revealed his old-fashioned prejudices more obviously than when he asked the jury: 'Is it a book you would wish your wife or servants to read?' The Greek junta laid its paranoia bare for all when, in 1967, it banned *Lysistrata*, Aristophanes's anti-war masterpiece.

Even China, so expert at banning, cannot hold back books for long. Recently two Chinese authors, Chen Guidi and Wu Chuntao, published the snappily titled *A Survey of Chinese Peasants*, an exposé of the plight of China's 800 million agricultural poor. It was banned by the government, promptly and inevitably, but has since gone on to sell an estimated eight million copies in thirty pirate editions. Chen and Wu were last year awarded the Lettres Ulysses Award in Berlin. (Yes, that is James Joyce's *Ulysses*: banned in Britain for fourteen years, as 'obscene, lewd, lascivious, filthy, indecent and disgusting'; recently selected by the Modern Library as the best novel of the twentieth century.) So, as the anti-Jerry Springer brigade seeks, once again, to ban the unbannable, let us remember Thomas Bowdler, who took all the rude and offensive bits out of Shakespeare: 'I regret that no parent could place the uncorrected book in the hands of his daughter, and therefore I have prepared the Family Shakespeare.'

Bowdler's Family Shakespeare prospered briefly, and then vanished utterly. Bowdler survives only as a pejorative term in the *OED*, a fitting epitaph for this literary King Canute (or Smoot), who tried, and failed, to hold back the unstoppable tide.

Angela simply could not decide whom to love: Edward Hyde or Henry Jekyll

'SHALL WE FOR EVER make new books, as apothecaries make new mixtures, by pouring only out of one vessel into another?' So wondered Laurence Sterne in *Tristram Shandy*, pondering on the way authors tend to rely, for inspiration, on their predecessors. Certainly, this year's Man Booker Prize line-up reveals a new wave of literary decantation:

Zadie Smith's *On Beauty* echoes the characters, plot shapes, themes and phrases of E.M. Forster's *Howards End*, while Julian Barnes's *Arthur and George* owes its inspiration to the life and works of Arthur Conan Doyle. Last year's Booker list was just awash with bits of Henry James Revisited.

Will Self's novel *Dorian* was, by his own account, 'an imitation . . . a complete and professed rewrite' of Oscar Wilde's *The Picture of Dorian Gray*. Julian Branston recently reworked the story of Don Quixote as *The Eternal Quest*. Jane Smiley retold King Lear as *A Thousand Acres*, and won the Pulitzer Prize for it in 1992.

This is the Hey Jude school of fiction: take an earlier book, and make it better.

I am all in favour. Homer, after all, was only retelling other people's stories, and the idea that a novel has to be novel is itself relatively new.

Call it 'homage' if you will; call it 'plagiarism' if you have a good lawyer; call it 'intertextuality' if you are an academic at a struggling English faculty. But Only Connect, and you have the makings of a Booker Prize on your hands.

Here are some examples:

The Sherlock Code by Dan Brown

IT WAS with some disquiet that I noticed my good friend Holmes had laid aside his violin and was now strapping a large belt studded with razor blades on to his thigh, while chanting 'Opus Dei'.

'This is quite a three-whip problem,' said the great detective, as he began to flagellate himself with a strip of rhino hide. 'It appears that the son of a well-known family has been, to put it bluntly, indiscreet, and has had a child out of wedlock. This has undermined the whole of Western culture.'

'But who is this errant young fellow?' I asked, fulfilling my role as dumb sidekick and plot-organising device.

'His name is Jesus Christ,' said Holmes.

'Jesus H. Christ,' I said.

'Quite.' The great man winced, as he drove a small penknife into his right buttock.

'Are you seriously telling me that you can take some half-baked medieval mythology, a smattering of art history, a little religious masochism and some French totty and sell millions of novels?'

'Elementary, my dear Watson.'

Dr Jekyll and the Aga of Love by Joanna Trollope
ANGELA was torn. She simply could not decide whom to love: Edward Hyde or Henry Jekyll. Dr Jekyll was so honourable, so rich, and he cooked a lovely soufflé. And yet there was something deliciously bestial about Edward, something about the way his knuckles scraped along the parquet when the Moon was high, that made her delightfully giddy.

As Angela pondered, the room suddenly turned cold, and she wrapped the silk negligee closer around her pale form. 'Henry, is that you?' she trilled. A guttural grunt came from the gloom, and suddenly she felt herself seized by two muscular arms and inhaled the heady, earthy scent of . . . what? Dead badger.

'Oh, Edward,' she moaned, burying her face in his exceptionally luxuriant chest hair.

'Grrrr,' said Mr Hyde.

Oliver Twisted by Hunter S. Thompson
WE WERE somewhere around Shoreditch on the edge of London when the drugs began to take hold. Myself and

my attorney, The Artful Dodger, had obtained twenty-five groats from Ye Olde Times, most of which had already been spent on extremely dangerous narcotics: four pints of unrefined gin, fifteen gallons of porter, a quart of laudanum, three bushels of raw opium, sixteen pints of chloroform and a chamberpot full of morphine.

The sky was full of what looked like huge bats, all swooping and screeching and diving around the hansom cab. Very soon, I knew, we would be completely twisted.

The only thing that really worried me was the laudanum. There is nothing in the world more helpless and irresponsible and depraved than a man in the depths of a laudanum binge.

I turned to my attorney: 'Please, sir, can I have some more?'

Emma Ramotswe by Alexander McCall Smith

EMMA RAMOTSWE, handsome, clever, and rich, with a comfortable home and happy disposition, seemed to unite some of the best blessings of existence. Yet the chief operative of The No.1 Ladies' Detective Agency knew this: it is a truth universally acknowledged that a single man in possession of a good fortune, such as J.L.B. Matekoni, owner of Tlokweng Road Speedy Motors, must be in want of a wife.

Emma made a pot of Bush tea and decided to discuss the matter with Mma Makutsi, plucky assistant detective and deputy manager of Tlokweng Road Speedy Motors. Even before Mma Makutsi had decided to establish the Kalahari Typing School for Men, the mildness of her temper had hardly allowed her to impose any restraint, and they had been living together as friend and friend, Emma Ramotswe doing just what she liked; highly esteeming Mma Makutsi's judgment, but directed chiefly by her own.

Moby Dickhead by Irvine Welsh
FUCKING BIG FISH. Och Aye. Huge, sleekit Fucking Fish. Guid wi' chips.

The film of the book

PATRICK SÜSKIND, THE FAMOUSLY introverted German writer, finally gave permission for the filming of his novel *Perfume* (*Das Parfum*), after twenty years of negotiations with film-makers. Many thought the extraordinary tale of a perfume-maker with no sense of smell in malodorous eighteenth-century France could never be made into a film, or at least not until someone invented smell-o-vision.

Süskind declared his novel to be 'unfilmable'.

Perfume has sold fifteen million copies in fifty languages and Hollywood smelt a hot property from the moment it was first published in 1985. Finally, Süskind has relented and given permission for Bernd Eichinger, producer of *Downfall*, to begin filming his masterwork. Even so, the novelist has insisted that as part of the contract (worth a reported £7 million), he will have nothing to do with the production and will not have to set foot on the set.

That this essentially olfactory work made it to the big screen may, finally, be proof that there is no such thing as an unfilmable book, but the episode is oddly illuminating of the strange, tortured relationship between books and films, between the writer and the film-maker.

Novelists are often intensely ambivalent at the prospect

of seeing their words translated into the blunter medium of film. As Gore Vidal once remarked, the camera cannot capture thought, and can thus only ever produce an approximation of the written word. On the other hand, writers need the money and crave the fame, not to mention the additional book sales and the opportunity to schmooze with the Paltrows and the Pitts. Rare is the novelist prepared to spurn the siren call of the movies. Hemingway eschewed Hollywood, and never once went near the place. But most writers, after some seemly hesitation and feigned insouciance, cash the cheque.

The passage from novel to screen was once slow and uncertain. It took seventy-seven years for Joseph Conrad's *Heart of Darkness* to become *Apocalypse Now*. But today some novelists sell their books to Hollywood before they are even books: a few lines on a scrap of paper written by John Grisham merits a multi-million-dollar contract.

But the hesitation on the part of more fastidious writers is understandable, for adaptation is one of the least predictable artistic lotteries. Hollywood cynics maintain that the better the book, the worse the film, but the real equation is not so simple. Certainly some of the very best books make the worst films (Louis de Bernières's *Captain Corelli's Mandolin*), while equally good or better books languish eternally in production purgatory (Donna Tartt's *The Secret History*).

Some dire books make marvellous films (Peter Benchley's *Jaws*), and very occasionally good books make even better films (the works of Roddy Doyle). Perhaps the oddest subcategory is that of entirely obscure books that become film classics (who has read *Red Alert* by Peter George, the book that was adapted into *Dr Strangelove*?).

Faced with this bizarre lottery, writers see their carefully honed treasures head off to the film factory and wonder if

they will come back stunted and deformed, faithfully repli-
cated, or, worst of all, transformed into something so much
better than the original book that no one remembers who
wrote it in the first place.

Films inevitably simplify and solidify, and there is the fear
of being reduced to a single, hilarious line in *Halliwell's Film
Guide*. How, I wonder, would Leo Tolstoy feel about seeing
his masterpiece described as 'a Russian family's adventures
at the time of the Napoleonic invasion'? James Joyce might
have balked at seeing 1,000 pages of protean prose exploring and subverting every aspect of the novel form described
as 'twenty-four hours in Dublin with a young poet and Jew-
ish newspaperman'.

Joyce himself believed that *Ulysses* 'could not be made
into a film with artistic propriety'. (He discussed the matter
with, of all people, Albert Einstein; now that's a conversation I would like to have heard.) That has not stopped the
film-makers. There are no fewer than three film versions
of *Ulysses* and one, even more ambitiously, of *Finnegans
Wake*. These have met with mixed critical responses, but
'The Dead', the last short story in *Dubliners*, was made
into a film by John Huston, a haunting and faithful tribute
to the original.

Lurking at the back of every writer's vanity is Woody
Allen's crushing observation: 'If I had my life to live again, I
would do it all exactly the same, but without seeing the film
version of *The Magus*.'

Hell has no fury like the writer who feels his book has
been traduced on film.

Bernardo Bertolucci surely winced when Paul Bowles told
him, after watching the film adaptation of *The Sheltering
Sky*: 'It should never have been filmed. The ending is idiotic,
and the rest is pretty bad.'

F. Scott Fitzgerald once complained that 'movies have taken away our dreams', but Italo Calvino maintained that great writing could not only withstand but required adaptation: 'The tale is not beautiful if nothing is added.'

Graham Greene, who knew the scriptwriter's trade from first-hand, took the most pragmatic position. 'One gets used to the corruptions of one's work . . . and it's a waste of time to resent them. You rake in the money, you go on writing for another year or two, you have no grounds for complaint. And the smile in the long run will be on your face. For the book has a longer life.' For my money, *The Third Man* remains the best book-to-film adaptation yet produced.

In spite of his reservations, there was surely a smile on Süskind's face as he signed the film deal for *Perfume*. The scent of Hollywood success is powerful, and only a writer with no sense of smell would turn his nose up at the prospect of celulloid celebrity.

Why books breed

BOOKS DO FURNISH A room. Over time, they begin to dominate a room. Finally, they utterly engulf a room, then the next room, then the entire house. Then they kill you. That, at least, was the fate of doomed Leonard Bast in E.M. Forster's *Howards End*, memorably crushed to death by a falling bookcase, obliterated by the sheer weight of middle-class literature.

Books have a self-hoarding, expanding quality. Unlike almost everything else in our society, they are enormously difficult to throw away. Once we have read them, they become part of our souls, a physical spur to memory. If we have not read them, they are even harder to jettison; they stand there on the shelf accusingly, worlds undiscovered.

Most books are – and should be – read only once. Only a very few are genuinely collectable or bear rereading. Yet instead of handing them on to someone else after we have read them, or selling them or using them for organic compost, we jealously guard them. Alberto Manguel, in *A History of Reading*, observed his own growing collection and admitted 'the main reason I hold on to this ever increasing hoard is a sort of voluptuous greed'.

There is also intellectual aspiration. No one, except Victoria Beckham, likes to be thought of as utterly illiterate. George W. Bush proudly tells us he is reading *Salt: A World History* by Mark Kurlansky. Our MPs shamelessly divulge that this year they have mostly been reading *The Da Vinci Code*. And when they have finished, instead of consigning Dan Brown to the dustbin with a snort, they will arrange him proudly on their bookshelves.

I write as one who has never been able to bring himself to get rid of a single book, old or new, read or unread. Long ago I gave up trying to order my shelves, and I now leave the books to multiply unhindered, double-stacked or wedged in horizontally. I wish I could claim to have read them all; but far from that, there are many, when I examine my shelves closely, that I have never even seen before.

Who, for example, invested in that copy of the feng shui for plants? When did I ever think I would read a biography of Barbara Cartland? Why are there three copies of *The Information* by Martin Amis? Is the little fellow magically self-replicating in there?

From time to time, I have attempted a page-purge. I scour the shelves looking for easy victims. Ah-ha, a Jeffrey Archer lurking on the top shelf. That, surely, can go. And what's this? Rilke's letters, trying to hide behind *The Bumper Book of Dinosaurs*. Life is too short for Rilke (about eighty years too short). Come to think of it, the dinosaurs have had their day too. But just as I am preparing to consign the books to oblivion, or Oxfam, I begin to feel like a Nazi. The books go into the attic. Heck, I might even get around to Rilke's letters one day.

Publishers remainder and pulp, so why can't I? I remain torn, and slightly foxed.

I blame Iris Murdoch. As a schoolboy, I remember visiting her home in Oxford, and picking my way through tottering canyons of books, some with plates or glasses balanced on top, great rivers of literature that streamed out of the rooms and stretched down every corridor. She never threw anything away, for one very simple reason: books had so completely taken over the house that the whereabouts of the rubbish bin had long since been forgotten. Her husband, John Bayley, explained that 'she depended for inspiration on the presence of her books'. But her presence also lent meaning to the sprawling library. A few years ago, after her death, Bayley decided to sell her personal collection. I thought that was the right thing to do. I also thought that, without those columns of books to hold it up, the house would probably fall down.

Even the least bookish of people seem to need books, or at least a facsimile of literature, if not for inspiration, then at least for effect. Anthony Powell's novel *Books Do Furnish a Room* deliciously mocked the bourgeois philistinism that confused reading with wallpaper. Powell would have been delighted by a modern California company, Book Decor (www.bookdecor.com), which sells books by the foot: 'Warm rich leathers and antique gilt accent any room ... designer books are an affordable and elegant way to add warmth and beauty to your decor.' The books come at $90 a foot for books of one colour, and $130 a foot for 'Designer Mix'. There is no danger of anyone reading these books, since they are printed in Danish. The company offers this baffling recommendation: 'Book Decor has supplied books for set decoration in four recent Mel Gibson films.' I am offering a second-hand copy of the letters of Rilke to anyone who can name a single Mel Gibson film with a book in it.

Mrs Beckham may never have read a book, but I feel sure that Beckingham Palace has its own library. For people too busy to browse, Waterstone's now offers a 'personal library shopper', an expert who will buy, on the client's behalf, the sort of books they ought to own, with no obligation to read. Say, a lovely shelf in matching Graham Greenes, with a modern fringe of Zadie Smith, and a nice fat Tolstoy as a focal point.

Suits you, sir, and if the jacket doesn't fit, you can always exchange it.

Maurice Sendak, author of *Where the Wild Things Are*, described a book as a 'love object', a thing of physical delight and aesthetic beauty as well as mental stimulation.

But love can be lethal, and I am haunted by the fate of Anthony Cima, an eighty-seven-year-old bibliomane who stuffed 10,000 books into his one-room flat in San Diego. Then came the earthquake of 1987, the shelves toppled and Cima was buried in books. He emerged barely alive, and as flat as a Bast.

The moral of this story is: throw the Jeffrey Archers away.

The bookshop at the edge of the world

THE CLOSURE OF THE Puff Inn on St Kilda is a cruel blow to thirsty ornithologists, rock-climbing naturalists, yachtsmen and other intrepid visitors to this storm-beaten rock in the Atlantic. But it will also be a source of sadness to book lovers, for the military building that houses Britain's most remote pub is also home to the country's most remote bookshop.

For years, tucked into a room behind the bar, the St Kilda Bookshop (run by the National Trust for Scotland) has stood as a testament to the extraordinary fascination of this romantic and windswept archipelago at the Edge of the World, once home to the most isolated community in Britain. One of the more peculiar pleasures of visiting St Kilda is to take a pint from the Puff and browse the shelves of books about the islands, a strange literary sub-genre flourishing more than 100 miles off the Scottish mainland.

For more than 400 years St Kilda has drawn writers of all sorts: romantics, reformers, historians, naturalists, missionaries and travellers. Journalists, from early Victorian times onwards, regularly descended on the islands like flocks of gannets to 'investigate' this lost tribe. Some seventy-six books have been written about St Kilda. Many of these remain in print; and most of those are stocked by the St Kilda Bookshop. Or they were, until the company that runs the island's radar tracking station announced, absurdly, that because of security concerns the prefabricated military huts should be reserved for the use of its personnel.

One of the earliest and most sympathetic chroniclers of the islands was Martin Martin, a canny, Gaelic-speaking minister who set out to describe life in the outer Outer Hebrides at the end of the seventeenth century. In 1697 Martin crossed the heaving seas to St Kilda in an open boat propelled by sixteen oarsmen from Skye, who had to be supplied with copious draughts of whisky. 'We plied them with plenty of Aqua Vitae,' wrote Martin. So much, in fact, 'that upon our arrival … there was scarce one of our Crew able to manage Cable or Anchor'.

In his *A Late Voyage to St Kilda*, Martin described a people wearing shoes made from the necks of gannets, nominally Christian but steeped in an older folklore, and surviving on the flesh of seabirds. Yet he was struck by the contented demeanour of these hardy souls, happily marooned in the middle of the ocean. 'The inhabitants of St Kilda … are much happier than the generality of mankind as being the only people in the world who feel the sweetness of true liberty.'

The conception of St Kilda as an insular utopia runs through literature from that day to this. The self-sufficient St Kildans fitted into romantic notions of the noble savage, isolated from the corruptions of modernity. The laird's factors visited annually, but for centuries the St Kildans had known little of war or peace, the rise and fall of kingdoms. In 1746, when a posse of redcoats arrived looking for the fugitive Bonnie Prince Charlie, the islanders responded, with perfect honesty, that they had never heard of any such person.

But alongside those who saw St Kilda as an Arcadia were writers who viewed the supposed ignorance and isolation of the islanders as a sin against civilisation.

Victorians and Edwardians, buoyed by the brutal self-confidence of that age, argued that advances in education, healthcare and religion must be brought to benighted St Kilda, just as they had been extended to other far-flung corners of the Empire. The tourists began to arrive by the boatload, to gawp at the lost Scottish tribe. They brought with them a sense of moral superiority, but also afflictions St Kilda had never known before: money and the common cold.

The best modern account of St Kilda's decline is Tom Steel's *The Life and Death of St Kilda*, as fresh and angry as when it was first published in 1975. For Steel, the St Kildan way of life was destroyed by the arrival of a harsh religion, well-meaning tourists and bureaucratic busybodies, rather than the effects of poverty or geography: 'When the island was evacuated in 1930, not only had Nature defeated man but, in a real sense, man had defeated fellow man.'

For Steel, the desertion of St Kilda represents 'a small human tragedy', an image reinforced by sepia photographs of the last of St Kilda's bearded men clinging to impossible rocks in the hunt for food, and the haunting pictures of deserted and overgrown houses. Anthony Trollope had also predicted that St Kilda could not survive 'progress': 'Though the life of a Robinson Crusoe or a few Robinson Crusoes may be very picturesque,' he wrote after visiting the islands in 1878, 'humanity will always desire to restore a Robinson Crusoe to the community of the world.'

St Kilda developed separately from the rest of the world: alongside a unique species of wren and mouse, it evolved a special literature, a complex and rich resource that says as much about the people who wrote it as about the St Kildans themselves. The island produced hardy breeds of people, birds and books, and the St Kilda literature continues to evolve today. Whatever happens to the island bookshop, for generations to come people will still be reading the Books at the Edge of the World.

Save the semicolon; please

PEOPLE HAVE BEEN GANGING up on the semicolon recently, even threatening to do away with it altogether. We must end this madness at once; right here, right now; full stop.

The bid to flush this vital punctuation mark out of our prose – let us call it semi-colonic irrigation – began, inevitably, in the US. Writing in the *Financial Times*, Trevor Butterworth reported: 'Americans see the semicolon as punctuation's axis of evil.' He quoted an essay by Donald Barthelme: 'Let me be plain: the semicolon is ugly, ugly as a tick on a dog's belly, I pinch them out of my prose.'

Americans have long regarded the semicolon with suspicion, as a genteel, self-conscious, neither-one-thing-nor-the-other sort of punctuation mark, with neither the butchness of a full colon nor the flighty promiscuity of the comma. Hemingway and Chandler and Stephen King wouldn't be seen dead in a ditch with a semicolon (though Truman Capote might). Real men, goes the unwritten rule of American punctuation, don't use semicolons.

Kurt Vonnegut was damning: 'If you really want to hurt your parents, and you don't have the nerve to be a homosexual, the least you can do is go into the arts. But do not use semicolons. They are transvestite hermaphrodites, standing for absolutely nothing. All they do is show you've been to college.'

The word comes from the Greek *Kôlon* (meaning 'limb', or 'clause'), but modern Greeks have virtually abandoned the semicolon, which no longer features on Greek keyboards and now appears only in articles lamenting the disappearance of the semicolon.

Sub-editors on *The Times* (though not in the Books section, obviously) have been known to whip them out in favour of something a little less fancy. I expect David Cameron wields a mean semicolon, but I somehow rather doubt whether John Prescott, a living exclamation mark, is much of a semicolon man.

Even Ian Jack, the editor of *Granta*, following up the

semicolon controversy in the *Guardian*, expressed doubts about deploying the little fellow. 'I came to the semicolon late,' he writes, 'and, like many people, I fret before using it in anything other than lists.'

Now you may think that a comma with a hat on is not worth busting your (Lynne) truss over, but you would be wrong. The semicolon is one of the most subtle and versatile tools in the language. Most punctuation marks were invented to aid speaking in public, but the semicolon is uniquely an aid to reading alone, in silence. The earliest general use of the semicolon in English was in 1591, Shakespeare's sonnets are full of them and Ben Jonson was a big fan. Despite its reputation as an effete English literary confection, the semicolon owes its modern inception to an Italian, the Venetian printer Aldus Manutius the elder, who came up with it as a way to separate words opposed in meaning and to mark off interdependent statements.

The beauty of the semicolon lies in its very vagueness. It indicates both connection and division. It is a gentle way of connecting thoughts, without applying the abrupt brake of a full stop or the breathiness of a comma. It implies a qualification or refinement of the idea stated in the first part of the sentence. Sometimes a string of semicolons shows an evolving idea or description, a string of interconnected ideas.

Virginia Woolf opens *Mrs Dalloway* with a lovely spray of semicolons: 'How fresh, how calm, stiller than this of course, the air was in the early morning; like the flap of a wave; the kiss of a wave; chill and sharp and yet (for a girl of eighteen as she was then) solemn, feeling as she did, standing there at the open window, that something awful was about to happen; looking at the trees with smoke winding off them and the rooks rising, falling; standing and looking . . .'

Everyone has fifteen minutes of fiction

YOU HAVE ATTAINED FULL celebrity status. You have the Hollywood agent, the trophy spouse, the swimming pool, the nose-job, the fashionable *chien du jour* and the original Damien Hirst hanging above the hot tub. Your friends run the gamut from Sienna to Salman. You can get a table at Sketch. And yet something is missing in your glittering life, the one distinction that would mark you out as a cut above the other, merely famous, people.

You need to write a novel.

One of the odder side effects of fame is a craving for the obscure satisfaction that only a slim volume of one's own can bring. Richard Tull in Martin Amis's *The Information* (1995) is enraged that people celebrated for 'news casting, cliff-scaling, acting, cooking, dress designing, javelin-throwing, and being related to the Queen' also presume to think they can write novels. Famous people do not usually imagine they can also paint a fresco, compose a symphony or write a sonnet.

Andy Warhol reckoned that everyone gets fifteen minutes of fame; the next stage, almost inevitably, is to try to parlay that fifteen minutes into 250 pages of fiction. Warhol himself 'wrote' *a: A Novel*, a transcript of a recording of twenty-four hours in the amphetamine-soaked life of his groupies. The book was produced soon after Valerie Solanas shot Warhol, and it reads like it. Speed was of the essence, so the book is full of typing errors. Warhol insisted that the mistakes stayed in, added some more, changed the names and arbitrarily altered anything else that caught his blood-shot eye. The result was profoundly, invincibly unreadable. But, heck, at least it was a novel.

It is easy to make fun of celebrity novelists. So we should. David Niven, Naomi Campbell, Kirk Douglas, Joan Collins and Dolly Parton have all felt impelled to show us the colour of their prose. Martina Navratilova was paid a huge sum of money to write a trilogy of novels about a tennis player who becomes a crime-fighting sleuth. Gene Hackman wrote *Wake of the Perdido Star*, which described itself as 'a novel of shipwreck'; perhaps the publisher meant 'a shipwreck of a novel'. Alan Titchmarsh wrote an unpickupable novel about a television gardener.

I have before me *Fan-Tan*; a novel by none other than the late Marlon Brando, published next month, 'a rollicking, swashbuckling, delectable romp of a novel – the last surprise from an ever-surprising legend'. I have read nine pages, but cannot get beyond the description of a man in prison having his fingers eaten by cockroaches ('oh, how delicately they chomped away at the husks of his fingertips'). Sadly, Brando did not live long enough to see the publication of his book. Sadly, I shall not live long enough to finish it.

Some famous people turn out to be rather fine novelists, but usually these tend to be those with an acute sense of irony: Steve Martin, Stephen Fry, Eric Idle and David Baddiel. Most celebrity fiction is ferociously bad because most celebrities, by definition, lack the essential ability to stand outside looking in. In John Updike's words, 'as soon as somebody is aware of being "somebody", of being watched and listened to with extra interest, input ceases, and the performer goes blind and deaf in his over-animation. One can either see or be seen.'

There are exceptions. In her first novel, Pamela Anderson, the ex-*Baywatch* star, looked inside to reflect her essence, the very core of her personality and fame: namely, two very remarkable breasts. Ms Anderson is a former waitress who went on to become a pin-up and actress with very remarkable breasts; her novel, entitled *Star*, is about a former waitress who goes on to become a pin-up and actress with very remarkable breasts. So far, so *roman-à-clef*, though I'm not sure Pammy would put it quite like that.

Mostly, the book is about tits, and what can be done to and with them. It is the story of two misunderstood glands and their journey in search of fulfilment in fullness: Cinderella, with silicone.

Initially, like many first-time novelists, Ms Anderson was daunted by the challenge: 'A book?' she told one interviewer. 'Like chapters, how many pages are in a chapter? How many chapters in a book? I needed some guidance.' She might have answered these questions by opening a book, any book, but instead she hired a ghost-writer, and in twenty-eight days he hammered out this classic of the genre, a confection as stiff, fake and perfect as Pammy herself, a monument to her monuments.

It reached number 13 on the *New York Times* bestseller list. This fact brings the intelligentsia out in vapours, but it does not represent the end of civilisation.

Rather, it might be taken as a backhanded compliment to fiction, an art so accessible and adaptable that it can bear any amount of abuse. People immeasurably famous in every other way crave the respectability that a novel carries. Stars who have probably never read a novel still want to write one. Anderson's oeuvre (a sequel comes out later this summer: *Starstruck*) might even be seen as affirmation of the cultural status of reading; there are many ways to make a name, but the book is what matters most. Pammy herself knows that books are sexy; her latest TV role is in a sitcom set in a bookshop entitled, wait for it, *Stacked*.

In a lyrical passage in *Star*, Ms Anderson ghost-writes that her heroine feels 'a sense that something was missing, like that feeling you get when you stand looking into the refrigerator, not really hungry, but unable to stop looking, the feeling that this time it might be there, right behind the ketchup and the pickled beets'.

That, of course, is how every celebrity novelist feels: out there somewhere lies literary immortality, that something missing, lurking behind the ketchup of life.

Amazon beckoned to the reviewer in all of us

ONE DAY IN 1995, a geeky and bookish young man retired to his garage in Seattle and began selling books on the internet. From these small and unpromising headwaters flowed the mighty Amazon.

Amazon has proved that the printed word can not only survive, but also profit hugely in the digital age. More than that, the online bookshop is one of the very few modern inventions that can be said, on balance, to have improved civilisation and enhanced world culture, profoundly altering the relationship between readers, reviewers and books. The online site launched by Jeff Bezos on 15 July 1995 was little more than a ropy website catalogue, but one with a revolutionary ethos, combining high-minded literary intentions with steel-nosed capitalism: Bezos believed that he could provide objective reviews about books and still sell them.

Despite several near-death experiences for the company, he was right.

Amazon sells every blockbuster on the block, but it has also been saviour to academic and small publishers. Catering for the most obscure interests, it is the bibliomaniac's paradise, a virtual bookshop that stocks everything, tells you about things that you never knew you wanted (but do) and delivers them at a discount without you ever having to leave the house.

Of course, the online retailer long ago moved on from simply selling books. Today Amazon markets, among other things, cars, garden shears, lobsters, DVDs, diamonds and dinner jackets for dogs. ('Top Dog Tuxedos are made of a comfortable Acetate/cotton blend,' the site declares brightly. 'Adjustable front Velcro closure with collar bow tie. Top hat has cardboard insert to maintain contour.') Huge and sprawling as it is, this vast online shopping centre still retains the flavour of its founder's intention in the customer reviews that accompany almost every product.

Initially, editorial staff wrote all the reviews on Amazon but, as time passed, the space was increasingly devoted to customers' opinions. Readers wanted room to hear themselves think. Some of the reviews were well-informed, intelligent critiques; some were quite barmy. But they poured in by the million, a testament to humanity's love of literature, and the accompanying urge to pass on what we think about what we have read.

Individual Amazon critics attained their own literary status, such as the indefatigable Harriet Klausner, the site's number-one reviewer with more than 9,000 reviews to date. The system developed its own self-regulating pecking order, with the most popular reviewers (that is, those deemed 'helpful' by other customers, which in practice meant 'gentle') rising to the top. Customer reviews could make or break a book. Publishers and authors took notice, and inevitably tried to abuse the system. Hiding behind anonymity or pseudonym, writers began giving their own works rave reviews and full marks, or encouraging their friends and family to tilt the ratings in their favour.

This has raised once more the issue of whether anonymous criticism is valid or valuable. T. S. Eliot, opposing the decision by the *TLS* to end unsigned reviews, wrote that by writing anonymously he had learnt to 'moderate my dislikes and crotchets, to write in a temperate and impartial way; I learnt that some things are permissible when they appear over one's name, which become tasteless eccentricity or unseemly violence when unsigned'. But the Amazon experience suggests that reviewers are more likely to put the boot in when the boot cannot be traced back. Despite Amazon's attempts to police the system, plenty of bile and bias (and plain ignorance) got through.

The anonymous customer-critic will never displace the expert book reviewer, but he has become a powerful and permanent figure on the literary landscape. Here is dumbing-up at its most democratic, for it is surely a mark of a healthy civilisation when millions feel not only compelled to buy and read books, but to write about them as well, to pass on their enthusiasms and aversions, to debate and discuss writing with complete strangers.

Amazon's tenth birthday party in Seattle will be celebrated with a concert and book-reading featuring authors, musicians and film-makers who have been selected on the basis of their popularity with customers over the past ten years. In some ways, this will be a celebration not of commercial success, but of the humble critic in the kitchen.

Amazon unleashed, or at least beckoned to, the reviewer in all of us. Today you can review anything on Amazon, and that has allowed a flowering of critical judgment on subjects and from people far outside the traditional critocracy.

Consider, for example, this heartfelt assessment of a new release on Amazon: 'It generates a multitude of feelings, a certain sense of security, yet also an empowering sense of freedom.'

That, delightfully, is one man's ode to his new underwear.

Useful language learn quick now!

I WAS RECENTLY WAITING for a flight in Delhi, when I overheard a conversation between a Spanish UN peacekeeper and an Indian soldier. The Indian spoke no Spanish; the Spaniard spoke no Punjabi. Yet they understood one another easily.

The language they spoke was a highly simplified form of English, without grammar or structure, but perfectly comprehensible, to them and to me. Only now do I realise that they were speaking 'Globish', the newest and most widely spoken language in the world.

Globish is not like Esperanto or Volapuk; this is not a formally constructed language, but rather an organic patois, constantly adapting, emerging solely from practical usage and spoken in some form or other by about 88 per cent of mankind.

Its chief promoter, astonishingly enough, is a Frenchman, Jean-Paul Nerrière, a linguist and retired computer executive who has earned the loathing of the French Establishment by insisting that Globish – simple, inelegant and almost universal – is the language of the present and the future. In his primer, *Parlez Globish*, Nerrière points out that Globish is not intended for writing poetry or telling jokes, but for communication at the most basic level. It is not a language in the traditional sense, freighted with cultural meaning, but a supremely useful and ingenious tool, the linguistic equivalent of a Swiss Army knife.

The Frenchman has calculated that the speaker of Globish needs to pronounce and understand no more than 1,500 words, starting with 'able' and ending in 'zero'.

The entire vocabulary of Globish amounts to less than one four-hundredth of the words in the *OED*. Starting from scratch, anyone in the world should be able to learn Globish in about one week. Nerrière's website (www.jpn-globish.com) also recommends that students use plenty of gesticulation when words fail, and listen to popular songs to aid pronunciation, including such unlikely language aids as 'What a Wonderful World' and 'The Great Pretender'. (What happens if one Globish speaker has an Elvis accent and the other speaks with a Satchmo twang? Will they understand one another, or do they need to simplify down to another level, and speak in Sex Pistols?) Language purists are naturally appalled by the emergence of this pidgin worldspeak, a mongrel tongue without structure and rules, pared down to its most rudimentary form. Facing the inevitable, the French government decreed last year that English lessons should be made compulsory for all French schoolchildren: better to have English taught correctly than allow 'airport English' to seep into French culture. But the central dilemma was summed up by a cartoon in *Le Monde*: 'If they force us to do English, then we'll speak only French,' one student says in French. 'Yeah,' replies his friend. Globish is already *le Must* among modish young Parisians.

If the French are anxious, how much more worried should the guardians of the English language be, faced by a spreading and debased version of our own tongue? As Nerrière points out: 'Globiphones are already at least seven times more populous than anglophones.' Is the mother tongue about to be overrun by her lumbering bastard offspring?

Not a bit of it, because commensurate with the explosion of Globish is an equally powerful and widely accepted determination to protect the central elements of real languages. Nerrière argues that the new global patois will actually protect French, by driving out franglais, thus leaving 'pure' French to survive unsullied.

Globish has been partly spread by the internet, yet the computer is also becoming the guardian of 'good' English. Everyone who writes using the Microsoft Word program (i.e. just about everyone who writes anything) is under constant surveillance by the inbuilt spell and grammar checker, wagging its electronic finger whenever we deviate from the rules. It is like having Lynne Truss living permanently inside your computer.

Microsoft Word is supposed to enforce correct English, but even the infallible computer gets it wrong. Type in 'I am agreeable with what this column say', and the grammar check does not object at all. But type in the first line of *Pride and Prejudice*, 'It is a truth universally acknowledged . . .', and it starts insisting you simplify, and add commas. Almost anything written by Henry James or Hunter S. Thompson sends it into a hissy fit.

This demonstrates the malleability of the language, as interesting English need not be correct English. The astonishing spread of English language in a single generation has allowed it to evolve more fascinatingly than any other: think of Indian-English, which is in many ways a more inventive and grammatically pure version of the language than the one spoken in Britain. 'Incorrect' English can be extraordinarily rich, and non-standard forms of the language are developing outside the West in ways that are as lively and diverse as Chaucerian or Dickensian English.

(Some French linguists argue that if Napoleon had not made the mistake of selling Louisiana to the US, we would all be speaking French today or, rather, a simplified version of it: Mondais, perhaps. I don't believe this, for French has never had English's adaptability and adoptability.) Globish is not the end of the language, but an important step on the evolutionary ladder, and for many an introduction to the world. The 1,500 basic words of Globish serve as an invitation to find the other 613,000 in the *OED*, as proven by the extraordinary and growing demand for English instruction worldwide. A recent British Council survey found that the language evolves ever faster as it spreads beyond traditional Anglo-Saxon usage: so far from threatening minority languages, Globish and its myriad local variants may serve to protect those threatened with extinction.

Jacques Chirac was right when he declared that nothing would be more damaging for humanity than for all its 7,000 languages to be reduced to one. He was referring to English. But Globish is not quite a language: it is a means to an end, a way of bringing millions into a global economy without the privilege of formal education, a world dialect, an international *über*-slang that, for the most part, leaves local languages intact. It may be a limited form of communication, but at least Globish means that we are talking to each other. 'Don't shoot, I'm Globish': now there is a phrase that needs no translation, anywhere.

A column of the purest bullshit

THE WRONG SORT OF snow finally pushed Yuri Luzhkov, the Mayor of Moscow, over the edge. Enraged with Russia's hopeless weather forecasters, he has vowed to fine them for any more inaccurate, misleading or unreliable predictions. As reported in *The Times*, he admonished them in the following, memorable terms: 'You are giving us bullshit.'

On the other side of the world, Harry G. Frankfurt, the moral philosopher and Professor Emeritus at Princeton University, would have smiled sagely at that remark. After decades of exploration in the thorniest thickets of philosophy, he has just published a slim treatise entitled *On Bullshit*, an earnest intellectual inquiry into this most pungent and slippery of philosophical concepts. His short theory of bullshit is a testament for our times.

We all think we can identify bullshit. We know when we are talking bullshit ourselves, and we have all been guilty of it at times, in the pub or the pulpit, though some of us produce more than others. Politics thrives on bullshit, while lawyers, advertisers, public relations consultants and talk show hosts produce the stuff in its purest form. Very occasionally, columnists have been known to lapse into it. Every language in the world has a word for it. But what is bullshit? The concept is universally recognised, yet as Professor Frankfurt writes, 'the most basic and preliminary questions about bullshit remain, after all, not only unanswered but unasked'.

He begins, like all good philosophers, by defining what bullshit is not. Bullshit is dishonest, yet it is not necessarily mendacious. The bullshit artist may not tell you the truth (though he may do so inadvertently), but he is not deliberately lying. This is because bullshit cares nothing for truth or falsehood, accuracy or error, and that is its force and danger.

Both the liar and the honest man must have regard for truth, the former to subvert it and the latter to propagate it. Bullshit, by contrast, is fundamentally unconcerned with truth or falsehood, but only with appearance, effect and persuasion, however transitory. Yuri Luzhkov was not accusing the Moscow weather forecasters of lying, or yet of trying to predict the weather and honestly failing; he was accusing them of not caring about the true weather. The essence of bullshit is getting away with it, with persuading listeners or readers of a sincerity that is, by definition, phoney. The bullshit artist simply does not care about truth: 'He pays no attention to it at all,' writes Professor Frankfurt. 'By virtue of this, bullshit is a greater enemy of truth than lies are.'

Yet we tolerate bullshit, even though we feign to disregard it. Lies make us morally enraged; mistakes, even honest ones, are unacceptable. The politician or businessman who lies to us, or fouls up, must go; but he can bullshit us with almost perfect impunity. We shrug, we may even grin ruefully, but in our craven hearts we know we are being fed a bluff, on-the-hoof hokum, and we do not care.

Perhaps our ancestors were just as susceptible to bullshit, purveying it and accepting it, as we are. Indeed, as the late Ronald Bell, the Tory MP, once observed, 'the connection between humbug and politics is too long established to be challenged'. Yet bullshit has surely expanded as fast, if not faster, than the growth of communications generally. The internet is a natural septic tank for it.

More than ever, public figures are required to opine on everything, even (and perhaps especially) when they have no idea what they are talking about. During the year when I was parliamentary sketch writer, I cannot remember a single occasion on which an MP conceded ignorance on any subject whatsoever. Professor Frankfurt is clinical and devastating: 'The production of bullshit is stimulated whenever a person's obligations or opportunities to speak about some topic exceed his knowledge of the facts that are relevant to that topic.'

In a sense, the quest to define bullshit is the oldest one in the philosopher's book. Socrates himself explored the tension between rhetoric or sophistry, arguments intended to persuade regardless of whether they were true, and the deeper quest for understanding through philosophy. In this respect, it is worth noting that the term 'bull', with a similar meaning, is probably far older, etymologically, than the modern 'bullshit': the original word seems to have come from the Latin *bullire*, to boil, bubble or froth. At its source, then, the term has nothing to do with barnyard excrement, but rather the appropriate evocation of pure hot air.

Bullshit makes quite good intellectual fertiliser. Indeed, the American term 'bull session' means an occasion to bat around outrageous ideas without concern for accuracy. But cumulatively, and unchecked, bullshit undermines what Professor Frankfurt calls 'the possibility of knowing how things really are'. Improvised, instantly disposable pseudo-knowledge becomes more important than reality. In a culture where bullshit is endemic, political debate, intellectual argument and appeals for our money and our votes are all judged on whether they are persuasive, rather than accurate, honest or realistic. Appearance becomes more important than objective fact; we hark to the purveyor of cogent humbug, and sceptically wonder whether anything is true.

If there is one aspect of Professor Frankfurt's thesis that does not go far enough, it is in exploring the distinctively public nature of the subject.

Bullshit is not a private matter, but a display, deployed to convey a specific, positive impression to others, regardless of accuracy. It is, in essence, spin.

When Tony Blair says he is a 'pretty straight kind of guy', he is implicitly asking his listeners to set aside notions of objective truth and believe in his sincerity. This has become the currency of our political culture. In a world of bullshit, truth seems unknowable, so we are asked to trust the persuasive authenticity of our leaders, who offer to be true, not to the facts, but to themselves. Yet human nature, moral philosophers agree, is impossible to know. In Professor Frankfurt's concluding words: 'Our natures are elusively insubstantial . . . and insofar as this is the case, sincerity itself is bullshit.'

At least the Moscow mayor and the Princeton philosopher have teamed up to prove that it is possible to cut the crap, and seize the bull by the horns.

Could do better

WINSTON CHURCHILL'S SCHOOL REPORTS are on display at a museum dedicated to his life. For those of us who still bitterly remember the sting of a bad report, they are as uplifting as any Churchillian oratory. 'Weak', was how his master at St George's School described nine-year-old Churchill's grasp of geography. His French was 'not very good', while his drawing was 'very elementary'. The behaviour of the future Prime Minister was also a problem: 'Troublesome . . . latterly has been very naughty.' This got worse over time, with another report lamenting that the young Winston 'cannot be trusted to behave himself anywhere', and that he was 'so regular in his irregularity that I really don't know what to do'.

The British school report – waspish, witty, frequently cruel and usually wrong – is an unjustly neglected literary genre, now sadly in decline. There was a time when extraordinary effort went into the writing of reports, as revealed in a recent collection entitled *Could Do Better*, edited by

Catherine Hurley (with profits to dyslexia research). Not only do these school reports provide a strange window into human development, they also reveal the pent-up frustrations of trying to teach recalcitrant little horrors, and the delight taken by some teachers in giving their pupils an end-of-term comeuppance.

Take this early assessment of Michael Heseltine: 'He is rebellious, objectionable, idle, imbecilic, inefficient, antagonising, untidy, lunatic, albino, conceited, inflated, impertinent, underhand, lazy and smug.' I particularly like 'albino'.

The report writer has plainly lost it. Mere invective cannot adequately express the depth of his contempt for young Heseltine. He needs a word that is completely out of the ordinary; he reaches out and in desperation he clutches . . . 'albino'.

There was a time when teachers treated the report as a form of literary caning, intended to inflict maximum salutary pain in the shortest space. Jilly Cooper's parents were told: 'She has set herself an extremely low standard, which she has failed to maintain.' The headmaster of Uppingham assessed Stephen Fry thus: 'He has glaring faults, and they have certainly glared at us this term.' Fry's English teacher was even more brusque: 'English: bottom, rightly.'

One almost feels pity for the pompous headmasters repeatedly missing the point of their most celebrated pupils. Robert Graves, poet, essayist, biographer and novelist, was offered this adieu on leaving Charterhouse: 'Well, goodbye Graves, and remember that your best friend is the waste-paper basket.' John Lennon's teacher offered the gloomiest forecast: 'Hopeless . . . certainly on the road to failure.' My favourite in the failed prediction category is Norman Wisdom's report: 'The boy is every inch the fool, but luckily for him he's not very tall.'

Occasionally, the teachers caught a glimmer of what was coming. Mr and Mrs Paxman were told that Jeremy had potential, but was not a natural diplomat: 'The stubbornness in his nature could be an asset when directed to sound ends. But his flying off the handle will only mar his efforts, and he must learn tact while not losing his outspokenness.' One of Michael Winner's teachers noticed his tendency to tell stories at dinner: 'There is a great demand to sit at his table.' Peter Ustinov's master at Westminster was adamant: 'He shows great originality, which must be curbed at all costs.'

It is impossible to imagine any teacher making so bold today, for school reports have become increasingly bland, winnowed of anything that might cause offence.

Political correctness and the threat of litigation have forced teachers to tone down their criticisms, or put them in oblique code, while the insistence that all children are equally gifted and comparisons are odious has ensured that any teacher who says what he or she really thinks will be swiftly brought into line, and probably sacked. The future philosopher A.J. Ayer was described by Eton in 1923 as 'a bumptious, aggressive, difficult boy, too pleased with his own cleverness'. Any parent receiving a report like that today would immediately reach for a lawyer.

Instead, modern teachers must use semantics, euphemism and circumlocution to get the message across. 'Tarquin is very lively in class.' Translation: 'The rowdy little bugger never shuts up.' 'Ethelreda has potential.' Translation: 'She's bone idle, or else quite thick, I haven't bothered to find out.' 'Janet's perseverance in the school production of *Swan Lake* did her credit.' Translation: 'This girl is vast. She needs liposuction, not ballet.'

How much heartache might have been prevented if, say,

Prince Harry's teachers had told it straight? 'History: Harry is not the brightest jewel in the crown; he has no grasp of history, and thinks that swastikas are funny.'

The defanged school report is only one aspect of a culture that shies away from direct criticism. As a society we would rather choke down a bottle of corked wine than send it back. Even literary and theatre criticism, once bastions of ferocious judgment, now tend more towards sniping than evisceration. Politics is just as vituperative as it ever was, but indirectly, the venom delivered behind closed doors and *sotto voce*.

Does anyone really believe that Gordon Brown squared up to Tony Blair and fired from the lip? 'There is nothing that you could ever say to me now that I could ever believe.' He might wish to have said that; he might even believe he said that; he certainly thinks that. But politicians do not speak this way to each other, and more's the pity.

It is time to bring back the barbed and unequivocal report, the blast of honest criticism, at schools, and in Westminster:

'Dear Mr and Mrs Brown, Gordon is a clever boy but moody and difficult. This term has seen yet more undignified feuding with the head boy. If he spent less time brooding on perceived slights, and more time on the mathematics at which he excels, he would go far. He should play more team sports. He is often rather untidy.'

'Dear Mr and Mrs Blair, Tony has allowed himself to become distracted far too easily, and there is a danger of him throwing away the good progress he has made in earlier terms. He appears to have fallen out again with his former chum Gordon, and I have given instructions that they should no longer be allowed to sit together, since their constant squabbling is seriously disrupting the rest of the class.'

Paradise is paper, vellum and dust

I HAVE A HALCYON library memory. I am sitting under a cherry tree in the tiny central courtyard of the Cambridge University Library, a book in one hand and an almond slice in the other. On the grass beside me is an incredibly pretty girl. We are surrounded by eight million books. Behind the walls on every side of the courtyard, the books stretch away in compact ranks hundred of yards deep, the shelves extending at the rate of two miles a year. There are books beneath us in the subterranean stacks, and they reach into the sky; we are entombed in words, an unimaginable volume of collected knowledge in cold storage, quiet and vast and waiting.

Perhaps that was the moment I fell in love with libraries. Or perhaps it was earlier, growing up in Scotland, when the mobile library would lurch up the road with stocks of Enid Blyton and bodice-rippers on the top shelf with saucy covers, to be giggled over when the driver-librarian was having his cup of tea.

Or perhaps the moment came earlier yet, when my father took me into the bowels of the Bodleian in Oxford and I inhaled, for the first time, that intoxicating mixture of vellum, paper and dust.

I have spent a substantial portion of my life since in libraries, and I still enter them with a mixture of excitement and awe. I am not alone in this.

Veneration for libraries is as old as writing itself, for a library is more to our culture than a collection of books: it is a temple, a symbol of power, the hushed core of civilisation, the citadel of memory, with its own mystique, social and sensual as well as intellectual. Even people who never enter libraries instinctively understand their symbolic power.

But now a revolution, widely compared to the invention of printing itself, is taking place among the stacks, and the library will never be the same again. This week Google announced plans to digitise fifteen million books from five great libraries, including the Bodleian. Google's founders, Sergey Brin and Larry Page, have declared their intention to collect all information online, an ambition that puts them up there with the Ptolomies, founders of the great library at Alexandria. What was once megalomaniac bibliomania is now a technological certainty.

Some fear that this total library, vast and invisible, could finally destroy traditional libraries, which will become mere warehouses for the physical objects, empty of people and life. The advantages for researchers of a single scholarly online catalogue are incalculable, but will we bother to browse the shelves when we can summon up any book in the world merely with the push of a button? Are the days of the library as a social organism over?

Almost certainly not, for reasons practical, psychological and, ultimately, spiritual. Locating a book online is one thing, reading it is quite another, for there is no aesthetic substitute for the physical object; the computer revolution rolls on inexorably, but the world is reading more paper books than ever. Indeed, so far from destroying libraries, the internet has protected the written word as never before, and rendered knowledge genuinely democratic. Fanatics always attack the libraries first, dictators seek to control the literature, elites hoard the knowledge that is power. Shi Huangdi, the Chinese Emperor of the third century BC, ordered that all literature, history and philosophy written before the founding of his dynasty should be destroyed. More books were burnt in the twentieth century than any other – in Nazi Germany, Bosnia and Afghanistan. With the online library, the books are finally safe, and the biblioclasts have been beaten, for ever.

But the traditional library will also survive, because a library is central to our understanding of what it is to be human. Ever since the first clay tablets were collected in Mesopotamia, Man has wanted not merely to obtain and master knowledge, but to preserve it, to hold it in his hand.

'I have always imagined that Paradise will be a kind of library,' wrote Jorge Luis Borges, poet, writer and librarian, who understood better than most the essential physicality of books. Borges was appointed director of Argentina's National Library in the year that he went blind:

'No one should read self-pity or reproach into this statement of the majesty of God, who with such splendid irony granted me books and blindness in one touch.'

Libraries are not places of dry scholarship but living sensuality. In *Love Story* Ali McGraw and Ryan O'Neal get together with the library as backdrop; in *Dr Zhivago*, Uri and Lara find one another in a library. I have a friend, now a well-known journalist, who became overcome by lust in the British Library and was discovered by a librarian making love behind the stacks in the empty quarter of Humanities with a woman he had met in the tea room. The librarian was apparently most understanding, and said it happened quite a lot.

Libraries are not just for reading in, but for sociable thinking, exploring, exchanging ideas and falling in love. They were never silent. Technology will not change that, for even in the starchiest heyday of Victorian self-improvement, libraries were intended to be meeting places of the mind, recreational as well as educational. The Openshaw branch of the Manchester public library was built complete with a billiard room.

Just as bookshops have become trendy, offering brain food and cappuccinos, so libraries, under financial and cultural pressure, will have to evolve by more actively welcoming people in to wander and explore. Finding a book online should be the beginning, not the end, of the process of discovery, a peeling back of the first layer: the word 'library', after all, comes from *liber*, the inner bark of a tree.

Bookish types have always feared change and technology, but the book, and the library, have adapted and endured, retaining the essential magic of these places.

Even Hollywood understood. In *Desk Set* (1957) Katharine Hepburn plays a librarian-researcher whose job is threatened by a computer expert (Spencer Tracy) introducing new technology. In the end, the computer turns out to be an asset, not a danger, Tracy and Hepburn end up smooching and everyone lives (and reads) happily ever after.

The marriage of Google and the Bodleian is, truly, a Tracy and Hepburn moment.

A message from the margins

HENRY VIII WAS FOREVER scribbling in the margins of his books. This most literate king collected an extensive library, and regarded the margins of his books as useful places to demonstrate his learning, pass billets-doux to his lovers or simply to vent the royal ire. Enraged or inspired by an author, he would pick up a pen and respond at once, in Latin; and, being a king, he didn't have to worry about being fined for returning a defaced book to the library. On the title page of a volume challenging his divorce of Catherine of Aragon he scrawled: 'The basic premise of this book is worthless,' and then threw the author in the Tower. (The poor man was later hanged, drawn and quartered at Smithfield, a forthright method of dealing with literary critics that is now, sadly, unavailable.) Perhaps the most important piece of marginalia ever written – revealed in Professor James Carley's book *The Books of King Henry VIII and His Wives* – appears in another of Henry's tomes, Augustinus de Ancona's *Compendium concerning Ecclesiastical Power*. When he read the book, Henry was actively scouring the scholarly texts for arguments to bolster his decision to divorce and declare himself head of the Church of England. Where Ancona had written: 'To have several wives was not against nature in the ancient fathers', Henry wrote approvingly: '*ergo nec in nobis*' (therefore neither in ours). And the rest, to coin a phrase, is history.

Many readers, thrilled or disgusted with a book, feel the overwhelming urge to reach for a pen (or, better, a pencil) to add their pennyworth in the margin: 'Oh yes!' or 'Oh yes???', 'Nooo', or something earthier. Most of us, however, disciplined by school librarians and awed by the sanctity of the written word, resist the temptation. This is a shame, for marginalia once formed a vital element in literature, a way of taking part in the otherwise one-sided conversation that is reading. Books are now so cheap, and the sharing of books so widespread, that the time has surely come to restore the digressive art of marginalia.

I am therefore launching today the Society for the Protection of Amateur Marginalia, or Spam.

The posthumous patron of Spam can only be Samuel Taylor Coleridge, who invented the term 'marginalia' and became so notorious for writing pithy remarks and asides in books that friends and rivals would send him their own works requesting that he scribble his thoughts in them. The marginalia became more important than the text, at least in Coleridge's estimation: in a volume belonging to fellow writer Charles Lamb, he wrote: 'I will not be long here, Charles! – & gone, you will not mind my having spoiled a book in order to leave a Relic.'

In the early manuscripts, space was left for the reader to add scholarly glosses or rubrics. Later editions might even be printed with these additions, with space left for more, the literature evolving with each edition. Between the middle of the eighteenth and the middle of the nineteenth centuries, with the spread of literacy and book ownership, notes written by readers and writers in their own books and those of their friends became a central part of the literary culture, a habit encouraged by new book designs offering wider margins. Few books were immune from the craze.

Thomas Hardy once annotated an entire book on billiards. Some of the best examples of marginalia have been collected by H.J. Jackson, including Mark Twain's comment on a botched translation of Tacitus: 'This book's English is the rottenest that was ever puked upon paper.'

Marginalia blurred distinctions between writer, reader and critic. Passed from one reader to another, the margins and flypapers of some books became a sort of message board for this unique form of intellectual graffiti, with brief accolades, argumentative asides, addenda and insults. Even the greatest writers could be deflated with a sharp jab from the margins. An anonymous reader who rebelled against Samuel Johnson's description of the weather as 'gloomy, frigid and ungenial' scrawled in exasperation: 'Why can't you say Cold like the rest of ye world?' Quite.

The growth of public libraries after 1850, with their ban on writing in books, changed all that: books became revered objects; to write in them was to violate them, and an offence to those who wanted to start reading with a clean sheet. Some fastidious arbiters of literature, such as Virginia Woolf, disdained marginalia, objecting to all the 'ohs' and 'wonderfuls' written by acerbic or admiring earlier readers. Yet the habit has persisted, almost guiltily. Nelson Mandela, imprisoned on Robben Island, wrote in the margins of his copy of Julius Caesar; while Nabokov, typically, complained in the margins about the quality of the translation in his edition of Kafka's *Metamorphosis*.

The psychology of marginalia is hard to pin down. When we make a remark in the margins, are we addressing the author? Fellow readers? Posterity? Or are we simply talking to ourselves, the literary equivalent of shouting at the television? Coleridge regarded his own marginal musings as a form of self-interrogation: 'A book I value I reason with and quarrel with, as with myself when I am reasoning.'

Whatever the reason, it is time the marginal note was rescued from Victorian disapproval and restored to its proper place in literature.

The rules of Spam are simple: no writing in library books, hardback books, illustrated books or books lent to us by people who haven't already written in them. No writing in pen, unless you have won a Nobel Prize for Literature. But any and every cheap paperback should henceforth be regarded also as a notebook to be written in and then passed on.

Books have properly wide margins because you are supposed to write your thoughts in them. Newspapers, regrettably, don't; which is why I am leaving a space at the bottom of this column.

Splash out on the great smell of Proust

SMELL CAN TRANSPORT US through memory like no other sense: see a face, hear a sound, and you may enjoy a fleeting jolt of déjà vu; but smell a redolent odour, catch a whiff of some half-forgotten perfume, and you are transported back to the moment itself.

Writers, most famously Marcel Proust, have often celebrated the power of smell and taste to summon the remembrance of things past, for smell is the fixative of memory. I can see my father's old study in my mind's eye, but I cannot truly remember it until I open one of his books, and inhale leather, musty paper and the preserved scent of Player's Navy Cut tobacco.

Smell is fleeting, by definition indefinable, leaving no trace in history, only reminiscence, but it brings a crucial, heightened sense of reality to fiction and experience. Nothing is more memorable than a smell. I will never forget the acrid, grey stench of the site at Ground Zero two weeks after 9/11, the very stink of Armageddon; I hope never to smell it again. The word 'scent' comes from the French *sentir*: meaning 'to smell', but also 'to feel'. Thus novelists deploy smells to describe ephemeral feeling, because neither can be bottled. Until now.

Beside me on the desk as I write is a small phial with an atomiser bearing the label: 'Marcel Proust: *Swann's Way*'. Spray it into the air and the room instantly fills with the odour of fresh pastry and vanilla, with an undercurrent tang of citrus and fresh tea. Here, indeed, is the translation into smell of Proust's evocation: 'And suddenly the memory appeared. That taste was the taste of the little piece of madeleine which on Sunday mornings in Combray ...

when I went to say good morning to her in her bedroom, my Aunt Léonie would give me after dipping it in her infusion of tea and lime blossom.'

The essence of Proust is one of five scents created by the Italian perfumer Laura Tonatto to evoke some of the most memorably smelly moments in literature. The stunt is part of a Waterstone's promotion, but more profoundly it points up the long and rich literary partnership between the nose and the mind, smell and memory, scents and sensibility.

Another of Signora Tonatto's literary pongs is Oscar Wilde's *The Picture of Dorian Gray*, 'violets that woke the memory of dead romances', a thick, cloying fragrance, heady, headachy and voluptuous. Then there is the scent dedicated to the moment in Flaubert's *Madame Bovary* when Emma secretly smells the inside of the Viscount's cigar case to 'breathe the scent of its lining – a mixture of tobacco and verbena'. For Emma, the smell suggests a world of grandeur and glamour from which she is excluded; I thought it smelt like an ashtray soaked in aftershave.

But undoubtedly the most pungent of Signora Tonatto's smells is that dedicated to Patrick Süskind's bestselling novel *Perfume*, the story of a murderous quest for the ultimate scent set amid the reeks of eighteenth-century Paris. The quotation from the book accompanying the bottle cautions: 'There reigned in the cities a stench barely conceivable to us modern men & women', and the resulting concoction is, indeed, truly disgusting: part musketeer's jockstrap, part fishpaste, all overlaid with odour of ancient abattoir; Charnel No. 5.

The experiment opens up an entirely new sub-genre of olfactory literary criticism, in which readers and critics will enjoy the great works while being suffused with the appropriate smell: scratch 'n' sniff classics. Many writers have

thought in aromatic terms. Since smells can now be reproduced digitally, we may one day be able to enjoy *Moby-Dick*
while suffused with the briny whiff of fish, tar and hemp;
hot strawberry essence could accompany the reading of *Tess
of the d'Urbervilles*; anything by Tom Clancy requires an
accompanying bouquet of cordite and male sweat; while
Jane Austen should be read to the smell of roses, powder
and port. We may, however, draw the line at trying to reproduce, in olfactory form, the passage from *Ulysses* where
Leopold Bloom goes to the jakes and then remains 'seated
calm above his own rising smell'.

Whether book buyers can be led by the nose remains to
be seen, but anything that increases our sense of smell, the
most unfairly neglected of the senses, should be applauded.
We have relatively few words to describe smell, and we are,
as a species, atrocious at smelling. Instead of enjoying and
celebrating the odours and malodours around us, we would
rather smother them in air freshener, one vast fake piney-
fruity stink.

It is no surprise that all the authors chosen for the smell
makeover at Waterstone's, with the exception of Süskind,
should be from earlier centuries.

Shakespeare revelled in the emotive power of smell;
Lady Macbeth knows that 'all the perfumes of Arabia /
Will not sweeten this little hand'; Claudius knows that his
'offence is rank, it smells to heaven'. Rudyard Kipling vividly evoked the thrilling stench of Lahore, 'the heat and
smell of oil and spices, and puffs of temple incense, and
sweat, and darkness, and dirt and lust and cruelty'. These
earlier writers delighted in the fragrances and flavours that
trigger emotion and are able, in Proust's words, to 'bear
unflinchingly, in the tiny and most impalpable drop of their
essence, the vast structure of recollection'.

By contrast, modern novelists seldom like to dwell on smell. This is not surprising, since natural smells are increasingly banished from the modern world, where mortality, dirt and decay must be cloaked in over-sweet, cloying deodorant.

Signora Tonatto's Eau de Flaubert is unlikely to be available at Boots anytime soon, but in poking her nose into the literary classics she offers a pungent reminder of the evocative power of pongs. Later writers should wake up and smell the coffee.

Why do Koreans say 'a biscuit would be nice' instead of 'I want a biscuit'?

THE AMAZONIAN PIRAHA TRIBE, as previously noted, cannot count up to four. They have a word for 'one' (which usually means 'roughly one'); and a word for two (which tends to mean 'not many', and sounds exactly like the word for 'one', only with a rising inflection); and they have a word for 'many'. A Piraha version of 'Ten Green Bottles' would not take long, then: one, two, a lot.

Linguists have long pondered the question of what evolutionary hiccup left the Piraha less numerate than ducks (apparently they can count to four), but research on the Piraha seems to reinforce the famous Sapir-Whorf hypothesis, which holds that every individual's perception of the world is directly moulded by language. We are what we speak or, as Wittgenstein put it: 'The limits of my language are the limits of my world.'

But does language determine thought, or the other way round? Do Koreans avoid the first person (seldom saying: 'I want a biscuit'; more usually: 'a biscuit would be nice') because they are naturally modest, or have they become unnaturally modest because arbitrary patterns of language have imposed that trait? Do Chinese eschew a direct 'yes' or 'no' out of an innate indecisiveness and unwillingness to give offence, or is the language doing the shaping? Inuits can describe snowfall in ways that we cannot imagine, because their language provides multiple words for snow; but on subjects other than frozen water, Inuit conversation can be rather restricted.

In a recent essay, the writer Amy Tan, who is of Chinese origin, wrote: 'It's a dangerous business this sorting out of language and behaviour.' For her own part, she was offended by the notion that the lack of definitive 'yes' and 'no' in the language made Chinese people more irresolute; yet she also wondered whether linguistic programming explained why she can't just tell those infuriating telephone salesmen to get stuffed.

Language does undoubtedly mould, and perhaps restrict, both national character and style of writing. English, for example, has many of the virtues associated with Britishness: expansive, flexible, eccentric. Yet compared with other languages it can seem inelegant and unromantic. The Czech novelist Josef Skvorecky complains that, for all its versatility, English lacks 'the sex appeal of feminine endings, the lure of verbal aspects, the capricious scherzo of prefixes'. Ours is a can-do language, but uptight with it.

It is this blend of national character and linguistic peculiarity that gives every language its central, untranslatable essence. The Piraha may have no word for 'three', but these hunter-gatherers have numerous other words and concepts that simply would not translate into our language. Conversely, the word 'googly' has no meaning in the lowland Amazon, the Piraha not being keen cricket players, probably on account of the scoring.

Trying to impose cross-cultural meaning can be disastrous, and hilarious. When Captain Cook arrived on the coast of north-west America in 1778, a group of Indians paddled out in canoes and shouted 'nootka', a form of greeting which roughly translates as: 'Why don't you take your big floating house around the other side of the bay where it's less windy?' Cook assumed they were referring to themselves, and the name stuck; even their language is known as Nootkan, based on a mistranslation from itself.

Some linguists fear that with the spread of English and the internet, the idiosyncratic essence of individual languages will gradually vanish, boiled into a soupy and debased universal tongue: to turn the Sapir-Whorf hypothesis on its head, our perceptions of the world will not vary much, since we will all speak the same language, becoming mutually comprehensible, and very dull.

But language, the greatest of all human inventions, is more resilient than that, constantly evolving and adapting. The internet has forged numerous, sometimes rather wonderful, mutant forms of English, just as the collision between languages in the past has produced some of the most remarkable literature. The great strength of English is its multiple borrowings from other languages and influences, layer on layer. Joseph Conrad's richly evocative, finely wrought prose, for example, owes much to his first language being Polish. Writing in another tongue forced him to think even harder about meaning: 'If I had not written in English, I would not have written at all,' he once said.

Language does condition thought, but also changes with behaviour and thinking.

Future generations of the Piraha will doubtless learn to count in the conventional way, but culturally they will probably continue to think: one, two, a lot. The numerically limited language of the Piraha may seem incomprehensible to us, but it has its own, inner coherence.

Which inevitably brings us to George W. Bush, who has brilliantly invented a language only he can truly understand, the perfect example of the fraught relationship between language, meaning and thought. As the President observed to an audience in Oregon last week: 'I hope you will leave here and walk out and say: "What did he say?"' And that is exactly what they did.

It is OK for the language to change

'I DON'T KNOW ENGLISH but I know very much Spanish and I suppose you don't know very Spanish but you know very English because you are American.' So wrote Fidel Castro (aged twelve) to Franklin D. Roosevelt in 1940. (Showing a precocious grasp of capitalism, the young Fidel also tried to touch the US President for 'a ten dollars bill green American'.)

British language purists might jib at the assumption that because FDR was American, he must therefore 'know very English'. Instead, we have always nourished the illusion that since 1776 the language, as deployed stateside, has been in steady decline, and infecting our own. Noah Webster, the American lexicographer, imagined a distinct national language for America, and predicted in 1789 that British-English and American-English would grow steadily apart until they were eventually as different as German and Dutch. Instead, to the annoyance of the Little England branch of English, America seized the language, joyfully adapted it and then sent back a raft of contagious new constructions, slang, euphemism, adult baby talk and linguistic shorthand, many examples of which were adopted wholesale.

'The English and American language and literature are both good things; but they are better apart than mixed,' observed the editors of *The King's English* in 1906.

Some hope. Guardians of the language did not like, but could do nothing to prevent, this reverse colonisation of the language.

Many American usages are so deeply part of our lexicon that their origin has been forgotten. Imagine trying to do without 'reckon', 'blurb', 'fix up', 'commuter', 'anyway', 'babysitter' or 'editorial'. Then there is the ubiquitous 'OK', arguably the most useful and adaptable word ever coined, which now exists formally in most languages of the world and informally in just about all of them. The word was first used in the *Boston Post* in 1839, as an abbreviation for 'orl korrect', there being a journalistic craze at the time for combining initials of misspelt words. The opposite of 'OK' was 'KY', meaning no use, from 'know yuse'. While OK leapt immediately into permanent parlance, KY inexplicably died at birth, unlamented and forgotten.

British writers have always felt uncomfortable at the spread of American English into the mother tongue. 'In his heart and however he may vote, no Englishman readily allows linguistic equality to an American,' wrote Kingsley Amis. Part of the discomfort comes from a sense that the linguistic traffic has been in one direction. The Briticism (a word which is itself an Americanism) did not go down well over there, being seen as a sign of snobbery: the American who referred to his 'university' rather than 'college', to 'ringing' rather than 'calling' a friend, to a 'queue' rather than a 'line', was displaying the linguistic equivalent of a bow-tie, for affectation and not for comfort or utility. On the other hand, Americans take pleasure in hearing British people using Anglicisms, the more out-moded the better, which explains why some long-term British residents in the US end up sounding like a cross between Prince Charles and Bertie Wooster.

But after two centuries in which the younger, brasher, American brand of the language has seeped steadily into the British way of speech, the tide may finally be turning. According to Ben Yagoda, Professor of Journalism at the University of Delaware, Briticisms are now cropping up in America as never before. He cites the example of 'gone missing', a construction that has a peculiarly British ring to American ears. In 1983, this formulation appeared nowhere in the *New York Times*, which preferred the more American terms 'disappear' or 'vanish'; in 1993, it was used just twice; in 2003, the term 'gone missing' and its variants appeared no fewer than fifty times in the newspaper.

Yagoda has identified numerous other identifiably British terms that have entered American speech and writing patterns: the British 'sell-by date' has so thoroughly replaced 'expiration date' as to become a American cliché; the lazy British term 'run-up', used when a writer or speaker cannot think of another way to describe the period before an event, is now endemic in the US, as in 'the run-up to the Iraq war'.

A more subtle Anglicisation of the American language is detectable in literature and the media. The *New Yorker* has adopted the British habit of doubling the final consonant of some verbs when adding 'ed' or 'ing': hence 'travelling', not 'traveling'.

Even more tellingly, American children are becoming more attuned to Briticisms: the early *Harry Potter* books had to be 'translated' into American English: 'crumpets' became 'English muffins', 'nutter' became 'maniac' and so on; but the latest edition, apart from a few spellings, was sold virtually unedited.

For years, Britain's cultural avatars have complained of the effects of American youth culture on the way we speak; now the reverse process is taking place.

American public figures may employ British words without pretension or heavy irony: Oprah Winfrey goes 'on holiday' rather than 'on vacation'; the actors on *Friends* have 'rows' and 'chat-up lines', Briticisms both; even George W. Bush 'takes' rather than 'makes' decisions.

The spread of British English into the American language may finally disprove the old myth of two countries divided by a common language. Languages pollinate one another, and efforts to stop them, such as the paranoid French attempts to expunge Anglicisms by state decree, are doomed. Americanisms flourish in Britain only to the extent that they are useful and fun; the same will be true of the recent spread of British usage in the US. It is the suppleness of British-English combined with the vigour of its American counterpart that helps to explain why the language dominates the world and continues to evolve.

English is not one language but many, constantly eliding and adapting, and providing the element of choice, which is its lifeblood. H.L. Mencken, the great scholar of the American language, once remarked: 'I can speak English, as in this sentence; or I can talk American, as in this one here.' And that, as far as I'm concerned, is perfectly OK.

The joys of writing while wearing a literary ball and chain

A FRENCH NOVEL. NO verbs. Just adjectival, noun-packed prose over 233 pages.

Staccato, well weird and a bit exhausting, but oddly inspiring. And very French.

Because amid all the verbless verbiage, no action, by definition. Enough parody already.

Michel Thaler, a French doctor of letters and novelist, has just published *Le Train de Nulle Part* (The Train from Nowhere) the first book ever written without a single verb in it. Monsieur Thaler did not just banish the verb, he buried it, with a formal ceremony at the Sorbonne. 'The verb is like a weed in a field of flowers,' he declared, momentarily lifting his own self-imposed rule for the sake of media attention. 'Verbs are invaders, dictators, usurpers of our literature.'

Quite why he hates verbs so much is not explained; perhaps he was bitten by a gerund as a child.

M. Thaler (not his real name) is in no doubt about his achievement: 'My book is a revolution in literature . . . it is to literature what the great Dada and Surrealist movements were to art.'

No, it isn't. *Le Train de Nulle Part* is a splendid grammatical stunt. Yet if one strips away the French pretension, such experiments do have a point, for they demonstrate that writing is about self-control and choice. Thaler's verb-free screed is a counterpoint to the bloated, over-egged prose of so much modern literature, the dyspepsia-inducing multiple ingredients of a Zadie Smith or a Dave Eggers, who must throw everything into the pot. Thaler is not really writing a novel, but making a point, and an important one, about self-control. What is poetry, after all, but writing to a formalised pattern?

Writers have often experimented with self-imposed rules. Most famously, in 1969, the great French writer Georges Perec wrote *La Disparition* (The Disappearance), a novel entirely without the letter E, the most common in the language; this was followed by *Les Revenentes* (The She-Ghosts) which used 'e' but no other vowels, even in its misspelt title. Applying almost mathematical principles to writing, Perec's prose is still a delight; every word is chosen, not merely with care, but with monumental precision. Perec's extraordinary achievement, dazzlingly reproduced by his translator Gilbert Adair, was to write a gripping detective story while wearing the literary equivalent of a ball and chain.

In a postscript, Perec wrote that the difficult exercise of eschewing 'e' had forced his writing down 'intriguing linguistic highways and byways', where he had discovered unexpected pleasures off the beaten track.

Some writers have taken lipography, the omission of certain words or letters in writing, to extremes. The German poet Gottlob Burmann (1737–1805) developed a morbid loathing for the letter 'r', and wrote 20,000 words of poetry in his lifetime, not one of which contained it. For the last seventeen years of his life, he even refused to use the hated letter in everyday speech, which made it impossible for him to introduce himself to anyone since his own name contained one.

Perec and Thaler are both in the tradition of the Ouvroir de Littérature Potentielle (Workshop of Potential Literature) or OuLiPo, the group of writers including Raymond Queneau and Italo Calvino, whose philosophy of writing required strict, restrictive and arbitrary rules, like mathematical templates. Queneau invented a sonnet machine: by creating fourteen sonnets with interchangeable lines, the user could create millions of poetic permutations, each with perfect rhyming and scansion. François Le Lionnais went in the other direction, paring his art to the limit with poems of only one word, such as his masterwork 'Fennel'. Here it is, in full: 'Fennel'.

Calvino wrote *The Castle of Crossed Destinies* using a

pack of Tarot cards, while another OuLiPo disciple, Richard Beard, wrote his 1998 novel *Damascus* using only nouns that had appeared in *The Times* on 1 November 1993. (All of us who contributed to the paper that day – I wrote a very boring article about the New York mayoral elections – can therefore consider ourselves novelists in a small way.) Some of the more extreme OuLiPo contortions are only for those with a higher degree in mathematics. Harry Mathews, the veteran word-player, wrote a short story according to the following, immutable rule, or chronogram: in each sentence, all letters corresponding to Roman numerals (c, d, i, l, m, v and x), when added together, should produce a number equivalent to a specific year of the Christian Calendar.

The story was entitled 'Clocking the World on Cue: The Chronogram for 2001' (which itself adds up 2001: c x 4, l x 2, d x 1, i x 1, m x 1).

Life is much too short to have to read a book with the aid of a calculator; the OuLiPo school has produced some works of pure brilliance, but also much that is mind-bending, time-wasting and borderline nuts. But the essential point about the mutability of language remains. Many of the greatest writers have deliberately bent the rules of writing, and so created their own. Marcel Proust and James Joyce forged sentences that sometimes extended for pages; Umberto Eco drops into Latin; José Saramago does not bother with paragraphs nor, more strikingly, with quotation marks.

At the very least, Thaler's experiment with verb-free writing may be seen as a plea to think harder about the way language is used, at a time when much of the bestseller list is crammed with intellectual fast food, larded with adjectives and additives, written to an utterly undemanding, conventional form. Readers enjoy being challenged by a book that is written under its own restrictions: for proof, look no further than the hugely successful *The Curious Incident of the Dog in the Night-time* by Mark Haddon, a novel written from the point of view of an autistic child.

In control, even sparseness, can be found the full potential of language; what is left out, deliberately, may be just as important as what is left in. Consider, then, the economy of this pair of poems that every would-be writer should pin to the wall, a lesson in self-restraint.

> There was a young man from Peru
> Whose limericks stopped at line two.

And the sequel . . .

> There was a young man from Verdun.

DIY book reviewing

AMAZON.COM RECENTLY POSTED A customer review of a book by the successful American novelist John Rechy. The reviewer ('a reader from Chicago') had awarded the maximum five stars, and the accompanying notice was glowing. The review had plainly been submitted by a reader who profoundly understood, and appreciated, John Rechy's writing. This was not all that surprising since it was written by John Rechy.

The world would never have discovered this minor act of self-puffery, had it not been for a temporary glitch in the online merchant's computer system, which accidentally stripped away the anonymity of its reviewers to reveal who was reviewing whom on Amazon's Canadian website. All under the cloak of anonymity, there were friends plugging friends, authors slugging their enemies and some loud admiration from relatives, cronies and other objective critics, all trying to boost ratings and sales under such noms de plume as 'a reader from Kansas' or 'bookcrazy'.

It is well known that authors will shamelessly use any opportunity to plug their own books. The American poet Walt Whitman wrote no fewer than three anonymous reviews of *Leaves of Grass*, and then quoted himself in the preface to the second edition: 'An American bard at last!' Anthony Burgess was fired from the *Yorkshire Post* after reviewing his own novel, and James Joyce collaborated on a review of *Finnegans Wake*. More recently Dave Eggers cut out the middleman, by titling his novel *A Heartbreaking Work of Staggering Genius*.

The unmasking of Amazon's reviewers was an illustration, not just of author vanity, but of the sheer power of online reviewing, and the democratisation of book criticism that has taken place in recent years. Offering opinions about books was once the preserve of a literary elite: Arnold Bennett, writing for the *Standard* in the 1920s, could make or break a book with a single review. Today Bennett's equivalent, in terms of literary clout, is Harriet Klausner, a Pennsylvania librarian who has written an estimated 9,000 online reviews to become Amazon's most prolific reviewer.

Bookselling websites now carry millions of reviews by readers, avidly followed by both nervous authors and their publishers. Consumer opinion of books is valued as never before. It used to be that everyone had a book in them; today everyone has a book critic in them. Online reviewers need not identify themselves, or demonstrate any expertise; they do not even need to have read the book under review, which is another long-standing literary tradition: 'I never read a book before reviewing it,' said Sydney Smith (1771–1845), 'it prejudices a man so.'

The tsunami of online literary judgments, ranging from the informed and thought-provoking to the obsessive and merely barking, is part of the phenomenon of mass opinion-broking in the book world. The proliferation of local reading groups, prizes in which readers select their favourite books at the push of a button and the spread of feedback sites are all proof that the literate many now rival the literary few as the arbiters of worth.

There are some who argue that by opening the gates to millions of reviewers, who may be incompetent, unedited and sometimes illiterate, the web has undermined the very idea of cultural authority. But this seems to misunderstand the nature of the new beast. At its best, internet reviewing provides a refreshing directness, a place where people say what they like and dislike without any of the baggage of literary criticism or knowledge of previous form, or grammar.

Books were supposed to be doomed in the internet age, but the explosion in the number of homespun reviewers proves otherwise. When people enjoy a book, they feel moved to pass on the tale to someone else, an ancient urge that has become hard-wired into our genes ever since Man first sat around the campfire relating the stories he had heard. The best online reviewers tell the story that they have read, add their own twist and take, and pass it on, creating a dialogue among readers that directly descends from the oral storytelling tradition.

It is no accident that the rise in amateur reviewing is mirrored by the growth of amateur writing; our interest in the written word has never been stronger; we like and need to hear our own voices, and so we should. That important cultural avatar, Bruce Willis, exercised the critic's right to get it profoundly wrong when he recently declared: 'Frankly, reviews are mostly for people who still read. Like most of the written word, it is going the way of the dinosaur.'

There will always be a quiet corner of the library where considered literary opinion is forged, according to the demanding disciplines of formal book reviewing; the DIY literary forum is something else, a huge, merry, noisy marketplace, full of competing voices, some worth buying, others not worth the cyberspace they are floating on.

It is not the quantity of online reviews that is the problem, nor even the patchy quality, but the anonymity. Only two things in the world are sufficiently powerful and omniscient to be permitted anonymity: God, and the leaders page of *The Times*.

'Anon' more often conceals cronyism than modesty. Everyone should be a critic, but named, since anonymity undermines credibility, with limitless opportunity for bias, backbiting and secrecy. Rechy defended his review of his own book by pointing out that, since others had anonymously attacked it, he should be allowed to defend his intellectual property in the same way. But Rechy was only the latest in the long and honourable literary tradition of enthusiastic auto-praise.

Hear about the Englishman who laughed at a French joke? No, me neither

AMID ALL THE BONHOMIE, back-slapping and *foie gras* at the Anglo-French celebration of the *entente cordiale*, there was something missing, although everyone was being far too polite to say so: there were no jokes. The *entente* was

100 years old in 2004, but the French and British have been misunderstanding one another's sense of humour for far, far longer than that. Britain and France are closer in culture than at any time in our shared histories, yet we remain for ever divided by a mutual refusal to find the same things funny: we will never get their jokes, and they will never get ours. This is the *mésentente cordiale*, which no amount of flag-waving and *foie gras* can obscure.

The struggle to get to grips with French humour was one of the hardest aspects of being a Paris correspondent. Even the locals seemed to need guidance; 'funny' articles in weekly magazines would be labelled *humoristique*, thus ensuring they were anything but. Jacques Tati left me cold; Jean-Marie Poiré's films were even worse. The only newspaper cartoonist in France that came anywhere near the British standard was Plantu in *Le Monde*; then again, Plantu is virtually the only newspaper cartoonist in France. The little Anglo-Saxon humour the French seemed to like, I hated. Benny Hill was considered hilarious. Jerry Lewis, quite possibly the unfunniest person on the planet, is known in France as *le roi de crazy*. Woody Allen has continued to be fêted and adored in France long after he stopped being amusing.

French humour often falls into one of two categories, neither of which is easily accessible to the British: elaborate, subtle, often highly intellectual word-play based on puns and allusion, and the Rabelaisian tradition of cuckoldry, slapstick and going to the toilet. (Here's a tip: if your children are going through the lavatorial phase, buy them a French children's book about a farting elephant entitled *Prout!*, in which the flatulent pachyderm is forced to leave the herd under a cloud. Read it to your children twice, and it kills toilet humour for ever, right down to the u-bend.) Chauvinists would argue that the French simply don't have a sense of humour. They have wit (*esprit*) in buckets, and the French invented farce, but a word to describe funniness did not officially enter the language until 1932 when the Acadèmie Française (an institution not noted for its comic qualities, at least not intentionally) reluctantly allowed the noun 'humour' into the dictionary.

In the seventeenth century European aristocracies broadly shared a sense of humour, but also the belief that uproarious laughter was best left to the lower classes. Jokes carried an unsettling hint of rebellion. Britain was the first to break out of the humour straitjacket to embrace satire, parody and, above all, eccentricity. Madame de Staël (a great social observer but a poor stand-up comic) caught the distinction precisely. 'The English language created a word, humour, to express a hilarity, which is in the blood almost as much as in the mind . . . What the English depict with great talent is bizarre characters because they have lots of those among them.'

As Theodore Zeldin, the great scholar of Frenchness, has observed: 'England, alone in Europe, raised humour to the status of a trait of national character, and dignified it with respectability.' The cult of English eccentricity grew up in conscious distinction to what was perceived as the rigidity and dourness of French social manners. The French responded by claiming that British jokiness concealed a deep underlying gloom, dark thoughts and sado-masochistic inclinations (*le vice anglais*).

Paradoxically, while regarding British humour with either bafflement or disdain, the French have long been concerned at the perceived decline of French humour.

More than a century ago, after hearing a poor excuse for

a joke, Émile Zola complained that France wasn't funny any more: 'It is not thus that people used to laugh, when they still laughed.' In 1939, according to one survey, French people laughed for an average of nineteen minutes a day (the rate probably dropped a bit the following year, when Germany invaded); by the 1970s the average amount of time devoted to laughter was apparently just five minutes. At that rate of decline, the average Frenchman must now be down to about one smirk a month.

Self-depreciation is not a big trait in French humour, while the strict rationalism of French education tends to militate against absurd or illogical jokes. Even the Iraqi sense of humour is probably closer to ours than the French variety. Take, for example, this joke that started doing the rounds in Baghdad within hours of the unsuccessful attempt to blow up Saddam Hussein during Operation Shock and Awe: the Iraqi Information Minister summons all Saddam's doubles to a meeting and tells them: 'The good news is that our glorious leader has survived this evil attack, so you all still have jobs. The bad news is that he has lost an arm.' I told this to a French friend who looked at me earnestly, before asking: 'What happened next?'

Humour inevitably tends to get lost in translation, yet there are aspects of French humour that easily outclass our own. *Astérix* in the original offers linguistic acrobatics and flights of fantasy that cannot be equalled in any of the seventy-two languages it has appeared in since. On TV, *Les Guignols* has long outlasted the *Spitting Image* idea that inspired it, being funnier, faster and crueller.

There will never be a Single European Humour, thank goodness, but at least the French and British agree in one important respect: what we have sniggeringly nicknamed a

French letter is *une lettre anglaise* in France, which just goes to show that there is one thing both countries find funnier than anything else: each other.

I drink, therefore I am

IMMANUEL KANT WAS A serious party animal. On the 200th anniversary of the great philosopher's death, a series of new biographies has revealed that, so far from being a stern Prussian egghead, Kant was a good-time boy who enjoyed playing billiards, telling jokes and, from time to time, getting plastered.

The author of the *Critique of Pure Reason* periodically drank so much red wine that he couldn't find his way home, which suggests that the Kantian categories of time and space are all very well when you're sober, but harder to put into practice when you can't walk in a straight line. Kant was strictly a wine man, and frowned on the lager lout. 'The beer drinking bout is associated with taciturn fantasies and frequently with impolite behaviour,' he wrote. 'Whereas a wine party is merry, boisterous and teeming with wit.'

The Monty Python team memorably identified the link between serious thought and serious drinking in 'The Philophers' Drinking Song': 'Immanuel Kant was a real *puissant* / Who was very rarely stable. Heidegger, Heidegger was a boozy begger / Who could think you under the table.' As so often, the Pythons identified a major philosophical truth, for thinkers have ever regarded wine not merely as an aid to profundity, health and conviviality, but as a source of philosophical speculation in itself.

Hippocrates, anticipating Thomas Stuttaford, *The Times*'s doctor, by about two and half millennia, reckoned that wine drunk in moderation could cure many ailments, including hunger, pains behind the eyes, fatigue, anxiety and yawning. For the ancients, wine drinking was a measure of civilised society, a ritual of intellectual life.

The original Greek symposium, deriving from their word for 'communal drinking', was an intellectual lock-in, at which the host would choose how much water to mix with the wine, a decision that would determine how riotous the evening should get.

Classical drinking produced some recognisable pub types. Socrates, for example, was the sort who somehow managed to stay sober and lucid while everyone else got blotto. As Alcibiades observes, Socrates 'could drink any quantity of wine and not be at all nearer being drunk'. Plato's pupil Aristotle noticed that while everyone got off their faces on such occasions, some also landed on them: 'Men who have been intoxicated with wine fall down face foremost, whereas they who have drunk barley beer lie outstretched on their backs; wine makes one top-heavy, but beer stupefies.' Heraclitus reckoned that bogus thinkers revealed themselves in their cups, pointing out that 'it is better to hide ignorance, but it is hard to do this when we relax over wine'. Diogenes, on the other hand, was another familiar figure at the bar: when asked what wine he most enjoyed, he replied: 'Someone else's.'

Inevitably, things could and did get out of hand. Chrysippus the Stoic once fed undiluted wine to his donkey, and then died of laughing at the hilarious spectacle of the tipsy animal trying to eat figs.

More modern thinkers have also enjoyed a drop. Karl Marx himself was a champagne Marxist, while Friedrich

Engels could sound like that most bourgeois of creatures, the wine snob. Sending a mixed case to the Marx family in 1859, he wrote: 'The champagne and the Bordeaux Château d'Arcin can be drunk at once, while the port wine should be rested a little.' Nietzsche was also something of a wine buff, declaring: 'We ought to have wine – that alone brings sudden recovery and unpremeditated health.'

But philosophers' interest in wine goes beyond merely drinking the stuff, for the craft of wine tasting directly addresses the tension between objectivity and subjectivity, one of the central questions of philosophy. The taste of wine is, obviously, a subjective matter, and yet wine writers strive to provide a systematic and objective vocabulary to describe different wines. In fact there are probably more words used to describe drinking wine than any other experience, except sex. Kant himself believed the effort was impossible, and that even the colour of wine was subjective.

A wine writer might insist that a particular claret was 'Kung-fu fighting Bob Dylan in a coffee and chocolate shop', but the description must necessarily fall short of objectivity. As Tim Crane, Professor of Philosophy at UCL, wrote recently, 'No matter how many wine books you had read, the descriptions would mean nothing to you if you had not tasted wine.' This in turn suggests that there are some subjective experiences that lie outside an objective reality and that, in Professor Crane's words, 'there are necessary limits to our scientific or objective knowledge of the world'. This year, a conference will be held in London on 'Philosophy and Wine' to explore the relativity of wine tasting and whether Einstein was right to assert that science cannot describe chicken soup or, for that matter, real ale or claret.

It is worth remembering then, as you head to the pub or uncork the Château Margaux, that in addition to enjoying the experience, you will be exploring the connection between science and subjectivity. And if you tend to get more philosophical by the fourth glass/pint and start putting the world to rights, you are following in the footsteps of Socrates, Plato and Aristotle. But philosophical drinking also has its limits, for as Pliny the Elder sagely remarked: *sapientiam vino adumbrari* – wisdom is overshadowed by wine. Or, to put it another way, philosophising under the influence often turns out to be the Critique of Pure Riesling.

We are the potato people: knobbly, chippy, a little grubby

THE OUTBREAK IN WALES of a highly contagious new potato disease has, we learn, sent 'panic' through the British countryside. This might seem an exaggeration, but the word is well chosen, for after the other successive blows that have recently befallen British agriculture, the threat of a fresh epidemic afflicting the once mighty potato seems, symbolically, the final straw.

The most important edible vegetable the world has known, the potato rose to power from the end of the eighteenth century to win iconic status in our fields, hearts and menus. We like to think of the oak as the plant that most accurately reflects the national character, but in truth, alongside the Irish, we are potato people: knobbly, adaptable, resilient and slightly grubby.

But now, just as the rural community seemed to be recovering, *Solanum tuberosum* is under attack from *Clavibacter michiganensis sepedonicus*, or ring rot, a bacterium that turns the common tattie to rotten slime. Townies may shrug; the chips around the fish seem unaffected. But the psychological impact of this latest agricultural disaster can be understood only when our rural history is seen, as it were, through the eyes of the potato.

Spuds have been eaten for 7,000 years, and often controversially. When first brought to Europe from South America by the Spanish in the late sixteenth century, the tuber was viewed with deep suspicion. Henry VIII believed it to be an aphrodisiac, but others looked less kindly on the root, associating it with madness, syphilis, chronic wind and leprosy. The Swiss botanist Gaspard Bauhin believed the potato, as a cousin to the evil mandrake root and deadly nightshade, possessed diabolical powers, while William Cobbett, the great rural reformer, loathed this 'lazy root', considering it the cause of 'all slovenliness, filth, misery and slavery'.

The population growth in England and Ireland between 1750 and 1850 was linked to the abundance of potatoes, and, like others, Cobbett feared that a crop so easy to cultivate would turn generations of workers into layabouts. Malthus rightly pointed out that a population dependent on a single crop was toying with calamity.

Initially the Catholic Church was also fiercely anti-spud, since the Bible makes no mention of potatoes; Russians spurned them as 'Satan's Apples' and until the middle of the ninteenth century the Japanese regarded potatoes as mere cattle fodder.

Gastronomes sneered: 'I appreciate the potato only as a protection against famine,' sniffed Anthelme Brillat-Savarin, arguably the first French foodie. 'I know of nothing more eminently tasteless.'

Even today, the potato gets a bad press, in the form of 'couch potatoes' and 'potato heads'. That former Vice-President Dan Quayle could not spell so modest and ubiquitous a word was redoubled evidence of stupidity. It is no accident that Robert Atkins, purveyor of the eponymous diet, should launch his broadside against the spud, the humble workhorse of nutrition, the vegetable fall-guy.

Yet the potato is a social force that has shaped history in profound and lasting ways. Easy to plant and harvestable with the bare hands, the potato provided cheap nutrition; but when the crop failed, as it did most dramatically in Ireland in 1845, it could bring famine, mass emigration and huge social dislocation.

Mostly, however, the potato was a force for good, the tuber that got things done: the American West was won by men and women fortified by potatoes; Napoleon's army marched on its stomach, which was often full of potatoes (*pommes frites* first appeared in 1818).

Potatoes, the largest single source of vitamin C in the twentieth century, affected working hours and the length of fingernails, changed patterns of housework, cuisine and agriculture. The spud was even, briefly, a fashion statement, when Marie Antoinette wore purple potato blossoms in her hair.

The potato is the most democratic and liberating of vegetables, for by providing cheap and nutritious food, it freed many men and women from the permanent anxiety over where the next meal might come from. Oats and corn could be fickle, but the versatile, all-weather potato offered independence.

The rural labourer with his potato patch was in some measure defended against both hunger and exploitation:

which is why many landowners bitterly opposed potato cultivation. 'Had the potato not existed,' writes Larry Zuckerman, the greatest historian of the potato, then 'nineteenth-century England would have been hungrier and harder-pressed.'

The ancient Andeans, who first cultivated potatoes, associated them with mystical, healing properties, and their descendants, the Incas, worshipped potato deities and developed a system for telling the time based on how long it took to cook a potato. The vegetable is still held in special reverence. Think of Van Gogh's *Potato Eaters*, painted in 1885: 'I have tried,' the painter wrote, 'to make clear how these people, eating their potatoes under the lamplight, have dug the earth with those very hands they put in the dish.' Van Gogh would never have painted broccoli or rocket.

The horror at the new outbreak of ring rot threatens an industry worth £580 million a year, but it should be understood in cultural as well as economic terms.

The British farming community is still reeling from BSE and foot-and-mouth, and deeply angered by a government that seems to understand the countryside little, and care less; now even the potato, hitherto a hardy and dependable ally, seems to be falling apart.

Farmers might feel that the Incan spud gods have turned against them, but perhaps they should take heart from the story of the potato itself: an unglamorous hero, the victim of superstition and fashion, disease and disdain, the potato has seen good times and bad, but it has always pulled through when the chips were down.

The only Gael in the village

AS A CHILD ON the West Coast of Scotland, I used to love listening to the island fishermen speaking in Gaelic, a tumbling rattle of consonants like pebbles in a wave. At the sheepdog trials and ceilidhs, some of the older folk chattered together in that raw, romantic language, but even the younger ones, who had travelled to Glasgow and owned television sets, occasionally reached for the Gaelic to describe local things that still eluded the steadily encroaching English: a fish, a plant or a joke.

That, of course, is the essence of language: to frame the world through individual eyes, and local words. Gaelic defined a specific way of looking at the world. The great eighteenth-century Gaelic poet Donnchadh Ban MacIntyre (not a direct ancestor, I am sorry to say), wrote of this vital cultural perspective: *chan fhaca tusa i leis na sùilean agamsa*; you have not seen her with my eyes.

Today the language spoken by St Columba is disappearing from much of Scotland. The language resisted numerous assaults over the centuries, including the infamous Act of 1616 ordering 'that the vulgar Inglishe toung be universallie plantit and the Irische language, quilk is ane of the chief and principall causis of the continewance of barbaritie abolisheit and removit'. Gaelic is still widely spoken on the islands, and here in Argyll there are efforts to rescue it from becoming merely an adornment to tea towels by teaching the language in schools. But in another generation, the idea that this was once a bilingual part of the world will seem bizarre, as mainland Scots Gaelic falls victim not to government fiat, but the crushing, brutal vitality of the vulgar Inglishe toung.

English has become entirely unstoppable. In a terrifying new examination of the spread of English, Andrew Dalby, author of *A Dictionary of Languages*, estimates that in 200 years the 5,000 languages that currently exist will be reduced to a mere 200. But only one will count. Unlike other, earlier world languages, modern English will never split off into distinct parallel forms, as the Romance languages evolved from Latin. For a new language to emerge requires a degree of cultural isolation, or at least independence, that has become impossible. The world is simply too interconnected, by global technology and a global economy, to think in new words. Intrusive, restless English has made cultural privacy a thing of the past.

The growing hegemony of English is not proof of any inherent flexibility and superiority, as some language imperialists argue, for the attraction of learning English is not linguistic, but economic and utilitarian. It is the language of advancement, the job-getting language, the status tongue. English is more useful than any other language, in the sense that it is more widely understood, but that does not make it more descriptive or appropriate than home-grown language, and often less so.

This was true of earlier language colonisations: according to some Classical scholars, concepts that were entirely easy to describe in Greek were far harder in Latin. My Gaelic dictionary offers five different words for 'rain'; given the climate, this seems hardly enough, but is still a lot better than the one, pallid English word we are left with.

Instead of growing broader as it spreads, English is becoming poorer, deprived of the competition from other languages that enriches vocabulary, lending flexibility and creativity. In the past, languages have intermingled, borrowed and grown: but modern English merely moves in, like the cuckoo or grey squirrel, and replaces the less aggressive species. Slang English is growing, to be sure, but such words are not so much additions to the language as imaginative reductions of it.

From the Bible to Esperanto, it has been argued that a single world language would contribute to peace and international understanding. In the beginning 'the whole world was of one language and one speech' (Genesis xi) but then God did 'confound the language of all the earth' at Babel, resulting in permanent disharmony.

Yet there is little evidence that the ability to communicate prevents conflict. Indeed, as Dalby observes in his new book *Language in Danger*, some of the most vicious wars of recent times, such as those in Rwanda and Bosnia, and the conflict between Iraq and Kuwait, have been between speakers of the same language.

Prince William is admirably teaching himself Swahili in order to work in Africa, but his may be the last generation to bother, for even Africa's lingua franca is retreating before the onslaught of English. Nation states forged uniform languages within their borders; the borderless world state may eventually ensure one, monolithic language, growing ever more arid and literal in its domination.

The cultural and epistemological damage done by the erosion of 'minority' languages is difficult to overestimate, and depressingly hard to stop. Ireland has made strenuous efforts to preserve and promote Gaelic, yet English spreads inexorably. The linguistic theorist Benjamin Whorf argued that the way a language is shaped both reflects and informs a specific view of the world; when the language goes, the organic culture it represents goes too.

Donnchadh Ban MacIntyre, 'Fair Duncan of the Songs'

as he was known, wrote a once-celebrated poem in praise of the remarkable spring, or 'pipe-well', that gushed to a height of several feet out of the stunning mountainside of Ben Dorain.

His songs have now been all but silenced by the deafening roar of English, and the spring has gone too.

According to George Calder, who edited a 1912 edition of MacIntyre's Gaelic poetry, the spring 'was a delight to others beside the poet, till a Sassenach wandering in these parts, and moved by what spirit it is not easy to say, rammed his stick into the orifice, and stopped the jet for ever'.

Where are the orators?

MODERN POLITICAL ORATORY IS in a parlous state: few political speeches are broadcast in their entirety; few people listen to those that are. What spoken words once achieved we now expect from pictures or pre-cooked 'quotes'; we may snatch a hurried sound bite in passing, but we seldom care to sit through the entire four-course rhetorical meal. This is perhaps unsurprising, since most modern oratory is fairly indigestible, if not actually emetic, and the low quality of most public speaking is steadily getting worse as interest in the debating chamber wanes.

Television has almost killed off the public meeting, confining public speaking to a small corner of political life. Politicians deliberately eschew high-flown rhetoric, which can look embarrassing on screen, in favour of the informal one-liner, which is better adapted to the brief attention span of the television news.

But oratory can change lives, and at its best can also make sense of life; a truly great speech can forge its own historical moment, soothe or stir the soul. The word 'oratory' is associated with the idea of prayer, and the best speeches are really prayers, summations of belief and significance, expressed in the declaimed word. Some speeches, such as Abraham Lincoln's Gettysburg Address, come to mean much more than the specific events that prompted them. In times of crisis and catastrophe, we still need oratory; we expect our leaders to articulate what we feel, hope or fear, but also to find the words to convince us that their beliefs and actions are the right ones.

War always produces a flood of oratory, for better or worse, and the quality of those speeches may be a vital determinant in the course of war, or its avoidance. The last week has seen two notable oratorical successes: Tony Blair's speech to the TUC and George W. Bush's address to the UN. But also one resounding disappointment, in the failure to frame the anniversary of 9/11 in oratory; there were many searing pictures of that event, and much fine writing, but no memorable speech to mark the moment and set it in historical context.

Winston Churchill knew the power of rhetoric better than any leader of modern times. What Roy Jenkins, in his recent biography, describes as the 'mesmerising quality of Churchill's oratory' produced a 'euphoria of irrational belief in ultimate victory' without which the war would not have been won. Blair's speech to the TUC was less than Churchillian in tone. 'I believe it is right to deal with Saddam' hardly measures up to 'We will fight them on the beaches'. But it was skilfully pitched, forceful and pungent, persuasive without being ingratiating. The very hostility of the audience seemed to give his speech an authentic urgency that Blair's set-pieces too often lack. There was even a flicker of wit, now so rare in political speeches.

Bush's speech to the UN was also a marked contrast to many of his earlier efforts. The President is much more at ease in informal settings, when he can josh and ad lib at will; unfortunately, those are also the moments he is most likely to produce one of those bizarrely mangled malapropisms that only he, if anyone, can understand. Bush is one of the very few politicians who is actually more persuasive with an autocue. Ronald Reagan had a special technique for engaging both with his audience and his cue cards: he would remove one long-sighted contact lens before ascending the podium, which allowed him to read the speech with one eye, and the audience with the other. Bush has now learnt the same technique, making eye contact even as he reads the script. He has also adopted the sort of rhetorical device he once disdained, repeatedly using the phrase 'If the Iraqi regime wishes peace . . .' to bolster the argument for war.

Some of the best speeches are short (the Gettysburg Address lasted two minutes) but some of the most effective oratory may be cumulative. In 1940 Churchill made not one broadcast, but an entire series; the power of Margaret Thatcher's public speaking lay less in its eloquence than its repetitive urgency. But the essence of great oratory is feeling. William Hazlitt once wrote that the point of a speech is 'not to inform, but to rouse the mind'. So far both Bush and Blair have been informative more than rousing and that, perhaps, is the defining characteristic of modern public speaking: that it tries to justify and explain more than it seeks to uplift or express.

Certainly this was true of the official words to mark the anniversary of the World Trade Center attacks. There was no great speech to adorn the memorials, no attempt to frame the events of 9/11 with ringing phrases for posterity.

Aristotle made a vital distinction between rhetoric, the art of persuasion, and philosophy, the pursuit of truth. Both Bush and Blair believe they have uncovered the truth of what needs to be done in Iraq, but the task of persuasion has only just begun. In Britain the rhetorical battle will be joined in earnest, and not before time, with the recall of Parliament. This will be the opportunity for those who oppose war as much as those who support it, to prove the power of words to move minds.

We have allowed oratory to be debased into the prolix ramblings of the inconsequential and the trite buzz words of professional speechwriters. But speeches do make a difference. Churchill's 'iron curtain', Reagan's 'evil empire' and Kennedy's 'new frontier' speeches were more than mere sound bites, but evidence that the declaimed word has the power to extract transcendental significance from the passage of events and political change.

War and tragedy do not just invite great oratory; they require it.

Sarah Palin, Sarah Palindromes and post-turtles

SARAH PALIN HAS ALREADY given so much to our political culture, but as she gears up for her 2012 presidential bid we must also celebrate her unique contribution to the language: the Sarah Palindrome.

This is a phrase, relevant to the Governor of Alaska, that reads the same backwards and forwards, as in 'Madam I'm

Adam'. The idea was invented by Alex Beam, of the *Boston Globe*, who sent out a call for Sarah Palindromes in the run-up to the election, and has since been swamped. Here is a selection:

> Dammit, I'm mad.
> Meet animals; laminate 'em.
> Evil deified live.
> Harass sensuousness, Sarah.
> Party boobytrap.
> God saw I was dog.
> No, son, onanism's a gross orgasm sin: a no-no, son.

But perhaps the most apt palindrome to emerge from the US election relates not to Palin but to Barack Obama: 'Obama Amabo' which in Latin can be translated as, 'I will love Obama.' (I can already hear the snorts of irate Latin scholars. If Obama is a first-declension noun, then as the object it should, I suppose, take an extra 'm'. Hence: Obamam Amabo. That is also a palindrome.)

Word of the week: post-turtle. A seventy-five-year-old Texas rancher recently explained this term to a country doctor. The conversation turned to the US election, and Sarah Palin's vice-presidential candidacy, and the old rancher observed: 'Well, ya know, Palin is a post-turtle.' The bemused doctor asked what a post-turtle was, and the old man replied: 'When you're driving down a country road and you come across a fence post with a turtle balanced on top, that's a post-turtle.' The rancher continued: 'You know she didn't get up there by herself, she doesn't belong up there, she doesn't know what to do while she is up there, and you just wonder what kind of dumb ass put her up there to begin with.'

In a war of words,
we'll always be top guns

NOT SINCE THE FIRST World War has our language been so radically and rapidly altered by the vocabulary of conflict, and whatever may be the long-term effects of the war against terrorism in Afghanistan and the wider world, we will never speak, or write, in quite the same way again. An entirely new jargon is slipping into the lexicon, words that seemed benign enough before September 11 are now freighted with additional meaning, and slang terms derived from recent events now pepper the spoken landscape like bomblets from a cluster bomb.

In our new 'weapons-grade' fighting talk, we speak of 'sleepers', 'bioterrorism' (or bioterrrism, as pronounced by George W. Bush), and 'daisy-cutters'. The tartars at work are now referred to as 'Taliban'; 'Ground Zero', once a specific term denoting the impact point of a nuclear weapon, has been expanded to mean not just the devastated downtown area of Manhattan, but anywhere that is the focus of attention or action. We talk of feeling "thraxy' and getting 'spored' when we have 'flu-like symptoms', and 'homeland', as in 'homeland security', has taken on a whole new meaning in American parlance, heavy with nationalism, patriotism and a tinge of paranoia.

The most powerful catchphrase to emerge from the trauma is 'Let's roll', the final words uttered by Todd Beamer before he and other passengers on board the doomed Flight 93 fought back against the hijackers, and the plane plummeted. The phrase itself has now been hijacked, as a catch-all to describe national resilience and a martyr's resolution in the face of danger. B52 crews now paint the words on their bombs, and the President himself has adopted them: 'We have our marching orders,' he declared in a televised address last month. 'My fellow Americans, let's roll.'

To 'take someone out', once an invitation to romance, now exclusively means to kill with maximum violence. 'I'll take him out,' Philip Marlowe declares in Raymond Chandler's *The Big Sleep*: Bush, Donald Rumsfeld, Tony Blair and even Dennis Hastert, the portly Speaker of the House, who doesn't look as if he could take out the rubbish without keeling over, have all been 'taking out' Taliban left and right. From the war-room, such words move swiftly to the boardroom, then the screen and then the playroom.

Wartime rules apply also to words, and politicians and commentators are currently getting away with the sort of misuse of language and Americanisms that would invite ridicule in peacetime. 'Enormity', a word thoroughly overused in the aftermath of the terrorist attacks, is now routinely used to describe something merely large; anyone using the term 'normalcy' without irony should be taken out. There is also some new self-censorship: politicians no longer 'target' the opposition, let alone 'carpet-bomb' them or launch a 'crusade', but the verb 'to plane' is gaining a slang currency, meaning to destroy in a sudden, unexpected attack.

The 'War on Terrorism' is a direct metaphorical descendant of Lyndon Johnson's 'War on Poverty' and the various 'Wars on Drugs'; but because the action against Osama bin Laden does not resemble any previous military engagement, being fought in large part off the battlefield and against individuals more than states, the very definition of the phrase is subtly changing.

In what is surely a sign of recovery, the events of the past few months have also developed an ironic usage. In the art world, pretentious critics have been heard to mutter that a work is 'sooo September 10', when it fails to reflect our newly minted wartime Zeitgeist.

This is the most intensive barrage of war-words to descend on the language since the war of 1914–18, when millions of literate civilians were exposed to the jargon and slang of war for the first time, and returned with 'over the top' and, of course, 'barrage'. Some of the most delightful words from that time relate not to the acts of war, but to moments of repose behind the lines: 'souvenir', 'boozy' (after the red wine from Buzy), and 'chatting', idle trench talk while crushing lice or 'chats' from the seams of infested uniforms.

The Second World War gave us 'Blitz', 'Jeep' and 'GI', while the Korean War gave rise to 'brainwashing' and 'flameout'. The Cold War popularised 'purges', 'fallout' and 'going ballistic'. Recent wars have seen a flourishing of euphemisms that have found their way into everyday speech: 'collateral damage' (killing civilians), 'friendly fire' (killing your own people) and 'redeployment' (running away). Saddam Hussein's signal contribution to language during the Gulf War was the 'mother of all . . .' construction, now the mother of all clichés.

We have yet to come up with a word or phrase to describe the event that gave word to the mushrooming (see Second World War) of language in the past four months. 'Tragedy' is too neutral, suggestive of the hand of God as much as man; 'crime' is diluted, lacking the political edge; 'terror attacks' lack scale, but 'atrocity', 'assault' and 'outrage' are overloaded words, which tire quickly. And so, as in all wars, we have tended to fall back on euphemism – 'the events of September 11' or merely 'September 11' – until time and distance furnish the right construction, as they will.

Our new lingo is violent, and often rather crass, but at least it is living; to compare this flourishing of words with the dead, obscure, rote language of Bin Laden's set-piece speeches is to gain another insight into his moribund, backward and unimaginative world. We are winning the war of words too.

It's all Geek to me . . .

SLANG, THOUGHT G.K. CHESTERTON, is 'the one stream of poetry which is continually flowing'. Today that stream is pouring out of the internet in a great tidal wave of new words, idioms and acronyms that amount to an entirely new language, revealing the richly inventive, cliquish and oddly defensive mind of the computer geek. Cyberspace now has its lingua franca – Geek-speak – and anyone visiting that vast place for the first time would be advised to pick up at least the rudiments of the argot.

Revolutionary new technologies, powering commerce, have repeatedly shaped language in the past. In the days of sail you got 'scuppered', or 'spliced' if someone liked the 'cut of your jib'. The railway age allowed us 'to pick up steam' or go 'off the rails'. When the automobile arrived we could 'rev up' and 'blow a gasket', but nuclear weapons offered the alternative of 'going ballistic'.

The industry and experience of war spawned a wide vocabulary, from 'going Awol' to 'over the top' to the way that anything even vaguely muddy is compared to the Somme.

To judge from the expanding range of hackers' dictionaries and cyberspeak lexicons now appearing in the US,

Geek-speak is evolving in a rather different way. Like the internet itself, the slang spin-offs are without limit and endlessly expanding; but this is also a self-conscious tongue, at once arrogant and repressed. Where other forms of cant swiftly spread into the general language and attain wider meaning there, cyberspeak delights in its own cultural isolation, as the tongue of the internet-initiated, the digerati.

The linguistic roots of Geek-speak can be traced to Seattle, headquarters of Microsoft Corp, where employees developed a tribal patois in the early days of the high-tech boom. What might be called Classical or Ancient Geek has since been diluted into a wider vernacular, borrowing heavily and ironically from popular culture, surf-speak, *Monty Python* and, inevitably, the jargon of American high tech.

The euthanasia campaigner Jack Kevorkian, for example, has become a verb in the new parlance; 'to kevork' is to kill off something, usually prematurely. To 'go granular' is a fine cyber-usage, meaning to delve into the gritty details of a project. The nerd-word 'nar' denotes disharmony or bad vibes, as in: 'The nar at the AGM was palpable.' An 'idea hamster' accurately summons up those people who trundle endlessly around the treadmill of inspiration.

The internet has invented several words that ought to have been around long ago. A 'triority' refers to the three things your boss wants you to do immediately and simultaneously; an 'overgrad' is someone in full-time, salaried employment who still talks about going to university. (Derived from the phrase 'Not over graduation yet'.) A 'thinko' is the mental counterpart of a typo, a minor and momentary lapse in cerebral processing, especially one involving a failure to recall information learnt by rote.

The new lingo loves an acronym – indeed, there is even an acronym within an acronym: a TLA (Three-Letter-

Acronym) department of a company is one without any apparent function. The language has been enriched by the arrival of the SLIRK (Spoiled Little Rich Kid), PANS (Pretty Amazing New Stuff) and the WOMBAT, a Waste Of Money Brains And Time.

OTOH (On The Other Hand), some of the new terminology is chippy, revealing and menacing. All slangs contain derogatory elements, but as the *New York Times* critic Michiko Kakutani recently observed, there is a disquietingly 'Nietzschean' ring to the way the new language denotes those in the charmed techno-circle as 'wizards' or '*über-geeks*', while the rest of us are 'sheeple', mere 'eyeballs' or 'drumps', a portmanteau of dreary and lump, 'typically, a middle-aged, pot-bellied, sexually frustrated single person who has given up on dating'.

The new language is rife with terms of abuse for a person who lacks the 'bandwidth' (intelligence) or inclination to get to grips with the new technology: a PONA (Person of No Account), a BDU (Brain Dead User) or a PEBCAK (Problem Exists Between Chair And Keyboard). Those who still get their information from books, newspapers or television are pathetic slaves to 'legacy media'.

The dictionaries also reveal an annoying tendency to over-complicate language to the point where it becomes quite incomprehensible, as anyone who has tried to read a software instruction manual will know.

This is particularly true of Microspeak, the subset of Geek-speak spoken at Microsoft, where workers tend to 'generate content' (write) about a 'taxonomy of options' (choices) which must then be 'disambiguated' (clarified). The geeks have a word for this too: 'Crufty', meaning unnecessarily complicated, from Cruft Hall, the old physics building at Harvard. The antidote is KISS: Keep It Simple, Stupid.

Alongside the narcissism of Geek-speak is a disdain for, or fear of human contact, as contrasted with the hygienic certainties of the cyberworld. 'Face-mail' is the mocking term for communicating with another human being in person rather than on e-mail; to 'touch skin' is to meet.

Our descendants may end up speaking Modern Geek as a first language, but they, in turn, will add their own variations. Slang is the enemy of pretension, and as we BDUs gradually wrest control of the web from the self-styled 'net.gods' who invented it, this emerging tongue will eventually be purged of its 'kubris' – 'an extreme form of arrogance found in multimedia *auteurs* who think they are Stanley Kubrick'.

Eurobabble bubbles from linguistic liquidiser

'IN SEINE BRUXEL OFFICE, Inspector Cabillot regarded la rain out des window while pensante aan quanto tempo und quanto work necessited ut Europa finalmently unita make.'

That stream of gobbledygook opens the first novel to be written in 'Europanto', a bizarre and free-form mixture of European languages that has been cooked up by a European Union translator as the linguistic answer to the single European currency.

The passage above translates, if that is the right word, as: 'In his Brussels office, Inspector Cabillot looked at the rain outside his window and thought how much time and effort it had taken to build a united Europe.'

Building a single European language is much simpler, it appears, for Europanto has no grammar, no punctuation, no pronunciation and only one firm rule: it should be at least vaguely comprehensible to every European.

The linguistic recipe used by Diego Marani, Europanto's Italian-born inventor, is broadly the following: take a firm grounding of English and French, toss in chunks of German, Spanish and Italian; garnish with a dash of Flemish and Euro-slang; pour the contents into a language liquidiser and serve when thoroughly pureed.

In *Las Adventures des Inspector Cabillot*, the Europanto novel just published in France, Signor Marani, thirty-nine, takes his language into new territory, having already given rise to a Europanto board game and a regular Belgian newspaper column.

The hero of Signor Marani's novel is the hapless Inspector Cabillot (a reference to *cabillaud* in French, meaning 'cod'), 'el autentico europeano polizero qui fighte contra al mal por eine Europa van pax und prosperity donde se speake eine sole lingua: de Europanto'. For those readers still getting to grips with the vocabulary that is 'a real European policeman who fights against evil for a Europe united in peace and prosperity where a single language is spoken: Europanto'.

The inspector tackles such varied euro-concerns as a mad cow disease terrorist cell (Demente Bovine Frakzion) that takes over London ('Die mad vaquas van all Europe sich united in Grosse Britannia und last noche taked el power in London') and the best chat-up line in a disco, 'Mayde trinke tu etwas?' ('Fancy a drink?')

President Clinton's domestic complications also get the Europanto treatment, beginning with this unlikely exchange between two world leaders: Jacques Chirac: 'Hallo Billy! Jacques speakante! Wat passe?' Bill Clinton: 'Ah! Jacques! Wat surprise! Ich passe gut! Todo in order. Und con toi?'

Signor Marani, who speaks about ten languages fluently and works at the EU Council of Ministers, came across the idea of inventing a hybrid tongue when he and his fellow interpreters found they were slipping into an odd multi-lingual argot after a hard day of high-speed translation in Brussels.

The pseudo-language has already attracted a large popular following and items in Europanto have begun appearing in the official Council of Ministers' *Gazette*, although not everyone gets the joke. Signor Marani has received a number of letters from Scandinavians wanting to sign up for Europanto lessons, and speakers of Esperanto, the universal language invented in 1887, are particularly unamused.

Signor Marani said he started speaking Europanto as a joke, but now actually thinks in Euro-pidgin.

'I adopted English structure because it is universally known and I tend to use words with a common root, usually Latin,' he said. 'International English is already a mixture of languages, polluted by foreign speakers like myself who put something of their own culture into it.'

As the author points out, many common words have already transcended national barriers to become part of universal parlance, such as 'pizza', 'espresso', 'chile con carne' and 'OK'.

'My language is more written than spoken, but then Dante's *Divine Comedy* was created when classical Italian was only a written language. It took two centuries before it became the language of Italy. I am developing artificially what happened naturally to languages in the past,' he said.

The blurb accompanying Signor Marani's project may have a familiarly earnest pan-European ring to it, offering to create 'a sort of humour that makes people from all countries laugh' and to 'facilitate the free movement of ideas'.

The only problem with Europanto is that, while some of it may be comprehensible to most Europeans, it seems unlikely that anyone, save Signor Marani, can follow every word of the linguistic hotchpotch he has created.

The *entente* and double entendre

EVERYTHING WAS GOING SWIMMINGLY at the bilingual outing in Sedgefield laid on by Tony Blair for Lionel Jospin, his French counterpart, until the two leaders were both treacherously betrayed, like so many before them, when they wandered too far into the perilous territory of a foreign tongue.

The Prime Minister had been airing his fluent French well up until that point, and M. Jospin was making a good fist of English, which he speaks badly. Both men, who have little in common, politically or personally, were stoutly expressing mutual admiration as they kicked a football around and drank a pint of Theakston's. Then a sneaky French double entendre came hurtling out of nowhere, and reduced the visiting and hitherto respectful French media to hysterical giggles.

'*J'ai toujours envie de Lionel de toutes les façons,*' said Mr Blair, intending to express his envy of the French leader's popularity and improving economy. M. Jospin's pinkish complexion went from langoustine to lobster and it was quietly explained to Mr Blair that what he had actually said was: 'I always desire Lionel in every way.'

A few moments later it was M. Jospin's turn to suffer a gust of mirth blowing in the opposite direction, as he emerged smacking his lips from the Dun Cow Inn and declared: 'The cook is delicious.' He swiftly corrected himself to 'cooking' only to be recorrected by Mr Blair, who pointed out that the pub cook was rather delicious, as it happened.

The situation will be familiar to many: you think you speak a foreign language pretty well; your interlocuter thinks he/she speaks your language better; you end up speaking each other's language. Result: linguistic mayhem.

Mr Blair and M. Jospin were not the first to discover that mixing languages, like metaphors, can be a double-edged sword of Damocles. Even the most crucial and carefully prepared speech in a foreign language may contain a lurking explosive, as demonstrated by John F. Kennedy's 'Ich bin ein Berliner', which can be translated, a little unfairly, as 'I am a doughnut' because he left the 'ein' in.

François Mitterrand often pretended not to understand English, knowing well that major pitfalls lie in appearing to understand more than you do, or believing you are being understood more than you are. Harold Macmillan's insistence on speaking what he thought was French to de Gaulle on the subject of nuclear weapons, and being roundly misunderstood, coloured Franco-British relations for years afterwards.

More recently Chris Patten, when interviewed in French about his book-writing sojourn in France, is reputed to have declared that his holiday home in the Tarn gave him 'une grande jouissance', a word suggesting rather more than merely cerebral pleasure, which seemed unlikely even for such a passionate Francophile.

Ronald Reagan never ventured into foreign languages after discovering, as a youth, that with prolonged rehearsal he was able to ask a question in French, but could never make head or tail of the answer. Even politicians able to speak another language well, like Jacques Chirac who learnt English while working in an American Howard Johnson's motel, are understandably cautious. When I interviewed the French President some time ago and asked him which language he would prefer to converse in, he replied pointedly: 'If I am discussing important matters, I speak in French.'

Getting the translation right, or intentionally wrong, can be a matter of life and death. On 17 August 1914, with the German Army marching towards Paris, the irascible French General Charles Lanrezac visited the equally crusty British Field Marshal Sir John French, on what would soon be the battlefields of northern France. Already poor relations between the two commanders deteriorated rapidly when they discovered that neither could speak the other's language intelligibly. The tension was near snapping point when Sir John, in badly wounded French, asked whether the Germans would cross the Meuse River at Huy (which he pronounced 'Ahoy!') and the General reponded in French, with swingeing sarcasm: 'Tell the Marshal I think the Germans have come to fish.'

'What does he say? What does he say?' demanded the Englishman.

'He says they are going to cross the river, sir,' replied General Henry Wilson, with a smooth piece of mistranslation that kept the two leaders on speaking terms and probably altered the course of the First World War.

As every Brussels diplomat knows, there are distinct advantages to working in two languages: without violating its basic import, a communiqué can be toned down or up, tweaked, flattened or sugared when translated into another language, giving invaluable room for nuance and often helping to keep negotiations moving.

A language gulf can also slow matters down, as on the occasion when a French member of the European Parliament laboriously congratulated one of his colleagues on his '*prudence Normande*'. The simultanous translator did his best, but for weeks afterwards English-speaking MEPs remained completely baffled as to why 'Norman Wisdom' had inexplicably been introduced into the proceedings.

However, perhaps the main advantage of being able to speak, or mis-speak another language, is the opportunity this provides for giving offence without apparently intending to. The master of this technique was Churchill, whose grinding accent in French belied his grasp of the language.

In one apocryphal address in French, Sir Winston was expected to reminisce about the contrasts of war and peace in his past. He began, surely more out of devilry than ignorance: '*Quand je regarde mon derrière, je le vois divisé en deux grandes parties...*', before a technician intervened to prevent a major diplomatic incident and cut off his microphone.

Languages can speak in unexpected ways

WE ARE FAMILIAR WITH the English word 'chary', meaning cautious or anxious. But if you were an elderly Siberian Chulym reindeer herder, and one of the handful of people left who speak the ancient language known as Middle Chulym or Tuvan, the word 'chary' would translate as 'a two-year-old castratable rideable reindeer'. (In Siberia, it seems, two-year-old uncastrated male reindeer have reason to be, well, chary.) The word tells us something specific about the ecology of reindeer herding in Siberia.

The linguist David Harrison cited this obscure word in a fascinating address to the American Association for the

Advancement of Science, as an example of the extraordinary interaction between language and biodiversity: the languages of ethnic groups, he pointed out, contain vitally important information about species often unknown to formal science. If the language is lost, so too will vanish the knowledge it contains about natural phenomena.

More than half of the world's 7,000 languages are expected to die out by the end of the century, taking with them irreplaceable knowledge about plants and animals.

Global warming, loss of habitat and pollution are not the only threats to the environment: lack of linguistic diversity poses a direct threat to biodiversity.

'Most of what humans know about eco-systems is not written down, it is in people's heads,' Harrison argues. Replace an old language with a new one that does not contain the same concepts and vocabulary, and the environment becomes literally indescribable – and far more vulnerable.

The tiny community of Chulym people, who live in central Siberia, roughly 2,000 miles from Moscow, speak a language that has evolved from the harsh environment, based on hunting and gathering, plants, animal behaviour, weather and the planets.

Modern languages long ago lost this organic fecundity.

But just as housing development encroaches on the forest, Middle Chulym is swiftly being eroded, like so many ancient languages. As nomadic people came under Soviet control, Russian spread, forcing out indigenous tongues and their preliterate oral tradition as surely as the grey squirrel displaced the red – there are now just 426 Chulym people left, of whom only thirty-five speak the ancient language fluently, all over the age of fifty.

In another generation, their language will be gone, preserved only in Harrison's digital archive: there will be no living person left to speak the multiple Middle Chulym words that evolved over the centuries to describe every single conceivable variety of reindeer.

Ancient languages reflect unique ways of seeing the world and interacting with it.

The Australian Aboriginal language of Guugu Yimithirr, for example, does not have a concept of 'left' and 'right', relying instead on the concepts of 'north', 'south', 'east' and 'west'. Your left hand, in other words, could be your north hand, unless you were facing 180 degrees in the opposite direction, in which case it would be your south hand. Guugu Yimithirr requires a constant awareness of where one stands within the landscape, geographically speaking – an alertness to one's surroundings utterly lost to modern speech.

Ancient language can also contain coded environmental information of which modern science may be unaware. The two-barred flasher butterfly of Central America, for example, was long assumed to be a single species. The Mexican Tzeltal tribe, however, knew better, and that knowledge was embedded in their language.

The tribe knew that although adult butterflies all looked the same, different types of larvae attacked different crops. Agriculture and survival depended on knowing, and naming, each distinct variety of larva. Scientists have only recently confirmed that there are at least ten species of two-barred flasher butterfly – something that the Tzeltal language could have told them all along.

Languages have always developed and expanded, withered and died, reflecting the ebb and flow of human politics, economics, nutrition and migration. Between 100 BC and AD 400, the number of languages spoken around the Mediterranean dropped from about sixty to ten, eliminated by the steady march of Latin and Greek. But today languages are disappearing faster – some linguists estimate that an old language dies every fortnight.

Linguists are racing to document the most endangered, such as the 'click' languages of South Africa, which may be the closest living descendants of the original human language that developed in Africa 100 millennia ago, and the 800 vanishing languages of Papua New Guinea, the most fertile language seed-bed on Earth.

When an animal species is declared extinct, we mourn, but world languages fade away with little fanfare. Preserving a language, as Harrison has done with Siberian Chulym, will not bring it back, but at least the ancient words will survive, like the DNA of the woolly mammoth preserved in permafrost, to tell us what the world we have lost was like.

Writer's ... um ... block

DAN BROWN, THE UBIQUITOUS author of the positively universal *The Da Vinci Code*, revealed this week that, when stuck for inspiration, he likes to dangle the wrong way up attached to a pair of 'gravity boots'.

'Hanging upside down seems to help me solve plot challenges by shifting my entire perspective,' he says. (Just for the legal record, this form of literary activity is entirely the inspiration of Dan Brown himself: he has not borrowed, adapted or plagiarised it in any way.) Writers have always resorted to strange habits to keep scribbling. Ernest Hemingway wrote while standing up – when he was not falling-down drunk; or in bed – when he was not fighting drunk. John Cheever would take the lift to the basement of his New York apartment block and write all day on a card table facing a blank wall.

George Bernard Shaw built a hut, 8ft square, on a rotating platform that could move to follow the sun's path across the sky. (He also installed a telephone but, crucially, one that could make only outward calls.) Edith Wharton wrote lying down and dropped each completed page on the floor to be collected by her maid when she finally got up. Graham Greene wrote exactly 500 words a day, stopping in mid-sentence if necessary, and James Joyce wrote in a corner, occasionally laughing out loud at his own jokes.

Every writer has his own peculiar rituals. For example, I require a certain amount of ambient noise, coffee in a bucket and the cricket score ticking over at the bottom of the screen; I cannot write if there are cooking smells in the vicinity, or if I am wearing a tie. (This last neurosis is probably a hangover from school: some subconscious but unbreakable link between wearing a tie and thinking nothing at all.) Behind Shaw's rotating room, Cheever's card table and Brown's gravity boots lies the dreadful spectre of writer's block; the fear of word-drought, the anxiety that without the empty wall to stare at, the sun on the desk or the blood pumping through the temples from dangling upside down, the writer will simply stop writing.

Writers like to imagine that their predecessors have always wrestled with a fickle muse. A blank page, sighs the blocked writer, is God's way of showing you how hard it is to be God. But in truth the concept of writer's block is comparatively new.

I can find no ancient writer who complained of the terrors of the blank papyrus.

Popular nineteenth-century writers such as Dickens and Walter Scott churned out prose at a prodigious rate. Trollope averaged 1,000 words an hour every morning, before going to work at the Post Office, producing forty-nine novels in thirty-five years. He dismissed the Romantic notion that words are elusive. The writer, he said, should treat writing as a job: 'No gigantic efforts will then be necessary. He need tie no wet towels round his brow, nor sit for 30 hours at his desk without moving.'

Stephen King is similarly businesslike. He recalls a dour Scottish interviewer once repeatedly asking him why he never ran out of ghoulish ideas. 'After several times trying to explain that it was really just a profession, I told her that, whenever I had writer's block, for inspiration I looked at a small jar that was always on my desk and held a pickled little slave boy's heart from before the Civil War.' She believed him, and the legend has followed King around since.

The romantic aura surrounding the modern writer is linked to the idea that he might, at any moment, simply cease writing and never start again. Scientists, in the US inevitably, are working on a 'cure' for writer's block that involves magnetic stimulation of the frontal lobes (do not try this at home – or, at least not before trying the gravity boots first).

Log on to www.unblock.org and there you will find Jerry Mundis, a specialist in unblocking blocked writers, promising a powerful literary laxative: 'I'll break writer's block for you immediately and for ever.'

Yet the number of proven cases of writers suddenly and inexplicably seizing up is small. In most cases of writer's block there is an explanation: drink, drugs, depression, insecurity or disillusion with the writing process. Writing is lonely, difficult and often badly paid. Like anyone else, writers can run out of steam, or inspiration, or the desire for success, but being both articulate and neurotic, they can dignify professional failure with an entire mythology.

Writer's block may be an Anglo-Saxon affliction for, as Joan Acocella pointed out in a recent *New Yorker* article, the term does not exist in French or German. This is odd, because the syndrome itself was invented by a Viennese psychiatrist named Edmund Bergler (who insisted that it was linked to breast-feeding), and France has produced an entire genre of writers who stopped. Success can put a spanner in a writer's works. Harper Lee, most famously, never published another novel after the huge success of *To Kill a Mockingbird*. Ten years separated Louis de Bernières's highly successful *Captain Corelli's Mandolin* from *Birds Without Wings* (although he denied any blockage). Rimbaud wrote *Une Saison en Enfer* at the age of nineteen to great acclaim, and never wrote anything again. Rimbaud also, exceptionally, did not seem to be remotely upset by the disappearance of his talent.

It was rumoured that Dan Brown himself had hit blockbuster block. Six years elapsed between the publication of *The Da Vinci Code*, which bust every sales record on the block, and the appearance of his next novel. In the fervid world of bestsellers, that is a long time to be left hanging around – particularly if you are hanging upside down.

BIBLIOGRAPHY

Adams, Jad, *Hideous Absinthe: A History of the Devil in a Bottle* (London: I.B. Tauris, 2003)

Ayto, John, *Wobbly Bits* (London: A&C Black, 2007)

Bergen, Peter L., *The Osama bin Laden I Know: An Oral History of Al-Qaeda's leader* (London: Simon & Schuster, 2006)

Croker, Charlie, *Still Lost in Translation: More Misadventures in English Abroad* (London: Random House, 2007)

Donald, Graeme, *Fighting Talk* (London: Osprey, 2008)

Engel, Matthew, *Extracts from the Red Notebooks* (London: Macmillan, 2007)

Everett, Daniel, *Don't Sleep There are Snakes: Life and Language in the Amazonian Jungle* (London: Profile Books, 2008)

Foyle, Christopher, *Foyle's Philavery: A Treasury of Unusual Words* (London: Chambers Harrap, 2007)

Goldwag, Arthur, *Isms and Ologies: 453 Difficult Doctrines You've Always Pretended to Understand* (London: Quercus, 2007)

Gross, John (ed.), *The New Oxford Book of Literary Anecdotes* (Oxford, Oxford University Press, 2007)

Harrison, K. David, *When Languages Die: The Extinction of the World's Languages and the Erosion of Human Knowledge* (Oxford: Oxford University Press, 2007)

Hitchings, Henry, *The Secret Life of Words* (London: John Murray, 2008)

Jack, Albert, *Pop Goes the Weasel: The Secret Meanings of Nursery Rhymes* (London: Penguin, 2008)

Jacot de Boinod, Adam, *Toujours Tingo: More Extraordinary Words to Change the Way We See the World* (London: Penguin, 2007)

Knight Bruce, Rory, *Timothy the Tortoise: the Remarkable Story of the World's Oldest Pet* (London: Orion, 2004)

Lawrence, Bruce (ed.), *Messages to the World: The Statements of Osama bin Laden* (London: Verso, 2005)

Leith, Sam, *Dead Pets: Stuff Them, Eat Them, Love Them* (Edinburgh: Canongate, 2005).

Maitland, Alexander, *Wilfred Thesiger: The Life of the Great Explorer* (London: HarperCollins, 2006)

Rees, Nigel, *A Man about a Dog: Euphemisms and other Examples of Verbal Squeamishness* (London: Collins, 2008)

Scroggie, Justin, *Tic-Tac, Teddy Bears & Teardrop Tattoos* (London: Hodder & Stoughton, 2008)

Taylor, Andrew, *A Plum in Your Mouth: Why the Way We Talk Speaks Volumes About Us* (London: HarperCollins, 2006)

Taylor, J.P.G., *A Fair Gate to Oblivion: A Celebration of the English Epitaph* (Wetherby: Oblong Creative, 2006)

Thesiger, Wilfred, *A Life of My Choice* (London: Flamingo, 1993)

——*The Marsh Arabs* (London: Penguin, 1983)

Thorne, Tony, *Shoot the Puppy: A Survival Guide to the Curious Jargon of Modern Life* (London: Penguin, 2006)

Tombs, Robert and Isabelle, *That Sweet Enemy: The French and the British from the Sun King to the Present* (London: William Heinemann, 2007)

OPERATION MINCEMEAT

THE TRUE SPY STORY THAT CHANGED
THE COURSE OF WORLD WAR II

One overcast April morning in 1943, a fisherman notices a corpse floating in the sea off the coast of Spain. When the body is brought ashore, he is identified as a British soldier, Major William Martin of the Royal Marines. A leather attaché case, secured to his belt, reveals an intelligence goldmine: top-secret Allied invasion plans.

But Major William Martin never existed. The body is that of a dead Welsh tramp and every single document is fake. *Operation Mincemeat* is the incredible true story of the most extraordinary deception ever planned by Churchill's spies – an outrageous lie that travelled from a Whitehall basement, all the way to Hitler's desk.

*

'With its fantastic plot and its cast of eccentric characters, the book reads like the most improbable of spy stories. It is a tribute to Macintyre's skill that we never for a moment forget that it is actually all true'
DAILY TELEGRAPH

'Macintyre has a journalist's nose for a great story, and a novelist's skill in its narration ... spellbinding ****'
CRAIG BROWN, MAIL ON SUNDAY

'Compelling'
WILLIAM BOYD, THE TIMES

*

ISBN 9781408809211 · PAPERBACK · £7.99

ORDER YOUR COPY: BY PHONE +44 (0)1256 302 699; BY EMAIL: DIRECT@MACMILLAN.CO.UK
DELIVERY IS USUALLY 3–5 WORKING DAYS. FREE POSTAGE AND PACKAGING FOR ORDERS OVER £20.

ONLINE: WWW.BLOOMSBURY.COM/BOOKSHOP
PRICES AND AVAILABILITY SUBJECT TO CHANGE WITHOUT NOTICE.

WWW.BLOOMSBURY.COM/BENMACINTYRE

B L O O M S B U R Y